**Evening Standard**

Weekend Breaks

DENISE ELPHICK &
ANNABEL FREEMAN

SIMON & SCHUSTER
A VIACOM COMPANY

First published in Great Britain by Simon & Schuster UK Ltd, 2000
A Viacom Company

1 3 5 7 9 10 8 6 4 2

Simon & Schuster UK Ltd
Africa House
64–78 Kingsway
London WC2B 6SX

Simon & Schuster Australia
Sydney

Text design: Rachel Hardman Carter
Typeset by: Stylize Digital Artwork
Printed and bound in Italy

A CIP catalogue record for this book is available from the British Library

ISBN 0 671 0 2911 8

Also published in this series:

All information was checked and correct at press time.
All foreign telephone numbers are given without international dialing codes.

CONTENTS

INTRODUCTION

Even the most confirmed urbanite needs a break from the smoke. London may well rock, but sometimes we all need the gentle roll of the English countryside. Moreover, it's too easy for Londoners to forget that there is more to Britain than the metropolis; there's a whole country out there waiting to be explored.

If you want rolling countryside, we've got it in plenty in the UK. If it's the bracing air of the seaside that you're after, don't forget that Britain has some of the most breathtaking and unspoilt coastline in the world, from sweeping sandy beaches to salt flats, from traditional Victorian resorts to wild estuaries and waterways. And, if the pull of urban life is too strong to give up even for a weekend, then some of Britain's other cities have just as much to offer.

People take weekend breaks away for many different reasons. It may be that you have young children who need a bit more space than a walk in the local park can offer or who are more familiar with seeing a tiger face to face at London Zoo than watching a field of Friesian cattle. Perhaps you're stressed out at work and need to unwind – with a bit of help from some professionals at a luxurious health farm? Maybe you've met the perfect partner and want to whisk them off to some romantic spot, or you're celebrating something special and want to do it in style? Or have you always wanted to try out a new sport or activity and don't have time or space in your life during the week to do so? Whether you're planning well in advance or acting on the spur of the moment, we've chosen some of our favourite places for weekends away.

Some of the places we mention are well known, and are here because we feel that they deserve their fame and really deliver what they promise. Others are here because they offer something special, or haven't been discovered by too many people yet.

A few of the establishments have been going for ages, whilst some are brand new and perhaps still finding their feet. We've tried to include something to appeal to all ages, tastes and wallets. There are a few jaw-droppingly expensive hotels, such as Cliveden, which makes the grade because it really is fabulous and perfect for a really special weekend, such as an important anniversary or even a honeymoon. On the other hand, we've also mentioned some very reasonable bed and breakfasts, which provide great value, sometimes in smarter surroundings than a hotel. And there are quirkier places: temples, a lighthouse, even a fort.

Of course, what makes up a good weekend is as personal as what you like for breakfast. Very often it's who you are with rather than where you are that makes it special. However, finding somewhere nice to go is a good starting point: a great place to stay, a fabulous meal or simply somewhere interesting to visit can all make a memorable weekend. It just depends what you're looking for. With that in mind, we've divided the book into chapters which roughly correspond to the kind of weekend you're after. Having said that, there is a lot of cross-fertilisation between chapters. Some of the venues for weekends on the coast might equally well suit a romantic interlude or a family trip away; some of the luxury breaks might be equally good for a health-and-beauty weekend.

This book doesn't pretend to be comprehensive – everyone will know pubs and hotels that they feel should have been included – but what it does do is provide some suggestions of places that we have visited and enjoyed and feel that others would too. The best starting point for using this book is probably to decide what kind of weekend you want and who you are going with. It may well not be appropriate to take an ageing aunt to somewhere with mirrored ceilings or a small child on a weekend of daredevil activity. However, it's worth looking at all the chapters as you might find that we've listed the perfect country pub in the Gourmet Weekends chapter, for example, because it serves exceptionally good scoff.

It's also well worth remembering that many places get booked up long in advance, especially during Bank Holiday weekends or holidays. Also, it's a good idea, if you are staying in a hotel with a spa, to book your appointments well in advance rather than waiting till you arrive. But if you are planning a weekend at the last minute, don't despair: you can sometimes find a lucky late vacancy by calling when hotels know they have had cancellations. If you have your heart set on going somewhere particular you may have to be creative – ask for a good local bed and breakfast or pub and go to the hotel for dinner or lunch, or ask for day rates for spas and health clubs and stay somewhere else.

Whatever your reason for going away, we hope that our suggestions will inspire you to venture out of London and enjoy a couple of days away from the smoke.

USEFUL INFORMATION

NATIONAL RAIL ENQUIRIES HELPLINE
☎ 0345 484950

For train times and fares information. Calls charged at local rate.

THE LANDMARK TRUST
☎ 01628 825925

The Landmark Trust is an independent charity that rescues architecturally interesting and historic buildings at risk and gives them a new lease of life by letting them for self-catering holidays. Handbook of all 166 properties £9.50 inc p&p, refundable against first booking. Exact location and directions are only given on booking.

ROMANTIC & LUXURY WEEKENDS

Some of the best romantic weekends are completely unplanned but, if you have set your heart on having a very special break away, it's probably best to give it a little planning and forethought.

Of course, everyone will have their own ideas about what makes the perfect romantic weekend for them but there are certain factors that can help to make or mar your stay. Location is obviously of prime importance. Whilst it is entirely possible to have the most romantic experience of your life in a Travel Lodge on the M1, a beautiful setting is more likely to put you in the right frame of mind! Whether it's an intimate pub in a secluded village, a grand country-house hotel or a simple but pretty cottage – if it's in the right spot it should help to do the trick.

However, even the most perfect location won't work its magic if everything else is wrong. Thick walls are clearly essential. If you're planning a weekend of passion you won't want to have to appear red-faced at breakfast the next morning, knowing that all the other guests have heard exactly what you've been up to. Equally, you won't want to be part of anyone else's romantic encounters.

Great service of the unobtrusive kind is also of paramount importance. If you need extra towels, room service, iced champagne or whatever, you don't want to be hanging around waiting for them but neither do you want to be constantly interrupted as you whisper sweet nothings over dinner.

A large and comfortable bed should be your next consideration. Two single beds pushed together so that one of you always slips down the gap simply won't do. And, of course, freshly laundered, crisp linen sheets are essential.

The ambient temperature must be right – a stifling bedroom with windows that won't open is not conducive to romance and nor is a freezing-cold room in which you need to keep your thermals on.

A good restaurant, either in the hotel or very close to where you are staying, will also make a big contribution to your enjoyment. You won't want to drive for miles after a good dinner, nor will you want to miss out on a decent bottle of wine because one of you is driving.

Of course, you may not be planning a romantic weekend but simply want to celebrate a special occasion, anniversary or birthday. If you are going to spend money on a really special weekend, you need to be sure that you're going to get your money's worth. Just because a hotel calls itself a country-house hotel and has knicker-blind curtains by the mile, it doesn't mean that it's automatically suitable – or any good.

Bearing in mind that not everyone has elastic pockets – even for a special event – we've included a wide range of properties, from bed and breakfast, self-catering cottages, castles, temples and lighthouses, up to the very grandest and most expensive hotels. If your chosen hotel seems out of reach, why not book up in low season, when rates can drop dramatically? Not only that but some hotels will upgrade you to a better room if there is space. So you might find yourself in a luxury suite at a knock-down price.

WHAT TO TAKE FOR A ROMANTIC BREAK
A partner
Glamorous underwear and night clothes
Scented, luxurious bath oils
A pair of wellies, for long walks
Candles, to create atmosphere
Exquisite morsels of easy-to-prepare food, and bottles of
    champagne, if you're going self-catering
A pashmina for cool evenings
Scent or aftershave
Shades, for clandestine weekends
Flattering swimwear
A racy novel, such as *Lady Chatterley's Lover* or the latest Jilly Cooper

WHAT NOT TO TAKE
The children or the in-laws
Winceyette pyjamas
Gardening or cookery books
Mobile phone
Laptop computer
Any tired-looking items of clothing or footwear, particularly
    grey underwear

If you do want a romantic weekend minus the kids you could always book them into:

PIPPA POP-INS

ADDRESS 430 Fulham Road, London SW6
☎ 0171 385 2458

If a reliable Granny or Auntie fails to materialise, make sure you still get your romantic weekend by giving the kids their own weekend break at Pippa Pop-Ins children's hotel. The hotel occupies a cheerful-looking town house at the Fulham Broadway end of Fulham Road and caters for children aged 2–12. Lots of jolly japes are organised to keep them happy, such as looking for fairies at the bottom of the garden or dinner parties, for the older ones. The children can be left from 5pm on Friday night, allowing you time to get to your destination calm and reassured that your children will be looked after and will have a good time in your absence.

- **COST** *£50 per night for Friday, Saturday or Sunday night*

BERKSHIRE

CLIVEDEN

ADDRESS Cliveden, Taplow, near Maidenhead, Berks SL6 0JF
☎ 01628 668561   **FAX** 01628 661837

Cliveden enjoys the almost-unheard-of distinction of being as good as it is cracked up to be. If you want a weekend of unparalleled luxury, this is the place to go. The erstwhile home of Nancy Astor, this small stately home is set in beautiful grounds, owned by the National Trust and overlooking the Thames and is only about a 30-minute drive out of London, provided that the traffic is on your side. As a guest, you really do feel that you are staying in a private house, albeit a very grand one, rather than paying to stay in a hotel. The bedrooms are prettily decorated with antique furniture as well as having all modern conveniences, such as fax machines and VCRs. Huge bathrooms have old fittings and enormously deep baths for wallowing in. Anyone over 40 will experience a certain frisson at being able to swim in the very pool where Christine Keeler so famously frolicked. There is also a smart indoor pool and a beauty centre, where you can indulge in treatments and massages.

- **MOST ROMANTIC ROOM** *Go for the luxurious Lady Astor Suite, which was Nancy's own bedroom when she lived in the house and has fantastic views over the river.*
- **WHERE TO DINE** *Either at Waldo's in the basement, which serves exceptionally good food, very reasonably priced for the standard, or the Terrace Restaurant on the ground floor*
- **WHAT TO DO** *Wander round the beautiful gardens, visit nearby Windsor, or just revel in the surroundings and lap up the luxury*

- **COST** *'The Cliveden Experience' weekend costs from £700 per couple for a two-night stay in a double room mid-week or from £795 at weekends, with breakfast and dinner in the Terrace Restaurant. The Lady Astor Suite costs £775 per night. Set dinner at Waldo's costs £52 per person and includes an amuse-gueule and four courses. Hungry foodies may like to dry the nine-course 'tasting menu' at £82 per head*
- **HOW TO GET THERE** *Take the M4 out of London and leave at Junction 7 (Slough West). Follow the A4, signposted Maidenhead. After 11½ miles you will come to a junction with the B476, signposted Taplow, Bourne End, Cliveden. The gates of Cliveden are on the left, after about 2½ miles*

SPRING COTTAGE (at Cliveden)

ADDRESS c/o National Trust Holiday Cottage Booking Office
☎ 01225 791199 The National Trust

If money is no object and you really want to hide away from it all, then book Spring Cottage, which is part of the hotel and was inhabited by Stephen Ward, the society osteopath at the centre of the Profumo scandal. Breakfast arrives fresh each morning from the hotel and you can choose to dine in the hotel itself or have your meals in total privacy in the cottage. Included in the price is a butler and use of the Belmont, a 1930s slipper launch.

- **COST** *A two-night stay costs £2,400 midweek or £2,800 at the weekend, for the cottage, butler and use of the boat*

NATIONAL TRUST COTTAGES (in the Cliveden grounds)

ADDRESS c/o National Trust Holiday Cottage Booking Office
☎ 01225 791199 The National Trust

If you can't manage the costs of Spring Cottage but like the idea of staying on the river bank, rent one of the two National Trust cottages within spitting distance of Spring Cottage and wander up to Waldo's (see page 144) for dinner.

NEW COTTAGE

ADDRESS c/o National Trust Holiday Cottage Booking Office
☎ 01225 791199 The National Trust

Two storeys with two twin bedrooms, sitting room with wood-burning stove and large kitchen.

- **COST** *From around £130 to £251 for two days, depending on season*

FERRY COTTAGE

ADDRESS c/o National Trust Holiday Cottage Booking Office
☎ 01225 791199 The National Trust

Single storey with one twin and one double bedroom, sitting room with open fire, kitchen/dining room with French windows to patio and bathroom.

- **COST** *From around £96 to £244 for two days, depending on season*

BUCKINGHAMSHIRE

THE GOTHIC TEMPLE (AT STOWE)
ADDRESS c/o The Landmark Trust, Shottesbrooke, Maidenhead, Berkshire SL6 3SW
☎ 01628 825925 The Landmark Trust

Gothic fantasists will go mad for this temple in the grounds of Stowe school. This is not the place to go if you want to skip about in a skimpy nightie or negligée, as the heating is somewhat erratic. However, the interior is stunning, with circular rooms and vaulted ceilings – the largest gorgeously painted with heraldic motifs. There are two double bedrooms on the first floor and a belvedere at the top of the staircase, with a great view over Capability Brown's gardens. This is also a great place for dog-owners to go, as you can bring the dog with you.

- **WHERE TO DINE** *Villiers Hotel, Buckingham*
- **WHAT TO DO** *Visit Oxford (see Cultural Weekends, page 175) or local stately homes, such as Claydon House, Winslow Hall or Wotton House*
- **COST** *Friday-to-Sunday lets cost from £389 to £600, depending on the season*
- **HOW TO GET THERE** *Take the M1 and come off at the A421, towards Buckingham. Then take the A422 towards Brackley and then follow signposts to Stowe School*

CUMBRIA

THE SAMLING
ADDRESS Dovenest, Ambleside Road, Windermere, Cumbria LA23
☎ 015394 31922 **FAX** 01539 430400

The ultimate luxury hideaway for a romantic weekend, much frequented by Tom and Nicole. The brainchild of Roger MacKechnie, known for being the creator of the Phileas Fogg snacks, it derives its name from an ancient Norse word for a gathering or celebration. Although not strictly a hotel, the house and 70-acre grounds have been restored for the sole purpose of providing a private and exclusive venue for small groups of people who either wish to confer, celebrate or simply relax, without any distractions. Unlike a hotel, you cannot just book a room but have to take over the whole house. This makes it perfect for family reunions or really extravagant romantic gestures. All of the ten suites have fantastic views of Lake Windermere and are stylishly decorated and equipped with CD players, faxes, TV and video. Best of all, there are no distractions, no prying strangers and your personal chef on duty 24 hours a day. If you want to wander lonely as a cloud then there are plenty of lovely walks, or you can fly away in a balloon or sample water activities on the lake. And, after a hectic day, relax with a glass of champagne or contemplate the view from the outdoor hot tub offering a spectacular view of Lake Windermere.

- **MOST ROMANTIC ROOM** *All are fabulous and individual and all have wonderful views of the lake. Presumably if you're taking over the whole house you could change rooms twice a night, if you so desired. Manmire is a particularly spectacular bedroom*
- **WHERE TO DINE** *Whenever and wherever you want. Your personal chef, Des Yare, will create menus for your stay but expect to find dishes such as: duck liver and confit terrine with a truffle salad; scallops braised in their shells, with Noilly-Prat sauce; roast guinea fowl with wild garlic, asparagus and truffle foam; pan-fried sea bass, with saffron mash and bouillabaisse sauce; oven-roasted rump of lamb, with a lime pickle and coriander sauce; nougat glacé, with raspberry and Sauternes coulis; crème brûlée, scented with lemon verbena and served with lavender cookies; fruit terrine with champagne jelly and fruit sorbet. Tom and Nicole used to bring their whole entourage, including their personal chef, but now prefer to come en famille and trust their meals to Des*
- **WHAT TO DO** *Boat trips on the lake, fishing for Windermere char. Visit John Ruskin or William Wordsworth's houses*
- **COST** *£395 per couple sharing, assuming there are six couples. For small groups a minimum fee of £2,370 per 24 hours applies. This includes dinner, accommodation, breakfast, morning coffee, lunch, afternoon tea and all beverages, wines/spirits on the list*
- **HOW TO GET THERE** *Although it's a bit of a hike, it's well worth the effort. It takes 4 hours by car and 1½ hours by helicopter. The Samling has its own helipad and guests can either come in their own or hire one for the trip. By car, take the M1, M62 and then M6 and turn off at Junction 36 onto the A65. Follow signs to Kendal, and then Windermere, then Ambleside. Before Ambleside, pass the Hotel Lowood and take the next right. The Samling is 50m up the hill*

ESSEX

MAISON TALBOOTH HOTEL AND LE TALBOOTH RESTAURANT

ADDRESS Stratford Road, Dedham, Colchester, Essex CO7 6HN
☎ 01206 322367 Hotel   01206 323150 Restaurant
The Maison Talbooth is a Victorian house with ten bedrooms, overlooking beautiful Dedham Vale. All the bedrooms are a decent

size and some have sumptuous bathrooms – The Keats Suite, for instance, has a round bath with marble pillars and mirrors. Those planning a romantic weekend might like to know that the Maison Talbooth has featured in the *Sex Maniac's Diary* and was given a five-star rating for sex! Breakfast and light meals are available in the hotel, but for dinner and lunch you need to visit Le Talbooth Restaurant. This is a pleasant walk down the road – or a minute's drive in a courtesy car.

Le Talbooth's cooking has won many awards but can be a little hit and miss. Some dishes are stunning, whilst some can be mediocre. However, what Le Talbooth really has in its favour is the setting. The half-timbered restaurant is right on the River Stour by a pretty bridge. On summer evenings you can take a pleasant stroll to the small bar. I have a lifelong affection for Le Talbooth, as one of my children was very nearly born there – early and after a very good dinner! From the end of May to the beginning of September they hold a barbecue instead of regular dinners on Sunday evenings. This may not be to everybody's taste, but it is nicely done and makes a relaxing and informal end to a weekend. If the weather's good you can sit out on the terrace by the river and enjoy the view.

- **MOST ROMANTIC ROOM** *The Shakespeare Suite*
- **WHERE TO DINE** *In the hotel's own restaurant half a mile down the road*
- **WHAT TO DO** *Visit Constable country, Colchester, Lavenham, Long Melford, Flatford Mill, Ipswich and Bury St Edmunds*
- **COST** *Principal suites £175 per night. Standard suites from £115 to £150 per night including continental breakfast*
- **HOW TO GET THERE** *Take the M11 and M25 (eastbound). From the M25, take the A12 past Colchester. Le Talbooth and Maison Talbooth are signposted from the A12. By train, take a direct train from Liverpool Street to Colchester and then a 15-minute taxi ride*

GLOUCESTERSHIRE

DREWS HOUSE
ADDRESS Leighterton, Glos GL8 8UN
☎ 01666 890230 **E-MAIL** proudlock@freeuk.com

A bed and breakfast may not be your first choice for a romantic weekend but, if you don't want to stay in a stuffy hotel, don't want to self-cater or are counting the cost, Lena Proudlock's traditional Cotswold farmhouse is the perfect solution. Straight out of the pages of a glossy magazine, Lena's house is decorated in chic Gustavian Swedish style. Lena herself is a designer – her house has recently featured in *Interiors* and *Country Living* and can often be seen as the backdrop for design features. Naturally, the six bedrooms are stylishly decked out – one with a four-poster bed designed by Lena herself. Lena's stylish touches include hand-crocheted bed-spreads and fresh flowers. Delicious breakfasts are served in the dining room, with blazing log fires. If you fall in love with the furniture you can buy the pieces from Lena's own range.

• **MOST ROMANTIC ROOM** Lena's own room with painted furniture, antique portraits, four-poster bed and ensuite bathroom

• **WHERE TO DINE** Lena can provide simple dinners in her Swedish kitchen or can direct you to lots of nice local pubs and restaurants

• **WHAT TO DO** Visit Tetbury, which is full of antique shops; 3 minutes to Westonbirt Arboretum for walks and the most beautiful trees; Bath; convenient for Badminton Horse Trials (5 minutes away) and Gatcombe Park Horse Trials

• **COST** If you want the whole house to yourself for complete privacy, or you want to take over the house for a family occasion or a house party, the total cost would be from £400 for two nights for up to 10 people. Bed and breakfast is £30 per person per night, excluding dinner

• **HOW TO GET THERE** Take the M4 to Junction 18 and then follow the A46 towards Stroud. After 10 miles, follow the signs to Leighterton

THE TEMPLE

ADDRESS Stancombe, near Wootton-under-Edge, Glos GL11 6AU
☎ 01386 701177 Rural Retreats

Legend has it that, in 1815, the Reverend Purnell-Edwards, the original owner of Stancombe House, fell in love with a local gypsy girl and built a temple as their love-nest. Access was via a labyrinth of tunnels which were too narrow for his portly wife to negotiate. You too can stay in this Grade-1-listed Doric temple, which is situated in the famous garden of Stancombe Park at the foot of the Cotswold escarpment. It has recently been extensively renovated and refurbished in an Etruscan-Chinois syle with the help of a grant from English Heritage. Set on the edge of a lake, it is utterly private with wonderful views and all mod cons. A dinner-delivery service is also available, so you can have dinner al fresco outside your temple by the lake in the moonlight. What bliss!

• **WHERE TO DINE** Why go anywhere?

• **WHAT TO DO** Lots of walks nearby; go swimming in the lake in the summer

• **COST** From £413 for 3 nights

• **HOW TO GET THERE** From the M5, take J14. Follow the B4059 to Wootton. At the crossroads, take the B4058 to Charfield for 3 miles. In Wootton-under-Edge, take the B4060 to Dursley, pass North Nibley, take the left hand side to Stinchcombe, take the lane past the lodge, turning to the temple on the right after the bend

HAMPSHIRE

CHEWTON GLEN HOTEL

ADDRESS Christchurch Road, New Milton, Hants BH25 6QS
☎ 01425 275341   **FAX** 01425 272310

A honeymooners' paradise, the Chewton Glen is the place to go to be pampered. On the edge of the New Forest, the 18th-century Georgian hotel has 70 acres of lawns and parkland. You are guaranteed plenty of personal attention and utterly luxurious surroundings. Scones and clotted cream are a must on the immaculately laid out lawns but the presence of Barbours, maps and wellies in the hall reminds you that you really ought to explore. When you do, wend your way down the hotel's private path to the sea.

• **MOST ROMANTIC ROOM** *The Marriot Suite – light and airy, it overlooks the croquet lawn and woodlands. The suite has its own balcony, where you can have breakfast, lunch or dinner à deux, and a lovely sitting room*

• **WHERE TO DINE** *The gourmet conservatory restaurant. Head chef Pierre Chevillard's typical menu might include: pistou of langoustine soup, garnished with mussels and pine kernels, and braised fillet of sea bass with shiitake mushrooms and beansprouts, flavoured with coriander and ginger*

• **WHAT TO DO** *Facilities at the hotel: turn into a body beautiful at the fabulous spa, which includes over 40 treatments; treatments for men; gym; personal training; hairdressing salon; 17m lap pool and indoor and outdoor tennis courts that, unlike those at some other hotels, are in tip-top condition, with a resident tennis pro*

• **LOCAL ATTRACTIONS** *Lymington, the New Forest, Beaulieu*

• **COST** *Rooms from £245 per night. Special breaks are sometimes available, especially in the winter*

• **HOW TO GET THERE** *By rail, London Waterloo to New Milton (1 hour 50 minutes) – the hotel can arrange a taxi to meet you at the station. By road, from the M25, take the M3 and then the M27(W). Follow directions for Bournemouth and then, at Junction 1, take the A337 as if going to Lymington. Turn onto the A35, following signs for New Milton. Follow signs for Walkford on the left*

THE LADYCROSS ESTATE

ADDRESS Beaulieu, Hants SO4 27QL
☎ 01590 622973   **FAX** 01590 622860

For those for whom a cosy country cottage with a blazing log fire is the ideal romantic location, the Ladycross Estate cottages are the perfect weekend venue. You get all the benefits of your own cottage, plus a few extras, without any of the hard work involved in the upkeep or maintenance.

Each of the fully self-contained cottages is individually furnished with a mixture of old and new furniture, prints, antiques and bric-a-brac, and has its own garden or patio. The 45-acre estate means that you are well away from hustle and bustle but still near enough to civilisation and the odd pub and restaurant.

Equipped with crisp linen and soft towels, the cottages are thoroughly cleaned and prepared before each visit by a team of caring housekeepers. There are thoughtful touches such as coffee filter machines, dishwashers and hairdryers.

Because Ladycross believes that breaks should be fun, most of the cottages have a four-poster bed and each one has a theme. Poop Deck has two sunken baths and a four-poster double bed, while the Crew's State Room has two single beds and a bathroom opening on to a walled atrium, with pool and fountain. There is a selection of nautical prints, a ship's lamp and even a ship in a bottle. Royal Box has a collection of theatre programmes and books on Royalty; Beaulieu Cottage and the Box have an automotive theme. Coachman's Halt has beams and horsebrasses and Fisherman's Tales a stuffed pike and river maps. All the cottages have a second colour TV in the master bedroom, magazines, books and selection of board games – should you run out of ideas of games of your own to play.

You can collect your own eggs for breakfast from the estate's hens, and there are pigs called Bunty and Grunty and a donkey called Dan. And you can book a continental breakfast hamper, champagne and flowers to get you started on the catering front.

• **MOST ROMANTIC ROOM** *Stars is a one-bedroomed apartment with a four-poster bed with a silver mirrored ceiling. It was originally the bachelor pad of the son of the family in the 1920s and is decorated in 20s-style silver, pink, black and white*

• **WHERE TO DINE** *If the thought of having to cook over the weekend has put you off going self-catering in the past, this needn't be a problem. Fish and chips and Chinese take-aways are available in Brockenhurst village 3 miles away and there are plenty of good local restaurants. Try Le Poussin or Le Blaireau in Brockenhurst, Chewton Glen, the Montague Arms at Beaulieu, The Master Builder's House at Buckler's Hard, the Red Lion at Boldre, or the Hobler at Lymington*

• **WHAT TO DO** *Riding at one of six local stables • Beaches only 4 miles away • Fishing, both fly and coarse, at Leominstead, also 4 miles away • Polo 2 miles away • Three golf courses • Sailing and windsurfing • Local attractions include: National Motor Museum at Beaulieu; Buckler's Hard; wagon rides; Paulton's Bird Park; Marwell Zoo; Isle of Wight; Palace House; Broadlands and Stratfield Say, the house of the Duke of Wellington*

• **COST** *From £99 plus VAT*

• **HOW TO GET THERE** *From the M25, take the M3, M27(W) and the A337 from Cadnam, through Lyndhurst to Brockenhurst. Turn left onto the B3055 towards Beaulieu and the Ladycross Estate is just off the B3055*

OXFORDSHIRE

LE MANOIR AUX QUAT' SAISONS

ADDRESS Church Road, Great Milton, Oxon OX44 7PD
☎ 01844 278881   **FAX** 01844 278847

Raymond Blanc's fabulous country-house hotel is the ideal location for a romantic tryst or for celebrating a milestone birthday or anniversary. 'It's all about celebration,' says Blanc, 'and creating fantasy.' The 15th-century manor house is just outside Oxford and lives up to expectations.

The rooms have been extended and updated by designer Emily Todhunter. The new rooms are themed so you can choose your own room according to the season or occasion. You could choose the grey-blue frosted Snow Room for ice maidens, the Opium Suite for hot passion, with its own private garden and pond, or the Vettriano Room for out-and-out romance. There are also some charming Provençal-inspired rooms in the converted barn.

- **MOST ROMANTIC ROOM** *Must be the Dovecote – ideal for honeymoon couples. Here you are removed from the main building in romantic seclusion*
- **WHERE TO DINE** *In Blanc's two-star, Michelin-award-winning restaurant. The new airy conservatory has tables well spaced out for private conversation and 'playing footsie' as Blanc so charmingly puts it. Choose from the £79 per head Menu Gourmand, which includes seasonal dishes using herbs and vegetables from the gardens. Sample dishes include: medley of asparagus spears and morels and pan-fried fillet and spit-roasted best-end or saddle of suckling pig with marjoram jus*
- **WHAT TO DO** *Wander round the Japanese water gardens and walled vegetable and herb gardens or take out a bike and explore the local villages of Great Milton and Little Milton. There is a soon-to-be-completed Givenchy spa and tennis courts. Visit the Swan pub and antique shop in Tetsworth. Newington Garden Centre, near Stadhampton, specialises in unusual plants*
- **COST** *Standard rooms from £230 per night. Special 'midweek escapes' available*
- **HOW TO GET THERE** *Take the M40 from London to Junction 7 (the A329) going towards Reading. About 3 miles later look for a signpost for Le Manoir*

THE CRAZY BEAR

ADDRESS Bear Lane, Stadhampton, Oxon OX44 7UR
☎ 01865 890714

The name ought to give you a bit of a clue but, as you approach the Crazy Bear along a country lane, you would be forgiven for thinking it was any old country pub. However, the minute you step through the door you realise that you could be entering a parallel universe. With overtones of Tom Sharpe there is a blow-up doll and a seven-foot stuffed bear in the bar, where, instead of the draught Hook Norton, you will find champagne on tap and a variety of exotic drinks, including frozen Mars Bar vodka. There are five bedrooms, each of which is decorated in a unique and totally over-the-top fashion.

• **MOST ROMANTIC ROOM** *Room 5, approached by an oversized Alice in Wonderland door which takes you into a large, loft-style room with an oversized bed, leopard-skin throw and carpet. It has a huge bedroom (with a bath big enough for six), giant TV and lots of Molton Brown toiletries. Big mirrors hang from the wall and even the ceiling. A wrought-iron, four-poster bed completes the picture*

• **WHERE TO DINE** *There's nothing weird about the Crazy Bear's cooking, which is seriously good. Try the newly opened Thai Brasserie. Breakfast is set up on a table by the fire. Very relaxed, stylish and informal*

• **WHAT TO DO** *A 10-minute drive to Oxford City Centre, or visit Blenheim Palace. Otherwise you can arrange to partake in Action Sports such as water-skiing, paragliding or shooting*

• **COST** *£100 per night for a double room, including continental breakfast*

• **HOW TO GET THERE** *Take Junction 7 (A329) off the M40 towards Reading and then turn right onto the B480 to Stadhampton*

BRUERN STABLE COTTAGES
ADDRESS Red Brick House, Bruern, Chipping Norton, Oxon OX7 6PY
☎ 01993 830415   **FAX** 01993 831750

Bruern Stable Cottages have been beautifully converted from a Victorian stable block built to accommodate the horses, carriages and groom of Bruern Abbey, a classical 18th-century house. Converted by Michael Astor's widow, Judy, in 1992, the cottages are much more luxurious than you would expect from a rented holiday cottage. If you are planning a romantic getaway but don't want to stay in a country-style hotel but equally don't feel that a Baby Belling and a kettle that doesn't boil don't add much to the general ambience, then this is definitely for you. Saratoga is reckoned to be everyone's favourite honeymoon cottage or the perfect choice for an autumn or winter romantic break. This perfect little love-nest is attractively decorated and furnished with proper grown-up furniture, including a blue and white painted faux-bamboo four-poster bed and a double-height drawing room with an open fire.

• **WHERE TO DINE** *No need to go anywhere. There is an exclusive range of frozen foods prepared by Mrs Astor's chef, Colin Bolam, made with fresh ingredients*

• **WHAT TO DO** *Lovely walks in rolling Cotswold countryside; fishing at Cornby Park; tennis; visits to Blenheim, Stratford and Burford; golf; horseriding*

- **COST** *Available at weekends from 5 Nov to 17 March, Saratoga costs £206 for a three-day break*
- **HOW TO GET THERE** *From the M40, take Junction 8 and then go west on the A40 to Oxford. Continue on the A40, following signs for Cheltenham and Whitney. Where the A40 crosses the A361 at Burford, turn right at the roundabout. Travel down the High Street to where the road crosses a single-lane bridge controlled by traffic lights. Just over the bridge, turn left at a mini-roundabout, following the signs for Stowe and the A424. After 3 miles, at a crest sign marked Bruern, turn right. The single-track road descends into Evenload valley. After ⅓ mile, turn right at a staggered crossroads and immediately left. Continue for 2 miles and you will see Bruern Abbey on the right and the stable cottages on your left*

SHROPSHIRE

THE TEMPLE

ADDRESS Badger, Badger Dingle, Bridgenorth, Shropshire WV6 7JP
☎ 0171 930 2212 Book via the Vivat Trust

The Temple is a honeymooners' hideaway, the perfect place in which to do a vanishing act. Lovingly restored by the Vivat Trust, a small charity devoted to rescuing interesting historic buildings, the Temple is a neo-classical pavillion and folly set in Badger Dingle, Badger, a romantic 40-acre landscape. Originally designed as a teahouse in 1782 by James Wyatt, the Temple gives you magnificent views of the wooded ravine. Inside, it has been converted and furnished in neo-classical style but with all modern amenities – Neff kitchen units, Farrow & Ball paintwork and Osborne & Little furnishings. Walk for miles in the woods where there are ornamental pools and waterfalls – all in all, a complete retreat from urban living.

- **WHERE TO DINE** *The Red Cow Inn; the Dartmouth Arms; or the Patshull Hotel*
- **WHAT TO DO** *Should you wish to escape from this paradise, you can visit the castle at Bridgnorth and take the cliff steam railway*
- **COST** *A 3-night mini-break costs from £260. Weekly rentals also available from £400*
- **HOW TO GET THERE** *From the M25, take the M40, M5(N), M6(W) and M54. Leave the M54 at Junction 3 and turn off the roundabout following the signs to the Aerospace Museum/RAF Cosford. Go straight through the traffic lights (less than ¼ mile), about 200 yards on from these, turn right into Albrighton. You will reach the village after about a mile. Continue into the village centre; on reaching the Crown Pub, turn right into Cross Road. Continue on this road for about a mile. At the main road, A464, turn right, signed to Telford. 100 yards on, turn left to Burnhill Green, which is 2 miles further on. Continue out of the village, past the tall trees on the left, and past the turn to Patshull. Take the next*

*right by a house on the corner, signed to Badger. Approaching
Badger village, drive beneath the bridge. To reach the Temple,
turn left and continue through the village until you reach a
T-junction. Turn right on to this road, then turn immediately right
by the church, in between the two pools. Opposite the church is
a small track to your right, leading to green double gates. The
Temple is through both sets of green double gates and about ½
mile along the Carriage Drive (keep driving till the end, a safety
light should come on when you are near)*

SOMERSET

BABINGTON HOUSE

ADDRESS Kilmersdon, near Frome, Somerset BA11 3RW
☎ 01373 812266   **FAX** 01373 813866

Babington house manages to be a country house whilst, at the
same time, being the antithesis of everything that country-house
hotels stand for. More like staying with friends than staying in a
hotel, a visit here gives you all the facilities of a hotel but provided
with a laid-back, informal air. The relaxed attitude extends to the
gardens: whereas in other hotels the loungers would be lined up
like hospital beds, here they are casually dotted all over the place
so that it is perfectly possible to spend an afternoon lying on a
lounger with Proust totally undisturbed. This place is very hip, so
don't expect traditional afternoon tea with silver teapots and
scones and cream: it's all very casual and relaxed.

• **MOST ROMANTIC ROOM** *Room 12 in the coachhouse has a 7-foot
bed, digital TV screen, DVD video and fabulous lighting. In the
enormous bathroom there is a freestanding bath, a TV and a large
walk-in shower – with room for a cast of thousands. The lights can
be dimmed and the excellent sound system piped through. And
there's no messing about with doll-sized bottles of Country Diary
of an Edwardian Lady potions and lotions: instead, you get giant
bottles of Babington's own range of fab shampoos, shower gels
and so on*

• **WHERE TO DINE** *The breakfast room is open 24 hours a day; you
can have a traditional pizza cooked in a kiln oven or eat in the
dining room for a slightly more formal affair. For romantics who
just can't leave their room, there is an all-day-breakfast room
service*

• **WHAT TO DO** *Babington has a really lovely spa in a converted
cowshed, called the Cowshed. Here you can have a massage
from the super-fit Assistant Manager, Roger. Choose your massage
oil to suit your mood – Stroppy Cow, Stressed Cow or even Horny
Cow are popular options. (See also entry in Health and Beauty
Weekends, page 135). There are super indoor and outdoor pools.
The outdoor pool is heated to 85°F and is surrounded by woodland*

• **COST** *From £210 per room per night*

- **HOW TO GET THERE** *Take the M3 to Junction 8 (A303). Then take the A36 towards Warminster and the A362 towards Frome. Head towards Radstock on the A362. Come to Brickland Dinham and take a left turn signposted to Mells. You will see Babington House on the left*

SUFFOLK

THE WHITE HART INN
ADDRESS 11 High Street, Nayland, Suffolk CO6 4JS
☎ 01206 263382

A reasonably priced and terrific-value romantic destination is the White Hart. Part-owned by Michel Roux, this local inn has just been refurbished. Pretty individually decorated rooms provide good-value accommodation whilst the bistro-style restaurant offers wholesome farmhouse fare with a French influence.

- **MOST ROMANTIC ROOM** *Caroline, which has a regal feel*
- **WHERE TO DINE** *At the inn itself, of course. Typical dishes include: Thai fish cakes with sweet and sour chilli relish; local game terrine with Cumberland sauce; breast of local wood pigeon and extremely good* crème brûlée
- **WHAT TO DO** *Dedham Vale; Flatford Mill*
- **COST** *Around £69.50 per night for a double room including full English breakfast. Starters, around £4.50; main courses, about £9; puddings £4*
- **HOW TO GET THERE** *From London, take the M11, M25 and then A12 as far as Colchester. From Colchester take the A134 towards Sudbury. Turn right at the first turning for Nayland off the A134 and the White Hart is on your left, in the centre of the village. By rail, take the train from Liverpool Street to Colchester and take a taxi from the station. Nayland is around 7 miles outside Colchester*

HOPE HOUSE
ADDRESS High Street, Yoxford, Saxmundham, Suffolk IP17 3HP
☎ 01728 668281

If you are looking for a romantic and luxurious weekend but cost is a consideration, then Hope is in sight. This beautiful Queen-Anne-style house has three *en-suite* bedrooms, all fabulously decorated with an eclectic mix of antiques and modern, comfortable pieces. The reception rooms have hand-made carpets and matching upholstery. There is a romantic walled garden through which to wander hand in hand. Owners Michael Block and Roger Mildren are welcoming without being intrusive. And, if you are planning a special celebration, you can take over the whole house exclusively, for a country-house-style party for between six and ten people – in which case Michael will also provide dinner for you and your guests. In winter, there are log fires in the drawing room and dining room to make you feel really cosy and at home.

- **MOST ROMANTIC ROOM** Co-owner Michael Block assures us that all the rooms are decorated to the same standard but, when pressed to express a preference, recommends the Blue Room, which overlooks a formal parterre and has pretty Colefax and Fowler wallpaper
- **WHERE TO DINE** Locally at: the Lighthouse at Aldeburgh; Hedgehogs at Kelsale; the Crown at Snape; or the Crown at Southwold. Good local pubs include the Mosaic and the Griffin, both in Yoxford. If you are taking over Hope House on a house-party basis, Michael's dinner menu might include such dishes as: warm Roquefort cheesecake, served with pears in balsamic dressing; crispy duck breast with cranberry juice and parsnip purée; and a fantastic lemon tart à la River Café
- **WHAT TO DO** Shops: Suffolk House Antiques, High Street, Yoxford, specialises in 17th- and early-18th-century furniture and accessories, wonderful oak dressers and refectory tables, candlesticks, tapestries, pictures and early Delftware. Open every day except Wednesday and Sunday, 10.00 to 13.00, 14.15 to 17.15. Visit Aldeburgh (page 43), Southwold (page 60) and Framlingham (page 103)
- **COST** Bed and breakfast is £90 per double room for a single night or £75 per double room per night for a minimum two-night stay. Country-house weekends are individually tailored but an approximate price is £70 per person per night, including dinner and drinks
- **HOW TO GET THERE** From London, take the M11, M25 (eastbound) and then the A12 past Woodbridge; Yoxford is on the A1120, off the A12

THE ANCIENT HOUSE (AT CLARE)

ADDRESS c/o The Landmark Trust, Shottesbrooke, Maidenhead, Berkshire SL6 3SW

☎ 01628 825925 The Landmark Trust

The Landmark Trust is an independent charity that rescues and restores architecturally interesting and historic buildings at risk, giving them a future and renewed life by letting them for self-catering holidays. Full details of all 166 properties are available in the handbook (price £9.50 including p&p which is refundable against the first booking). Anyone who hankers after a perfect English country cottage will find that the Ancient House fits the bill. This pretty half-timbered building bears the date 1473 in the pargeting (raised plaster decoration) so typical of East Anglia. The house was bought in the early 1930s by a local farmer to save it from being dismantled and transported to the States, where it would probably now be called Ye Olde Englishe House. Half of the house is now a local museum for local agricultural artefacts and items relating to the wool trade. Fortunately for guests, the museum is staffed on a voluntary basis, so is not open all of the time. The other half provides very cosy accommodation, with beamed ceilings and sloping floors. The sitting room has an inglenook fireplace and a bay window with views over the neighbouring churchyard. If you want to sit outside and sniff the fresh country air, there is a small, walled, private garden.

• **WHERE TO DINE** *The Bull at Cavendish; the Chimneys Restaurant at Long Melford*

• **WHAT TO DO** *The castle at Castle Hedingham; Kentwell Hall and Long Melford Hall at Long Melford; Gainsborough's house at Sudbury. Long Melford is famous for its antique shops, which are well worth a browse. Also worth visiting is the factory shop at Vanners Silk Mills in Sudbury, for Turnbull & Asser silk ties and Margaret Howell and Liberty silk scarves at knock-down prices*

• **COST** *Friday to Sunday lets from £237 to £331, depending on the season*

• **HOW TO GET THERE** *Take the M11 out of London, come off at the Bishops Stortford exit (Junction 8). Take the A120 towards Braintree. Turn off on to the A131 towards Sudbury. At Halstead, take the A604 towards Haverhill and then turn on to the A1092, which will take you into Clare*

THE SWAN

ADDRESS High Street, Lavenham, Suffolk CO10 9QA
☎ 0870 4008116 **FAX** 01787 248286

Lavenham is one of the country's most perfectly preserved and unspoilt Tudor towns, and has featured in countless period dramas. The Swan has a cosy atmosphere – loads of heavily timbered public rooms and inglenook fireplaces that house blazing fires in winter. The dining room was added in the 1960s but blends in with the rest of the original building extremely well. At the time of writing, the hotel is about to undergo a major refurbishment at the hands of Ann Boyd, who has worked in the past for Ralph Lauren. The bedrooms are kitted out with dark oak furniture and many have their own fireplaces. The bedrooms are all going to be redone in the refurbishment and the bathrooms improved and updated. Many of the beams are rather low, and anyone over 5 feet 2 inches may find themselves having to duck – padding has been thoughtfully provided on some of the low areas on staircases, to prevent guests from nutting themselves.

The Old Bar was a favourite for US Army Air Corps, based locally during the Second World War, and the bandleader Glenn Miller allegedly had a drink here before his last, fateful flight.

The hotel is very popular with Americans – both veterans who knew it in the 1940s and tourists soaking up Ye Olde Englande.

• **MOST ROMANTIC ROOM** *The Lindsay Room or the Kersey Room which both have four-poster beds*

• **WHERE TO DINE** *The Swan's menu is surprisingly modern and includes such dishes as: cep risotto served with a madeira sauce, £4.50; pan-fried terrine of guinea fowl with sweetbreads £7.50; salad of char-grilled vegetables with truffle dressing £7.25; pan-fried sea bass on potatoes £17.25 and poached cannon of lamb with cabbage farci £17.25*

- **WHAT TO DO** *Gainsborough's house in Sudbury; Lavenham Guildhall; Ickworth House at Bury St Edmunds; Vanner's Silk Mill Factory Shop in Sudbury; loads of antique shops in Long Melford*
- **COST** *From £120 for a double room or £70 per person per night including dinner, bed and breakfast. Weekend breaks available*
- **HOW TO GET THERE** *Take the M11, M25 and A12 to Colchester. From Colchester take the A134 towards Sudbury. From Sudbury, take the B1071 to Lavenham. By train, go from Liverpool Street to Colchester and take a taxi to Lavenham*

HINTLESHAM HALL
ADDRESS Hintlesham, near Ipswich, Suffolk IP8 3NS
☎ 01473 652334   **FAX** 01473 652463

Hintlesham Hall was converted to a restaurant and cookery school from a private house by Robert Carrier. After he sold it in 1984, it was turned into a fully fledged hotel. A beautiful Tudor mansion with an attractive Georgian façade, the house is approached by a long, sweeping drive. This is particularly appealing in darkness, when the lights from the windows and the outdoor illuminations make it look magical. The staff were utterly charming from the minute we arrived. Casually dressed for our weekend dinner, we were sent back to our rooms to change, as no jeans are allowed in the restaurant. However, this was charmingly done so as not to cause the least offence or embarrassment. Our room was in the converted stable block and was ballroom-size, with an opulent, well stocked bathroom. The dining room is architecturally fabulous although we weren't too sure about the lilac walls and multicoloured curtains.

The hotel backs on to a very pretty garden, perfect for romantic strolls before dinner. Hintlesham has its own golf course and leisure club with a work-out room and a heated outdoor swimming pool.

- **MOST ROMANTIC ROOM** *Rosette, with a four-poster bed, an open fire and a view of the lake*
- **WHERE TO DINE** *In the hotel. Our meal started with seared scallops with deep-fried salsify and orange marmalade, followed by fillet of sea bass with chargrilled radicchio and endive, with a Sauternes essence. A good selection of English cheeses and excellent coffee and home-made petits fours finished us off*
- **WHAT TO DO** *Flatford Mill, Dedham; Lavenham; Long Melford*
- **COST** *Small double rooms, £115 per night; good-sized double rooms £150 per night; principal double room, £180 per night; large principal double room, £220. All rates include a generous continental breakfast, newspaper and VAT. A la carte English breakfast is available from £7.50*
- **HOW TO GET THERE** *Take the M11, M25 and then A12 out of London. Proceed towards Ipswich town centre at the A12/A14 interchange roundabout. Turn left at the first set of traffic lights onto the A1071. Continue straight over the next roundabout and you will enter Hintlesham village after about 2 miles. The entrance to*

the hotel is just past the church, on the right-hand side. By rail, take the train to Ipswich from Liverpool Street and then a short taxi ride to the hotel

SUSSEX

THE LIGHTHOUSE

ADDRESS Belle Toute Lighthouse, Beachy Head, East Sussex BN20 0AE
☎ 01323 423520
England's only residential lighthouse, this B&B is very romantic. Situated at Beachy Head, it has two oval-shaped bedrooms and a dining room, with exceptional views. Hearty breakfasts of porridge, pancakes, sausages, and kippers.

• **WHERE TO DINE** *The Tiger, an unspoilt traditional pub, and the Hungry Monk at Jevington*

• **WHAT TO DO** *Energetic walks, kite-powered go-karts or take a luxury boat trip along the coast*

• **COST** *The rooms are from £35 per person per night*

• **HOW TO GET THERE** *From the M25, take Junction 7 (M23) and then the A23. Turn left on to the A27 towards Lewes and follow the signs to Beachy Head*

FOX HALL (AT CHARLTON)

ADDRESS c/o The Landmark Trust, Shottesbrooke, Maidenhead, Berkshire SL6 3SW
☎ 01628 825925 The Landmark Trust
Fox Hall was built for carousing huntsmen, as a place where they could behave as badly as they wished away from the constraints of home. You too can behave badly at this small Palladian building. The magnificent bedroom contains a gilded alcove for the bed and in the pediment over the fireplace is an indicator to show the direction of the wind – vital information for the fox hunter. The bedroom/sitting room is incredibly opulent, with walls clad in hunting-pink damask, lots of elaborate gilding and moulding and antique rugs thrown over wooden floorboards.

• **WHERE TO DINE** *The Angel or the Spread Eagle at Midhurst*

• **WHAT TO DO** *Chichester; Goodwood; Arundel*

• **COST** *Friday to Sunday lets from £359 to £500, depending on the season*

• **HOW TO GET THERE** *Take the A3 out of London. At Petersfield, take the A272 towards Midhurst then the A286 towards Chichester. Charlton is signposted to your left*

AMBERLEY CASTLE

ADDRESS Amberley, near Arundel, Sussex BN18 9ND
☎ 01798 831992 **FAX** 01798 831998
If you've always had a Sleeping Beauty fantasy, take a knight in shining armour (with a platinum charge card rather than a

snow-white charger) to Amberley Castle. This really is a castle with all the toys – portcullis, moat, turrets – and 15 bedrooms, all decorated in 'medieval' style with unmedieval jacuzzis. The approach is a driveway, bordered by two lakes, which crosses the bridge over a grassy moat. Each night, the portcullis is lowered so there is no escape.

- **MOST ROMANTIC ROOM** *The Chichester Room, decorated in rich reds and deep blues. There's a 6-foot-wide four-poster bed and the bathroom has a double jacuzzi. Views from this third-floor room are out over the Amberley Wildbrook conservation wetland*
- **WHERE TO DINE** *The 12th-century Queens Room restaurant – the barrel-vaulted, first-floor hall with a mural of Catherine of Braganza's visit (Charles II's wife). Head chef Sam Mahoney cooks traditional food with natural ingredients, such as wild South Down rabbit and warm savoury mushroom quiche with creamed leeks, which form part of a seven-course menu*
- **WHAT TO DO** *Stroll hand-in-hand on the beautiful South Downs and visit Arundel Castle and Petworth*
- **COST** *From £300 per room per night, including breakfast*
- **HOW TO GET THERE** *From the M25, take Junction 9 (A24) and head south. Turn right on to the A283 towards Storrington and then take the B2139 and head for Amberley. Go past the turning for Amberley and, after two more bends, you are at the castle*

WILTSHIRE

LUCKNAM PARK
ADDRESS Colerne, Chippenham, Wilts SN14 8AZ
☎ 01225 742777   **FAX** 01225 743536
Surely the most heavenly approach to any hotel in England must be the one-mile-long, tree-lined drive that leads to this Palladian mansion set in 500 acres of grounds. The hotel itself is ultra-swish and glamorous, with some luxurious additions – a leisure spa, beauty salon and equestrian centre. And, better still, there's a chance to make a really romantic gesture or celebrate an anniversary or the birth of a child by having your names inscribed on a newly planted tree in an arboretum of 600 trees created to celebrate the hotel's 10th anniversary. With any luck, if you come back to the hotel in 20 years' time you will find a flourishing tree rather than a shrivelled twig.

- **MOST ROMANTIC ROOM** *The Orchid Room. A very large, beautifully furnished room in a profusion of pink, with wonderful views down the tree-lined drive. Although Pavarotti stayed in the Blue Suite down the hall, the Orchid Suite is more romantic by far*
- **WHERE TO DINE** *The hotel has an elegant restaurant with faultless service. Chef Paul Collins serves up dishes such as ravioli of mushrooms and quail and best end of spring lamb with tarragon and garlic, with stuffed courgettes*

- **WHAT TO DO** *As well as chilling out at the spa you can clock up several miles by cycling up and down the drive, take out a horse for a spin, or do as we did: we sent my daughter off for an hour on a pony as a real treat for her and an hour's rest for us*
- **COST** *From £180 for a standard room. Leisure break rates available*
- **HOW TO GET THERE** *From the M25, take the M4 to Junction 17, signposted Chippenham (A350). Take the A420 to Bristol/Castle Combe at Bumpers Farm roundabout. Continue to the village of Ford and then take the first left, signposted to Colerne*

BISHOPSTROWE HOUSE

ADDRESS Warminster, Wilts BA12 9HH
☎ 01985 212312 **FAX** 01985 216769

A charming Georgian country house, it is very comfortable and remarkably peaceful, being set well off from the main road. And though other hotels boast acres of grounds, at Bishopstrowe there really are some lovely walks to be had in the 27 acres of countryside. Walk down to the river and there are sheep, horses, lots of little bridges to cross and even a rotunda temple in the grounds. The reception rooms are all flower-filled and stuffed with antiques and there are always piles of newspapers to read. You will love the spa, which has one of the nicest indoor pools you'll find anywhere – kept at a lovely warm temperature. There is an outdoor pool, and a Michaeljohn hairdresser's and beauty treatments are also available.

- **MOST ROMANTIC ROOM** *The Oval Room, with a large, oval-shaped bed and door. Lovely views across to Longleat and beyond. The hotel will provide cots or beds to accommodate children*
- **WHERE TO DINE** *The Mulberry Restaurant – very attractive, serving wonderful fresh food with an emphasis on light eating*
- **WHAT TO DO** *Facilities at the hotel: bikes to hire; shooting can be arranged; etc. Local attractions: Woburn Abbey; Longleat Safari Park; Stourhead National Trust Gardens; Stonehenge; Bath and Salisbury*
- **COST** *From £170 per night for a double room, including breakfast; weekend offers available*
- **HOW TO GET THERE** *By train, Warminster from Waterloo takes about 2 hours. Then take a 5-minute taxi ride to the hotel. By road, from the M25, take the M3 to Junction 8 (A303), and follow signs for Warminster. Then take the A36 to Warminster and continue to a roundabout. Take the fourth exit (B3414): Bishopstowe House is 1½ miles along on the right*

WORCESTERSHIRE

THE LYGON ARMS

ADDRESS Broadway, Worcs WR12 7DU

☎ 01386 852255

If it's a case of 'love me love my dog' with you and you simply can't bear to be parted from your pooch, then for the most romantic of weekends the Lygon Arms is your answer. While this is probably one of the most obvious hotels for a weekend away in the country, their new dog-friendly service and facilities give it a new slant. Canine guests will be welcomed with complimentary dog biscuits, the dog food of their choice, a water bowl, and a dog bed (changed daily). If you let them know in advance, the hotel will ship in your dog's favourite blend of food or prepare special meals to meet any specific dietary requirements. And, if the thought of taking Fido for a bracing walk in the glorious Cotswold countryside is far too much like hard work, they operate a complimentary dog-walking service.

But even without the luxury of being able to take your dog, the Lygon Arms provides a romantic setting for a weekend away. It is ideally located for visiting pretty Cotswold villages and has all the right ingredients – four-poster beds, ample bathrooms, open fires and plenty of history. The Patio Restaurant is surrounded by wisteria and honeysuckle and serves late breakfasts, light lunches and afternoon tea in the warm summer months, while the main dining room in the Great Hall has a vaulted ceiling and an original 17-th century minstrel's gallery.

When you want a bit of pampering or you've overdone the eating, head for the Lygon Arms Country Club, with its stylish indoor pool, spa bath, plunge pool and health and beauty rooms. You can treat yourself to a range of beauty therapies from aromatherapy, thalgo Cosmetic or Decleor treatments, sauna, steam room, solarium, water aerobics or circuit training.

- **MOST ROMANTIC ROOM** *The King Charles I Suite and the Great Chamber*
- **WHERE TO DINE** *The Great Hall, the hotel's main restaurant, Oliver's Brasserie, or the Cotswold Bar for less formal dining*
- **WHAT TO DO** *Hidcote Manor Garden; Upton House; Snowshill Manor, Banbury, home of an eccentric collector; Snowshill Manor golf; clay-pigeon shooting; fishing; croquet; riding or take a helicopter or hot-air balloon flight for a totally different view of the Cotswolds. Alternatively, take a romantic landau carriage trip or go to the RSC in Stratford and come back for a candlelit supper in the Great Hall*
- **COST** *A double room costs from £178 per night, including continental breakfast. A room with a four-poster costs from £255 per night; a large suite from £385*
- **HOW TO GET THERE** *Take the M25 and turn off on to the M40 towards Oxford, and then the A40 to Burford. Take the A424*

*through Stow-on-the-Wold and pick up the A44 to Broadway. The
hotel is situated on the main street in Broadway itself. By rail, take
the train from Paddington to Moreton-in-the-Marsh, which is 9 miles
from the hotel*

SCOTLAND

INVERLOCHY CASTLE

ADDRESS Torlundy, Fort William PH33 6SN
☎ 01397 702177   **FAX** 01397 702953

A little further afield than most other places featured so far,
Inverlochy is nevertheless one of our absolute favourites. To say
Inverlochy is old-fashioned is true but in the nicest sense of the
word. There is no spa and no swimming pool because it doesn't
need them. People come to Inverlochy to admire the awesome
views. If your room faces one side of the house you get the loch,
if it faces the other you get a giant picture-postcard view of Ben
Nevis. Who could ask for more or say which is better? Old-
fashioned it may be but that doesn't stop it being elegant and
luxurious – there are beautiful trappings – frescoed ceilings,
chandeliers and antiques, squashy sofas to sink into – but
everywhere is decorated in a very low-key way that doesn't
intrude on the beauty of the surroundings. Inverlochy is small,
just 17 bedrooms, so you do feel like a favoured few gathered
together for a shooting party. The staff are very friendly and nice
and the manager, Michael Leonard, who has been at Inverlochy
for over 30 years, is utterly charming and oversees the whole
place with considerable aplomb. All the staff seem genuinely to
love him and so did we. Doors are thrown open, log fires lit even
in the warm weather and scones and home-made biscuits are
served on the terrace overlooking the loch. After tea, we walked
down to the loch and took a boat out for a gentle row, feeling that
we had found heaven.

- **MOST ROMANTIC ROOM** *Room 1 or Room 5. Huge, airy rooms,
exquisitely furnished, overlooking Ben Nevis*
- **WHERE TO DINE** *In the hotel. Our dinner was cooked to perfection
by young chef Simon Haigh. Dinners are staggered, which gives
the chef the opportunity to prepare each dish personally, from
scratch. Sample dishes include: ravioli of Skye mussels with garlic
butter on a bed of artichoke and asparagus; grilled Angus beef
laced with foie gras; followed by Scottish cheeses and home-made
oatcakes*
- **WHAT TO DO** *Naturally, lots of walks such as walking to Ben
Nevis, about 3 hours; to the Caledonian Canal Walk with a series
of steps called the Neptune Staircase, 2–3 hours. The hotel can
also arrange shooting; falconry; visits to the local distillery; grouse
shooting; and skiing in January and February*
- **COST** *From £165 per person per night for dinner, bed and full*

Scottish breakfast in the low season (£135 if booked through the Internet, www.inverlochy.co.uk, plus a free bottle of champagne). In high season, double rooms go from £315, including full Scottish breakfast

- **HOW TO GET THERE** *By helicopter or by plane. BA fly to Inverness (☎ 0345 222 111) or go by Easyjet (☎ 0870 600 000). Car hire can be arranged through Avis (☎ 0990 900 500). or fly to Edinburgh on Go (☎ 0845 605 4321), BA's new low-cost airline that flies out of Stansted and take the West Highland line, to Fort William. The hotel is then a short taxi ride away. The scenery is stunning, especially the views of Loch Lomond. Book through Scotrail (☎ 0345 484950). The train takes about 3½ hours so you may need a long weekend for this, although even if you were only at Inverlochy for a night it would be worth it. By road, on leaving Inverness, take the A382 for Fort William. Pass the villages of Drumnochit, Fort Augustus and Spear Bridge. Inverlochy Castle is 6 miles further on, in the village of Torlundy. The hotel is clearly signposted from the main road*

WALES

GARTHMYL HALL

ADDRESS Garthmyl, Montgomery, Powys SY15 6RS
☎ 01686 640550   **FAX** 01686 640609

Quite a way to travel for a romantic weekend but, if you are on a tight budget, this place is worth it. 'Some people from London even say they think we are too reasonable', says owner Nancy Morrow. Informal and friendly, Garthmyl is in a lovely location with some very stylish rooms in which to plight your troth. Log fires and fresh flowers and a lovely relaxed atmosphere.

- **MOST ROMANTIC ROOM** *Room 10 – the Honeymoon Suite – with muslin draping the antique carved four-poster bed. Lots of crisp Irish linen sheets. Wonderful double-ended bath downstairs*
- **WHERE TO DINE** *Simple but delicious food – a typical £18.50 menu might include: sea bass with fennel risotto; fillet of Welsh lamb served with mint and basil pesto and roast Mediterranean vegetables; and elderflower and gooseberry fool*
- **WHAT TO DO** *Powys castle, with fab gardens; Montgomery, with traditional ironmongers and craft shop and ruined castle; village of Berriew; light railway at Welshpool; plenty of walks*
- **COST** *From £50 per room, including breakfast*
- **HOW TO GET THERE** *By train, to Welshpool from Euston. By car, take the M40, M42, M54 and, from Shrewsbury, mid-Wales is signposted. Follow signs to Welshpool and after 6 miles come to Garthmyl. Take a right-hand bend past a pub called the Nag's Head; the hotel is 100 yards on, on the right. Take the left-hand fork up the driveway*

DUBLIN

Whereas Paris is strictly for romantic lovers, Dublin is for fun-loving lovers. Bursting full of life and enthusiasm, with everyone clutching a bottle of Guinness rather than the Londoner's saintly bottle of Evian, Dublin has a dangerous streak – just right for a weekend of fun and frolics, whether it's for a naughty romantic weekend or for sightseeing. There are fantastic shops, bars and restaurants that take you to a world away from London living. It's a city that attracts pop stars, writers, thespians, who are drawn to the city by its easy tax laws and louche living, with bars and restaurants open till all hours.

You can stay in the luxurious Merrion hotel, a restored Georgian town house just off elegant Merrion Square or hip hop to the Clarence – part-owned by Bono and The Edge – which is funky and minimalist, with a back entrance that thrusts you right on to Temple Bar, the youngest and grooviest area of the city.

WHERE TO STAY

THE CLARENCE
ADDRESS 6–8 Wellington Quay, Dublin 2
☎ 407 0800 **FAX** 670 7800

Forget chintz curtains and country-house hotels. When you walk into the Clarence, you enter a luxurious hotel that is utterly modern. The staff are dressed in monastic-looking Armani-style suitès and, indeed, the hotel itself has a vaguely ecclesiastical feel, which is slightly odd when you think that it is part-owned by Bono and The Edge and that outside, through the back of the hotel, is the hippest part of Dublin – Temple Bar. They may look austere but the staff are anything but – they are warm and hospitable and refreshingly informal. The 50 rooms have every little luxury – TV, mini-bar, squashy leather sofas, and a fab sound system. There is even a helpful collection of Irish CDs but, surprisingly, none by U2. Everywhere, including the doors, is covered in oak panelling; a further stylish touch is the insides of the cupboards and drawers, in bright shades to offset the otherwise-sober exterior. Expect a blissfully comfortable bed and cool linen sheets. Ask for a front room with a view on to the River Liffey.

• **MOST ROMANTIC ROOM** *Even if you're not Robbie Williams, who recently spent a few nights here, for an extra-special occasion book the Penthouse Suite, where Bono stays when he is in town. There are two master bedrooms, plus baby grand, state-of-the-art stereo system, outside terrace and a fabulous hot-tub for a candlelit night-time soak with a wonderful view over the rooftops of Dublin*

• **WHERE TO DINE** *The Tea Room, the Merrion's excellent restaurant. But remember to book well in advance. Chef Michael Martin trained under the Roux brothers. Typical dishes include: sautéed foie gras and salad of mango and beans; confit of duck with*

braised garlic potatoes and madeira and cèpe jus. And don't forget to check out the ultra-cool Octagon Bar
- **COST** *Rooms from £155 and the Penthouse Suite is £1240. Dinner around £20–£30 a head*

THE MERRION HOTEL
ADDRESS Upper Merrion Street, Dublin 2
☎ 603 0600   **FAX** 603 0700
The hotel is, in fact, four Georgian town houses joined together and the building has preserved some of the best aspects of its 18th-century heritage. There are 125 rooms and 20 suites. The main rooms are elegant and traditional, with lots of open fires, and there is a wonderful collection of 19th- and 20th-century Irish art. Wander round the beautiful gardens, reproduced to the designs of Lady Mornington's original garden with box-hedged beds and bay trees and then visit the Tethra Spa which has a super 18m pool. There is also a marble steam room and beauty-treatment room.

Rooms are large and airy, with front rooms looking out on to the Parliament buildings. The rooms again reflect the period feel but with every little hi-tech feature, including luxuriously fitted marble bathrooms.
- **MOST ROMANTIC ROOM** *The Monk Suite, which was originally created for Lady Monk who lived there in the 1760s. It has a wonderful ornate carved ceiling and is very spacious, with views overlooking the hotel's private garden. Very popular with honeymooners as there is a 7-foot bed, dressing room, study and beautiful Italian marble bathroom*
- **WHERE TO DINE** *Even jaded London palates will be impressed with the two-Michelin-star Patrick Guilbaud restaurant, for divine food in the most romantic setting. Tables are well spaced out and service discreet but attentive. You will need to book the restaurant well ahead. The Merrion also has two bars, The Cellar Bar in the original 18th-century wine vaults and No. 23, the hotel's cocktail bar*
- **COST** *£217 per night for a double room. Breakfast is £13 per person for continental or £17 for full Irish breakfast. Dinner for two in the Patrick Guilbaud restaurant is about £75*

THE MERRION SQUARE MANOR
ADDRESS 31 Merrion Square, Dublin 2
☎ 662 8551
A fabulous bed and breakfast.
- **COST** *£45 per person sharing a room*

THE MORRISON
ADDRESS Lower Ormond Quay, Dublin 1
☎ 878 2999   **FAX** 878 3185
A chic new hotel designed by John Rocha. Its Pravda bar is the hip new place to meet.
- **COST** *£175 per room, £350 for a suite*

WHERE TO EAT

EDEN AT MEETING HOUSE SQUARE

ADDRESS Temple Bar, Dublin 2

☎ 670 5372

Opened in 1997, this is the city's hot new restaurant. It is decorated like a tiled swimming pool with lots of blue mosaics and cool white tablecloths and Eleanor Walsh's cooking continues to be admired. There is lots of seafood and breast of corn-fed chicken with mashed potatoes is one of the favourites.

- **COST** £30–£35

PEACOCK ALLEY

ADDRESS Fitzwilliam's Hotel, St Stephen's Green, Dublin 2

☎ 478 7015

Peacock Alley is owned by Conrad Gallagher, the well known Irish restaurateur.

- **COST** £45 for the set menu

LA STAMPA

ADDRESS 35 Dawson Street, Dublin 2

☎ 677 8611

A large restaurant which seats up to 200. Always full, the food is brilliant and the atmosphere lively and fun.

- **COST** A la carte from £35 for dinner, from £20 for lunch

BAILEY

ADDRESS 2–4 Duke Street, Dublin 2

☎ 670 4939

Dublin's trendiest watering-hole – a great place to stop off for a Guinness near to the shops in Grafton Street.

WHAT TO DO

NATIONAL GALLERY OF IRELAND

ADDRESS Merrion Square, Dublin 2

☎ 661 5133

Works by Yeats, Osborne, Hone and Lavery as well as old masters such as Goya, El Greco and Titian.

- **OPENING TIMES** Mon–Sat 10.00–17.00; Thurs 10.00–20.00; Sunday 14.00–17.00
- **COST** Free, but donations welcomed

IRISH MUSEUM OF MODERN ART

ADDRESS Royal Hospital, Kilmaiham, Dublin 8

☎ 612 9900

There is a good restaurant and shop in this museum which features works by Irish and contemporary artists.

• **OPENING TIMES** *Tues–Sat 10.00–17.00; Sun 12.00–17.30; (closed Mon)*

• **COST** *Free*

SHOPPING

If you are staying at the Merrion, just a few minutes walk away you will find the Louise Kennedy lifestyle shop at 56 Merrion Square, ☎ 662 0056. Louise Kennedy is one of Ireland's best known and most successful designers. A wonderful Georgian town house sells her vast clothing collection – popular with ex-Irish president Mary Robinson – but also a range of accessories including fabrics from Andrew Martin and Hodsoll McKenzie, antique furniture, and gifts such as wooden bowls and scented candles.

Also check out Minama on St Stephen's Green, a wonderful emporium of modern kitchen and living equipment, which stocks everything from Alessi, and the famous Grafton Street, which seems to be full of far too many of the run of the mill shops you might find anywhere, but does have a great department store – Brown Thomas – a sort of outpost of Harvey Nicks. Here you will find Jil Sander, Jean-Paul Gaultier and Buckle My Shoe for kids as well as lots of young Irish designers. John Farrington, 88–95 Grafton St, ☎ 679 5666, is a famous art deco jewellery shop for those in the know. This is where Adam Clayton bought Naomi Campbell her ill-fated engagement ring and where models flock when they are in the area. Also visit Designyard, 12 East Essex St, ☎ 677 8453 for lots of Irish and international designers. The ground floor is devoted to jewellery whilst the first floor is an interior-design gallery selling furniture and ceramics.

PARIS

Paris has to be the number-one romantic city in the universe. Spring, of course, is the perfect time to go but a visit at any time will have you singing *chansons d'amour*. Walk hand in hand down the banks of the Seine, take a *bâteau mouche* when the sun is setting over the city and eat your dinner as Paris glides by. Linger over a *kir royale* or a *café crème* at a boulevard café and, when you are tired of staring into each others' eyes, there is plenty to see: museums, art galleries, flea markets and, of course, thousands of fabulous shops.

• **HOW TO GET THERE** *The Eurostar lovetrain pulls out of Waterloo at 19.54 for Paris. Lots of snuggling couples can be seen getting*

*into the mood, guzzling champagne with their heads on each
others' shoulders. Long queues for the buffet bar might suggest
that lovers should bring their own champagne and caviar
with them*

WHERE TO STAY

HOTEL DU JEU DE PAUME

ADDRESS 54 rue Saint-Louis-en-l'Ile, 75004 Paris
☎ 01 43 26 14 18
If you are looking for a truly authentic and reasonable prices
French hotel, then look no further than the Hotel du Jeu de Paume.
A converted old palm tennis court, this beautiful 17th-century hotel
is situated on the island in the centre of Paris. Charming and small,
with a pretty private garden, it is close to Notre Dame and has a
plentiful supply of excellent classic French restaurants and brilliant
brasseries running along the same street. Such is the popularity
of this hotel that you will need to book at least six weeks ahead
for a weekend.
• **MOST ROMANTIC ROOM** *Suite 701, which comes at the standard
room rate but is located at the top of the hotel, with sloping ceilings
and a lovely view*
• **COST** *1900F per night per room, not including breakfast*

HOTEL TROCADERO DOKHAN'S

ADDRESS 117 rue Lauriston, 75116 Paris
☎ 01 53 65 66 99   **FAX** 01 53 65 66 88
Situated between the Trocadéro and the Arc de Triomphe, the
hotel has a strong neo-classical look. Straight out of the pages of
Elle Deco, it is serious chic: with stylish wallpaper, classical statues
and moulded ceilings, heavy wood doors and interesting period
furniture. The lift – which looks like the inside of a Louis Vuitton
trunk – snaps shut to transport you to your love nest. Rooms are
decorated in strong stripes, with fabric-covered walls and lots of
marble in the bathroom. The loos are hidden away in a discreet
little corner of the room but even the loo rolls are tied in black
ribbon – a neat little touch.
   There's a gorgeous moss green and gold breakfast room, with
surprisingly nice, friendly staff. There is also a library of arty books
and exquisite arrangements of flowers everywhere.
• **MOST ROMANTIC ROOM** *Suite 608, which is like having your own
Parisian apartment with a private terrace, a view of the Eiffel Tower
and a jacuzzi*
• **COST** *From 1950F per room per night, excluding breakfast.
Suite 608 costs 4500F*

SOFITEL LE FAUBOURG

ADDRESS 15 rue Boissy-d'Anglas, 75008 Paris
☎ 01 44 94 1400   **FAX** 01 44 94 14 28

If shopping forms part of your romantic agenda, then this new hotel – built from two 18th- and 19th-century mansions – is the shopaholic's choice. Situated between the Place de la Concorde, the Faubourg St-Honoré and the Champs Elysées, it is bang in the middle of and, in some cases, next door to all the best department stores and designer shops. It has a light, airy lobby, 30s-style bar and a library full of books and plenty of interesting *objets d'art*. Lots of fashion plates and original drawings in the corridors. And, if your suitor loves you enough to buy you a designer creation, then neighbouring shops – such as Thierry Mugler, Hermès and Lanvin – will arrange to give you a private show.

- **MOST ROMANTIC ROOM** *Suite 701, which comes at the standard room rate but is located at the top of the hotel, with sloping ceilings and a lovely view*
- **COST** *1900F per night per room, not including breakfast*

THE LANCASTER

ADDRESS 7 rue de Berri, Champs Elysées, 75008 Paris
☎ 01 40 76 40 76   **FAX** 01 40 76 40 00

If you want to be utterly private and untroubled by the hoi polloi then be prepared to pay the price to stay at the Lancaster. Recently given a Grace Leo-Andrien facelift, the hotel personifies discreet charm and is amazingly quiet, despite being so close to the bustling Champs Elysées. Only guests are allowed to use the facilities, so celebrities such as Posh and David Beckham can sip their champagne in peace. Each bedroom is completely individual, with an opulent bathroom, and some have terraces overlooking the Paris rooftops.

- **MOST ROMANTIC ROOM** *No.80, the only room on the top floor, with two terraces and a huge bed*
- **COST** *2350F per night for a double room. Breakfast is 120F*

PRINCE DE CONDE

ADDRESS 39 rue de la Seine, 75006 Paris
☎ 01 43 26 71   **FAX** 01 43 26 71 56

Or stay at a slightly cheaper but equally charming twelve-bedroom Prince de Condé on the rue de la Seine in St Germain.

- **MOST ROMANTIC ROOM** *No. 601, chintzy suite with its own jacuzzi*
- **COST** *There is usually a winter rate of 395F a night for a double. Libertel, the chain that owns the Prince de Condé, is well known for its charming but reasonably priced hotels and also has other bed and breakfasts in Paris:* ☎ *0800 895950 for details*

WHERE TO WINE AND DINE

ANGELINA

ADDRESS 226 rue de Rivoli, Paris
☎ 01 42 60 82 00
Excellent for tea and famous for their Chocolat l'Africain, 36F and Mont Blanc meringue – whipped cream and chestnut purée, for a really sweet tooth, 36F.

BUDDHA BAR

ADDRESS Opposite the new Sofitel Le Faubourg, Paris
A great place to go for drinks. Well worth a visit, if only to see the giant Buddha that looms over this oversized galleried bar. Interesting range of eclectic dishes: wok-fried salt and pepper calamari and frogs' legs; spicy salmon cakes on sugar cane; crispy bass sweet and sour; liquid-centred chocolate cake with vanilla ice cream; or red fruit platter.
• **COST** 390F for champagne and nibbles range from 60F to 320F.

JULES VERNE

ADDRESS 2nd Floor, Eiffel Tower, Paris
If it's a really special romantic occasion, or if you just want a real treat, go to this Michelin starred restaurant. It is precided over by top chef Alan Reix and serves up wonderful fare – lobster, caviar and sole etc. Go for the view alone. Gentlemen must wear jacket and tie. Book three months ahead for dinner and two weeks ahead for lunch.
• **COST** Dinner from 1000F

WHAT TO DO

When in Paris for just a weekend, you could feel overwhelmed by all there is to see and do but you mustn't miss the romantic cruise on the Seine and it's a good idea to explore some of the smaller museums and galleries.

BATEAUX MOUCHES

ADDRESS Pont de l'Alma, Paris 8
☎ 42 25 96 10
You can buy your tickets in the Eurostar station before you even leave or you can buy them at the boat. The boats leave from cours Albert (nearest metro: Champs Elysées – Clemenceau). A must for any romantic trip to Paris, the 1 hour trip takes in the Louvre, Notre Dame, quai d'Orsay, la Saint Chapelle, but remember to take your earplugs – the sound of noisy Americans is bound to take the edge off your romantic leanings. Better

still, go for dinner on the boat. It leaves at 8.30pm and the trip lasts for 2¼ hours.
• **COST** *40F per person, Menu Gourmet 500F*

JEU DE PAUME

ADDRESS Place de la Concorde, Paris
☎ 01 42 60 69 69 or 01 47 03 12 50
This delightful little museum is on the corner of rue de Rivoli and is dedicated to modern works and the visual arts. There are always top-quality exhibitions.
• **COST** *38F for adults, 28F for children*

MUSEUM OF MODERN ART

ADDRESS Centre Georges Pompidou Place, Beoubourg, Paris 4
☎ 01 44 78 12 33
Paintings by Matisse, Léger, Miró, etc. It has a very good and interesting gift shop. Buy a stone paperweight 'Le Baiser' by Brancusi, which depicts a couple embracing.

THE PICASSO MUSEUM

ADDRESS Hotel Sale, 5 rue de Thorigny, Paris 3
☎ 01 42 71 25 21
A very popular, small museum dedicated to the works of Picasso just off the rue de Franc-Bourgeois, in the Marais district.
• **COST** *30F for adults, 20F for ages 18–25, free for under-18's and on Sunday adults pay 20F*

SHOPS

For fab chocolates go to Paul B, 4 rue Marbeuf (☎ 47 20 86 26) Among the bizarre chocolate creations on sale is an all-chocolate replica of a high-heeled shoe, all edible, 220F. Also visit the shop owned by Karl Lagerfeld's former muse Inès de la Fréssange in the avenue Montaigne. Buy glasses that spell love, ashtrays that say 'je t'aime' or a boxed gift of four ashtrays saying 'I love you'. Beautiful handbags, scarves and belts with signature leaf design and other love tokens are also on sale. If you are an Agnès B fan, then you should go to rue de Jour, (1st arrondissement). Here she has her flagship stores, one each *pour les enfants*, for the home, *pour l'homme* and *pour la femme*. On Sunday morning, explore rue de Franc-Bourgeois, in Le Marais (4th arrondissement). Shops open at around 11 in the morning. Halfway down there's a quirky little toy shop, Marais Plus, with an excellent café at the back of the shop. Lots of French teddies, French-made dolls and small inexpensive items. Across the road look out for Why? a crazy shop selling mauve wigs, inflatable chairs, soap novelties, etc. Amongst these offbeat, quirky shops you can also find some seriously chic designer clothes stores like Ventilo and Et Vous. For a hundred and one variations on a ladies' white shirt go to Big Ben. They also have a men's shop next door, with shirts in strong, vibrant shapes from just 290F. There are also lots of interesting homeware stores like La Rochère, selling beautiful Tiffany-style lamps, glasses and salad bowls.

NICE

The advent of ultra-cheap flights has put destinations such as the South of France within reach of most of us. Nice and the surrounding area is great for a weekend, not least because the airport is so central to the town that you don't waste hours and hours getting to where you want to be. The flight to Nice is only around 1 hour and 20 minutes, so it is eminently possible for a weekend. Not only that but hotels and restaurants in France – even in this rather glitzy area – offer tremendous value for money. Add to this better weather than here and you have the perfect ingredients for a luxurious and glamorous break.

• **HOW TO GET THERE** *Easyjet from Luton to Nice, British Midlands and British Airways from Heathrow, AB Airlines from Gatwick or BA Cityflyer from City Airport. Taxis are easy to find at Nice Airport, or you can hire a car. The following companies have desks at the airport: (*Terminal 1, **Terminal 2)*
Avis ☎ 04 93 21 36 33*, 04 93 21 41 80**
Budget ☎ 04 93 21 36 50*, 04 93 21 42 51**
Europcar ☎ 04 93 21 36 44*, 04 93 21 42 53**
Hertz ☎ 04 93 21 36 72*, 04 93 21 42 72**

• **COST** *At about £80, the Easyjet flight is probably cheapest*

WHERE TO STAY

LA COLOMBE D'OR
ADDRESS Place de General de Gaulle, Saint Paul de Vence 06570
☎ 04 93 32 80 02
Unassuming from the outside, this is one of the most fantastic places to stay. The bedrooms are comfortable but basic but the walls are hung with original works of art by the likes of Chagall. The outdoor swimming pool is stunning, with huge modern sculptures, and the terrace dining area is very romantic with views over the hills. It must be said that the menu does not seem to change very frequently and the food can sometimes be a little hit or miss. It's also sometimes difficult to get a drink or a cup of coffee outside mealtimes. The service is friendly and fun – Stefan the waiter asks you if you would like Spanish coffee for breakfast ('*café olé*'). The whole place is rather like a very upmarket student hostel, with interesting, off-beat people as well as the plain wealthy. Great friendships are formed in the bar during late-night carousing, although the barman might treat you like a naughty child and tell you that it's time you went to bed. If you want to keep yourself to yourself it's perfectly possible,

but you might miss out on a lot of fun. The restaurant is much frequented by celebs during Cannes Film Festival. Be sure to ask for a room in the main hotel rather than the annexe.

- **MOST ROMANTIC ROOM** *All those in the main hotel are lovely; the most romantic ones are probably those overlooking the pool*
- **WHERE TO DINE** *In the hotel, at Le Diamant Rose (which is on the outskirts of St Paul de Vence) or Maxima (see page 41)*
- **WHAT TO DO** *Fondation Maeght art gallery; walk round the pretty village of St Paul; watch the games of* pétanque *with players who look as though they have been supplied by Central Casting*
- **COST** *1820F for a double room and dinner, or for the room alone, 1400F*
- **HOW TO GET THERE** *Take the N202 and turn off onto the D2210. Take care to follow the signs to St Paul, as there is also a village called St Paul de Vence*

LA CHEVRE D'OR

ADDRESS Rue du Barri, 06360 Eze
☎ 04 92 10 66 66

A truly beautiful and extravagant place to stay. The hotel is part of this tiny medieval village set into the rock above the Côte d'Azur. No cars are allowed up the narrow cobbled streets, so your baggage has to be carried up by hotel staff. Sip cocktails on the terrace overlooking what must be one of the world's most amazing coastlines and dine in the fabulous hotel restaurant. The food is superb – particularly the set menu. Make sure you order the hot soufflé, even if you don't think that you'll have room, and do leave a small place for the amazing cheese board, which is kept in absolute peak condition. The hotel is Swiss-run so the service is impeccable and probably more friendly than if it were French. Fantastic for a short honeymoon or a really special break.

- **MOST ROMANTIC ROOM** *The hotel never reserves a specific room number, but they suggest you book a deluxe room or a junior suite*
- **WHERE TO DINE** *In the hotel restaurant or the grill/bistro*
- **WHAT TO DO** *Visit Monte Carlo and its casinos; go for a drink in the very grand Hôtel de Paris*
- **COST** *Between 1800F and 3800F per night for a double room*
- **HOW TO GET THERE** *Take the Corniche from Nice towards Monaco and follow signs to Eze Village. You have to park your car at the bottom of the village and walk up to the hotel*

THE GRIMALDI

ADDRESS 15 rue Grimaldi, 06000 Nice
☎ 04 93 16 00 24

A beautiful 1930s *belle-époque*-style town house in the centre of Nice, just a few minutes from the promenade des Anglais and a short drive from the airport. It has 24 air-conditioned rooms, each decorated in Souleiado fabrics. But best of all its prices are so reasonable for the South of France.

- **MOST ROMANTIC ROOM** *If you can stretch to it, the suite is the most romantic since you can have breakfast on the balcony (costs from 1100F per night)*
- **COST** *Double rooms are from 410F to 690F – what could be better value?*

WHERE TO DINE

LE GRAND HOTEL
ADDRESS Cap Ferrat, 71 Boulevard du General de Gaulle, 06230 Nice
☎ 04 93 76 50 50
Highly recommended for dinner. There is a stunning bar decorated with lilac leather bar stools and an aquarium of exotic tropical fish. Great martinis and the hotel's own delicious champagne cocktail. The set menu – at around 420F per head for what seemed like about 20 courses, all exquisitely tiny portions, beautifully presented – was fantastic value and superbly cooked. Hotel food is often not on a par with top-class restaurants but this was a truly memorable meal. The dining room is grand, with painted murals, and would be a very good place for a celebratory meal. You can of course stay here, but it is on the pricey side. Better to go for dinner which is fantastic.

MAXIMA
ADDRESS 689 Chemin de la Gaude, 06140 Vence
☎ 04 93 58 90 75
Fantastic food produced by a young chef in a small but stylish restaurant 10 minutes drive from the Colombe D'Or. Eat in the nasturtium-filled garden in the summer, or in the small dining room when it's chilly. There are two modern works of art hanging in the dining room constructed from forks and spoons. The set-price menus are very reasonable, from 350F to 650F per person, and are all equally delicious.

WEEKENDS BY THE SEA

As a nation, we do like to be beside the seaside. However, unlike France – where it's easy to find a chic little hotel to stay in and there are rafts of small, family-run restaurants serving delicious, reasonably priced food – English seaside towns can be a bit of a nightmare. This is a shame, as we have some of the best beaches and most beautiful coastlines in Europe. What is unfortunate is the preponderance of cheap burger bars and tacky shops selling useless souvenirs which don't even have kitsch appeal. Where our French cousins have *moules marinière* we have fish and chips, which ranges from the fantastically good to the truly abysmal. Where the Italians have rows of attractive sun umbrellas and loungers, with beautiful-bodied families reclining on them, we tend to have a few lardies sheltering behind a windbreak, wriggling to get undressed under a towel. However, as with lots of things in Britain, when we get it right, we do it really well. Nothing could be better than the beach at Southwold, with its much photographed beach huts and effortless, laid-back charm. And who but we Brits could have come up with the beach hut as a concept? The coastline of north Suffolk is some of the most attractive and unspoilt, with rivers and inlets and small yachts pottering about. Our fresh seafood, when you can get it, is superb, and our lobsters and crabs tastier than those from just about anywhere else.

For this chapter, we've chosen hotels, pubs and restaurants where we actually like to go; some might be best on a hot summer's day with a pint or a Pimms in one hand, whilst some might be best appreciated off-season, when they're empty of people and open to the elements. Nothing could be more invigorating than a walk along a British beach in mid-December, for instance. Some are mainstream and some are slightly offbeat but they are all places we would be reluctant to leave on Sunday evening.

ALDEBURGH

Aldeburgh is just down the coast from Thorpeness and is a 'proper town' instead of a purpose-built holiday resort. Famously the home of Benjamin Britten and Laurens van der Post, it is an attractive spot with a life of its own outside the holiday season. Rather genteel and respectable, it can get a bit 'hoorayish' during Regatta Week in August, when a younger and noisier element arrives from London. To expect there to be loads of things to do is to miss the point of Aldeburgh completely. Go here for a break if you want to potter about the town or beach – in all weathers – or just chill out. This is not the place for you if you want exotic nightlife and a wild time.

• **HOW TO GET THERE** *Take the A12 exit from the M25 and turn off onto the A1094. By train, leave from Liverpool Street to Saxmundham, changing at Ipswich*

WHERE TO STAY

THE BRUNDENELL HOTEL
ADDRESS The Parade, Aldeburgh, Suffolk IP15 5BU
☎ 01728 452071   **FAX** 01728 454082
This is probably the poshest place to stay in Aldeburgh. 'It's where everyone has their funerals', said one local. The hotel is right on the seafront and a lot of the rooms have dramatic views of the sea. It does have a rather old-fashioned feel, but that is not necessarily a bad thing. Starters include smoked salmon, prawn basket or sautéed black pudding and you can choose from dishes such as venison casserole or smoked haddock and bacon.
• **COST** *A double room at a weekend costs from £90 for two. Bed and breakfast ranges from £34 to £52 per person per night. Dinner, bed and breakfast costs from £44 to £62 per person per night. There is a £10 supplement for rooms with a sea view. Dinner costs £15.95 per head for two courses and £17.95 for three courses*

WENTWORTH HOTEL
ADDRESS Wentworth Road, Aldeburgh, Suffolk IP15 5BD
☎ 01728 452312   **FAX** 01728 454343
The Wentworth is towards the edge of Aldeburgh and is the nearest Aldeburgh gets to a country-house hotel. Family run, it has been under the same ownership since 1920. There are open fires, antique furniture, cosy drawing rooms and comfy bedrooms, many with sea views. The food is cooked using only fresh produce. A typical menu would contain warmed mushroom soufflés set on a tomato roundel with tomato dressing; local asparagus tips, drizzled with vinaigrette; Adnam's pork casserole, braised in a rich tomato sauce; mixed seafood crêpes; followed by lemon

steamed pudding, topped with a liqueur syrup; or summer-fruit parfait with a fruit coulis.

• **COST** *A double room with a sea view costs between £68 and £80, depending on the season for a two-night break per person per night, including dinner, bed and breakfast. Dinner alone costs £14.50 per person, Sunday to Friday, or £15.95 per person on Saturday*

MARTELLO TOWER (AT ALDEBURGH)

ADDRESS c/o The Landmark Trust, Shottesbrooke, Maidenhead, Berkshire SL6 3SW

☎ 01628 8225925 The Landmark Trust

The Martello Towers were built against the threat of a French invasion during the Napoleonic Wars by the Board of Ordnance, and this one at Aldeburgh is the largest and most northerly in the chain. It was bought by The Landmark Trust in 1971 and has been sympathetically restored to provide sleeping accommodation for up to four people. It's best to go with your own family, or those that you know really well, as the bedrooms are screened off from the living area but not fully divided. This is the place to go if you want a real sense of being beside the sea, and at the right time of the year you'll be able to hear the waves beating on the nearby shore and the wind howling round the thick walls of the tower. Beachcombing is a favourite activity at Aldeburgh; look out for amber and bloodstones brought from Scandinavia by glaciers, as well as cornelians, shells and other interesting driftwood to take home.

• **COST** *Between £423 and £600 for a Friday-to-Sunday let, depending on the season (sleeps four)*

• **HOW TO GET THERE** *Full details are supplied by The Landmark Trust when you book*

WHERE TO EAT

THE LIGHTHOUSE

ADDRESS 77 High Street, Aldeburgh, Suffolk IP15 4AU

☎ 01728 453377

The Lighthouse is co-owned by Peter Hill and Sara Fox and is probably the best restaurant in Aldeburgh. 'A huge amount of our bookings at weekends are 0171 or 0181 numbers' says Peter. 'Regardless of the current fashion for holidaying in this country, Aldeburgh has always been fashionable in a low-key sort of way with professional and affluent people.' Lunch is à la carte and, although the menus change daily, might include dishes such as: potted shrimps from the Norfolk coast, £4.50; duck confit, puy lentils and new potatoes, £7.75; or plaice in beer batter, hand-made chips and mushy peas, £6.95. Puddings like lemon-balm crème brûlée or coconut tart with passion-fruit mascarpone are all

£3.25. Things are slightly different in the evening, when guests pay a set price but can choose what they like. There is a daily menu and a list of Lighthouse classics from which to make your selection. Go for duck-liver parfait with sweet and sour figs; griddled tuna loin on a spicy mixed bean and coriander salad and similar puddings to lunchtime. 'Our philosophy is to produce great food using the finest ingredients at a reasonable price' says Peter Hill. Booking is essential as they obviously do what they say!

• **COST** *(Dinner) two courses £13.50; three courses £15.75*

REGATTA

ADDRESS 171 High Street, Aldeburgh IP15 5AN

☎ 01728 452011

A very jolly and friendly restaurant, decorated in blue and yellow with lots of flags hanging around the walls. There is a chalk-board menu for fresh fish dishes as well as the *à la carte* menu. You can choose all the dishes in either starter or main-course size, the latter coming with potatoes or chips and a Regatta salad. Crayfish cocktail with real Marie Rose sauce, £5.50 or £8.50; smoked haddock fishcakes, with watercress tartare sauce, £4 or £8; chilled couscous with roast tomatoes and baked goats' cheese, £5 or £8. Nibbles at £2 each include black-olive tapenade with croûtons; sun-dried tomato tapenade with croûtons; and mixed marinated black and green olives. Closed Monday to Wednesday.

• **COST** *Between £10 and £15 per head*

THE FISH AND CHIP SHOP

ADDRESS at the Yacht Club end of the main street

If you fancy eating al fresco on the beach, this does fantastic fish and chips. Expect to queue during the summer, as it is very popular.

WHAT TO DO

THE YACHT POND

Not to be missed, and as much enjoyed by parents as any child, this is a traditional, old-fashioned model boating pond which is hugely popular. Bring your own boat, or buy one at the nearest newsagents or Orlando's Antique Shop.

LIFEBOAT AND MUSEUM

ADDRESS situated on the beach

Going round this will probably occupy all of 10 minutes but there is normally some friendly, gnarled old sea salt who can regale you with tales of the lifeboat.

• **OPENING TIMES** *Staffed on a voluntary ad hoc basis*

• **COST** *Free*

MOOT HALL MUSEUM
ADDRESS Aldeburgh, Suffolk IP15 5DS
A pretty building, with exhibits about the history of Aldeburgh.
- **OPENING TIMES** *Sat-Sun, Bank Holidays, 3 April–31 May 14.30–17.30; Daily, June 2.30–17.00; Daily, July &Aug 10.30–12.30, 14.30–17.00; Sat & Sun, Sept 14.30–17.00*
- **COST** *Adults and concessions 50p, children free*

CATCH OF THE DAY
Another must, particularly if you are self-catering or perhaps as you head off back to London, is to buy fresh wet fish direct from the fishermen on the beach. What's available is whatever the catch has been that day, and you couldn't find fresher fish anywhere.

THE AMBER SHOP, STEPHENSONS JEWELLERS
ADDRESS 122–142 High Street, Aldeburgh, Suffolk IP15 5AB
The oldest amber shop in Great Britain, the Amber Shop has been polishing and shaping amber for over 150 years. The amber is all found on the local coast, and the display of over 1,000 pieces of jewellery of all descriptions is worth a look.

ALDERNEY

TOURIST INFORMATION CENTRE
ADDRESS Victoria Street, St Anne GY9 3TA
☎ 01481 823737

Although the main reason for including this is the offbeat Fort Clonque, Alderney is a charming island with a distinctly Gallic flavour. The island is only three miles long by one and a half miles wide, with unspoilt countryside and fabulous sandy beaches. The main town of St Anne has narrow, cobbled streets and is packed with cafés and restaurants, many with fresh seafood specialities. The Alderney Museum is worth a look and contains armaments and personal belongings recovered from an Elizabethan warship which was discovered in 1991 just off the coast, or you could take a guided tour of the Mannez Lighthouse. The Tourist Board produces a good local map with suggested walking routes.

WHERE TO STAY

FORT CLONQUE
ADDRESS c/o The Landmark Trust, Shottesbrooke, Maidenhead, Berkshire SL6 3SW
☎ 01628 825925 The Landmark Trust
If you want a really off-the-wall weekend away, particularly for a large group of friends – say for a school reunion or a stag

weekend – then Fort Clonque would be perfect. This Victorian fort, which was disarmed in 1886 but left standing, clings to a group of large rocks off the steep south-west tip of Alderney. It was refortified in 1940 when the Germans invaded the Channel Islands but is not nearly as grim as it sounds. It is small and picturesque, with stretches of grass and samphire (delicious steamed or boiled and served with melted butter or hollandaise sauce) and colonies of the gannets which fish off the coast. The fort sleeps up to 11 people and, with walls up to 19 feet thick in places and nothing much around you but sea, you can have as rowdy a party as you would wish.

• **COST** *Short breaks between £99 and £210 per night for a minimum of 3 nights (sleeps 11)*

• **HOW TO GET THERE** *The quickest way to get to Alderney is to fly from Southampton to Aurigny (£139 return). A taxi from the airport to Fort Clonque will take 15 minutes. Otherwise, take the ferry from Southampton on Friday evening, returning on Sunday evening, for £49*

WHAT TO DO

The island of Alderney has fantastic beaches at the north end and is small enough to be explored on foot or by bike. Take your sketch book or camera if you are feeling artistic or run around as you used to in the playground shouting 'Achtung, Englischer Schweinhund' as loudly as you wish.

BEAULIEU

WHERE TO STAY

THE MASTER BUILDER'S HOUSE

ADDRESS Buckler's Hard, Beaulieu, Hants SO42 7XB
☎ 01590 616253   **FAX** 01590 616297

Situated on the west bank of Beaulieu River at the village of Buckler's Hard in the New Forest, the hotel overlooks the slips where hundreds were employed to prepare the New Forest oak for Nelson's fleet. The man who was the designer and master-builder of great ships such as the *Agamemnon* was one Henry Adams. This was his home and workplace. The hotel was lovingly refurbished by new owners Jeremy Willcock and John Illsley of Dire Straits fame. The nautical design theme gives just the right atmosphere to the hotel. The bedrooms, twenty-five in all, comprise seventeen standard and eight superior rooms in the main house. The Riverview Restaurant and adjoining terrace overlook the river and private gardens. The cooking is modern with lots of seafood, naturally. This is a great place for keen sailors, with hundreds of sailing boats moored on the banks of the river. The hotel also owns the *Master George*, a graceful 36-foot gentleman's motor yacht, which can be chartered by guests at a cost of £500 for half a day during the summer season.

- **COST** *Double rooms cost £120 per night including full English breakfast*
- **HOW TO GET THERE** *Take the M3 and M27 (West) and come off at Junction 1 (A337). At Brockenhurst, take the B3055 to Beaulieu and follow the signs to Buckler's Hard on the left*

BRIGHTON

Brighton has always had rather a saucy reputation. The outrageously ornate Royal Pavilion was built by George IV to house his then mistress and, over the centuries, illicit liaisons have always been conducted of a weekend between the piers. Brighton still has a slightly louche and bohemian feel to it, and as well as that, is also a great centre for arts and crafts. Brighton University has a great art faculty and graduates often stay on in the town and set up shops or market stalls selling their creations.

Another thing about Brighton that makes it so colourful is the thriving gay scene. Gay bars and clubs abound and, of course, members of the community add to the number of impressive interiors shops.

Look out for Elephant, in The Lanes, which sells glamorous and eclectic objects and furniture from around the world. Nearby is England at Home, which stocks funkier items, such as the Alessi range of kitchenware and clever clocks and watches.

- **HOW TO GET THERE** *It takes an hour by train to get from London to Brighton. Trains go every hour or half hour from Victoria Station. By car, take the M23 (Junction 7 off the M25) and then the A23 to Brighton*

WHERE TO STAY

THE SUSSEX ARTS CLUB
ADDRESS 7 Ship Street, Brighton, Sussex BN1 1AD
☎ 01273 727371
Regular live bands and other arty evenings. This is a real arts club with only seven rooms. Try the Wilde Room, full of art deco mirrors. The staff are happy and friendly and full of local information. Nice informal, relaxed atmosphere.

- **COST** *Bed and breakfast £80 per room per night. The Arts Club suites are £100 per night per room*

WHAT TO DO

THE ROYAL PAVILION

ADDRESS Brighton, Sussex BN1 1EE
☎ 01273 290900
This is an obvious half-day visit as is the Palace Pier (good for fish and chips) and a tour of the West Pier complete with hard hat and wellingtons.

PRESTON PARK

ADDRESS off London Road, Brighton
Very pleasant and surrounded by pretty gardens.

BRIGHTON MUSEUM AND ART GALLERY

ADDRESS Church Street, Brighton, Sussex BN1 1EE
☎ 01273 290900
Next to the Dome and the Pavilion, and the streets of Kemptown, which is slowly becoming upmarket and houses some interesting designer and antique shops.

THE BRIGHTON FESTIVAL

ADDRESS www.brighton-festival.org.uk
The festival is held in May. To find out more, see the web site.

SHOPS

A Lot of Gaul, 32 Kensington Gardens (☎ 01273 621135) sells Tintin, Asterix and Barbar merchandise. England at Home, 22B & 32 Ship Street (☎ 01273 205544) is a shop with up-to-the-minute designs for both large and small items. Grains of Gold, 52 Meeting House Lane (☎ 01273 77197) sells classic jewellery and exclusive designs. Jezebel, 14 Prince Albert Street (☎ 01273 20609) specialises in art deco and nouveau clothes, furniture and various objects. Near the Palace Pier, under the esplanade, there are several little craft shops selling miniature lighthouses, paintings, prints and mirrors made of driftwood. Down the hill, east of the station, there are several shops selling outlandish fashions, antiques, and crafts, which are well worth a look. This was where Anita Roddick set up her first Body Shop, with cosmetics in medical bottles. The Lanes, just off the seafront, are rather more establishment, with a mixture of brand-name stores and a few craft and designer shops sprinkled among them. On a Saturday it's hard to squeeze yourself through the narrow passages but on Sundays it is clearer and quite a few shops are open and doing brisk business. If you like markets, the car park by the station has a car-boot sale and flea market on Sundays, where you can pick up anything from a pile of rubbish to a priceless antique for a couple of quid.

WHERE TO EAT AND DRINK

THE SQUID
ADDRESS 78 Middle Street, Brighton BN1 1AL
A good place for pre-club drinks and an interesting mix of retro, hi-tech and Latin American décor, with loads of Warholesque artwork. Drinks are inexpensive.

CLUB AT THE BEACH
ADDRESS Kings Road Arches, Brighton BN1
This is one of several clubs in the Kings Road Arches playing a mix of happy House music and has occasional guest appearances by Fat Boy Slim.

PETER'S CAFE
ADDRESS Shop Street Gardens, between Middle Street and Ship Street, Brighton BN1 1AJ
Ideal for a good cooked breakfast. Open seven days a week.

1 PASTON PLACE
ADDRESS 1 Paston Place, Brighton BN2 1HA
For fancy fare, try this ultra-cool restaurant. An interesting menu, combining fresh fish, game and seasonal vegetables, is complemented by a very good and varied wine list.
- **COST** *Expensive at about £50 per head without wine but worth it*

CLIMPING

Climping is a tiny village, eight miles east of Chichester and 30 minutes' drive from Brighton. Although you might want to go to Bailiffscourt Hotel just to chill out and enjoy the seaside position, there is lots to do and see locally. Beautiful Goodwood House and its famous racecourse are an easy 20 minutes' drive to the north and the pretty town of Midhurst is only half an hour away. Nearer still is Arundel, with its magnificent castle, and a host of antique shops.
- **HOW TO GET THERE** *From London, take the A3 to Portsmouth and then the A259 going east; or take the A23 to Brighton and then the A259 going west. Climping is signposted from the main road*

WHERE TO STAY

BAILIFFSCOURT HOTEL
ADDRESS Climping, West Sussex BN17 5RW
☎ 01903 723511   **FAX** 01903 723107

Bailiffscourt Hotel is a 'perfectly preserved medieval manor house' that isn't. It belonged to Lord and Lady Moyne, of the Guinness brewing family, who had it built from architectural salvage in the 1920s and 1930s. They employed Amyas Phillips, who described himself as an 'antiquarian', to design the house and locate the 'salvage'.

Lady Moyne then spent a lot of time and effort furnishing her house with suitable decorations and furniture – some manufactured from old pieces of oak. She asked Phillips to design two-pronged forks and 'medieval' plates, which the chauffeur hammered out in his spare time. Chips Channon, the famous diarist, described Bailiffscourt as 'decorated to resemble the cell of a rather "pansy" monk'. The Moynes' desire for a medieval paradise didn't finish with the house; dozens of trees were uprooted from the Downs and re-planted in the grounds. Travelling down by train, Lady Moyne would open a carriage window and scatter wild flower seeds along the way.

The house is now the perfect hotel for a romantic break by the sea, which is literally a stone's throw away. Pretty bedrooms, many with four-poster beds and open fires, are comfy. The restaurant is informal, with excellent food and very good service. We shared the restaurant with, among others, a party of American ladies – good for eavesdropping – and Nick Berry and his family. The atmosphere is relaxed and, surprisingly for the surroundings, you don't feel as though you have to be on your best behaviour. However, whilst the ambience is informal, you do still feel as though you are somewhere special.

The dinner menu includes dishes such as: smoked chicken and mango terrine; cream of asparagus soup; fillet of pork wrapped in pastry with a prune and madeira *jus*; supreme of salmon with saffron couscous, with baby asparagus and pesto; duo of chocolate terrines with fresh raspberries, and pecan-brownie pudding with honey ice-cream.

• **COST** *Standard bedrooms are £145 per room per night for bed and breakfast or £100 per person for dinner, bed and breakfast, but you can pay up to £315 per room per night for the master bedroom – Baylies – for bed and breakfast or £175 per person per night for dinner, bed and breakfast. Alternatively, 'Romantic Weekend' breaks cost between £125 and £170 per person per night for a minimum of two nights, including dinner, a room with a four-poster bed, full English breakfast, champagne on arrival, flowers and hand-made chocolates*

WHAT TO DO

The beach is 3 minutes' walk from the hotel and, although pebbly, is very clean and uncrowded. There's lots to do locally, such as antique shopping in Arundel, which is 4 miles away. Chichester, Brighton, Midhurst and Goodwood are all within easy reach.

FOLKESTONE

Most of us race through Folkestone as fast as possible on our way to the Continent. However, in its heyday, Folkestone was one of *the* places for Edwardians to spend their summer holidays. Because of this, Folkestone has some attractive buildings and a pretty shopping area known as The Lanterns. The Victorian Bandstand on the promenade still hosts outdoor concerts and for a real 'period experience' you can take a ride on the Leas Cliff Lift, which connects the promenade to the seafront. Sandgate, on the edge of Folkestone itself, has a raft of antique shops, wine bars and bistros as well as six Martello towers.

• **HOW TO GET THERE** *Take the M20 (Junction 3 off the M25) until Junction 11 and then follow signs for Hythe on the A261. Then follow signs for Folkestone along the A259 coastal road. By rail, take a train from Victoria to Folkestone Town*

WHERE TO STAY

THE SANDGATE HOTEL
ADDRESS The Esplanade, Folkestone, Kent CT20 3DY
☎ 01303 220444 **FAX** 01303 220496
Go to the Sandgate Hotel for its food if nothing else. Chef Samuel Gicquear, who, together with his wife Zara, owns and runs the Sandgate, is an alumnus of Raymond Blanc's Manoir aux Quat' Saisons. La Terrasse, the hotel restaurant, has an extensive *à la carte* menu as well as a three-course set menu available from Tuesday to Thursday lunchtimes and evenings and Friday lunchtime only, at £20.50. There is a five-course set menu on Friday evenings, Saturday lunchtimes and evenings and Sunday lunchtimes, at £29.50. A typical £29.50 menu might comprise: salade de coquilles Saint Jacques grillés et gazpacho; ravioli de homard de la baie de Hythe et son fumet emulsionné a l'estragon; sorbet au champagne et son marc; canon d'agneau de Romney Marsh rôti, jus simple à la fleur de thym et tian de légumes; le plateau de fromages de maître fromager Philippe Olivier de Boulogne sur Mer; or giboulée [shower] des cerises with glace à la vanille de Bourbon.

The hotel itself dates back to the mid-19th-century, the days when Folkestone was a fashionable venue and was frequented by resting officers and gentlefolk. Today, it is sympathetically decorated and all bedrooms have en-suite facilities. In warm weather, you can take your breakfast on the balcony, overlooking the sea – choose a full English version, or warm petits croissants, pains au chocolat or brioches.

- **COST** *A double or twin room with en suite bathroom and balcony costs from £74 per night and includes either English or continental breakfast*

- **HOW TO GET THERE** *The hotel is situated on the left-hand side of the A259 coastal road, travelling from Hythe towards Folkestone. Sandgate is on the edge of Folkestone*

WHAT TO DO

From the Sandgate Hotel, you can visit Canterbury and its cathedral, the charming fishing village of Rye, and Leeds Castle.

HARWICH

The old town boasts an attractive Old Customs House in use from 1795 up until 1935 and a Guildhall rebuilt in 1769, where you can still see graffiti carved by prisoners in its gaol. The town is steeped in maritime history. Nearby Mistley is worth a visit, with its towers which were remodelled by Robert Adam in 1776 from the remains of a medieval church, as is the Essex Secret Bunker, the former Essex County Council HQ in the event of a nuclear war.

WHERE TO STAY

THE PIER AT HARWICH

ADDRESS The Quay, Harwich, Essex CO12 3HH
☎ 01255 241212   **FAX** 01255 551922

Harwich may make you think of the container port and cross-channel ferries, and indeed, the Pier Hotel was built to serve intrepid passengers to the Continent. However, Old Harwich is actually quite attractive, with a lighthouse and old maritime buildings. There is also a wonderful old cinema, which has been lovingly restored to its original glory. Watching something like *Brief Encounter* there is an atmospheric experience. The first floor of the Pier Hotel houses the Harbourside Restaurant, whilst the ground floor is devoted to the modestly priced Ha'penny Pier. The Harbourside specialises in top-quality fish and seafood – any smoked items on the menu are smoked at the restaurant and their own salt-water tanks allow them to serve the freshest of lobsters. Dishes include: flash-fried scallops, £6.75; cold poached lobster, £9.75; New England clam chowder, £5.25; mixed grill of seafood, £12.95; and *fruits de mer* £22.50. Puddings such as baklava or strawberry shortcake gâteau are all £5.25. The Ha'penny Pier has more bistro-style fishy food, such as excellent fish and chips. A children's menu of soup, fish and chips and ice cream is good value at £5.50.

There are six pretty bedrooms, some with stunning views over the estuary. The hotel is in the same stable as the Maison Talbooth and Le Talbooth Restaurant in Dedham (see Romantic Weekends, page 12).

- **COST** *Double rooms are between £75 and £85 per night per room, including continental breakfast*
- **HOW TO GET THERE** *From the M11 and M25, take the A12 as far as Colchester and then take the A120 to Harwich. The Pier Hotel is on the seafront. By train, you can go direct from Liverpool Street to Harwich*

WHAT TO DO

THE REDOUBT AND BATHSIDE BATTERY

ADDRESS Behind 29 Main Road, Harwich, Essex CO1Z 3LT
☎ 01255 503429
Built during the Napoleonic Wars as a defence against a French invasion.

- **OPENING TIMES** *Daily, May–Aug 10.00–17.00; Sun, Sept–Apr 10.00–16.00*
- **COST** *£1 for adults and concessions; accompanied children free*

CLACTON SHOPPING VILLAGE

ADDRESS Stephenson Road West, Clacton-on-Sea, Essex
☎ 01255 479595
For shopaholics, the latest factory-outlet centre.

- **OPENING TIMES** *Mon–Wed, Thurs–Sat 10.00–18.00; Thurs 10.00–20.00; Sun 11.00–17.00*

THE ISLE OF WIGHT

There is something rather magical about visiting an island and now the catamaran can whisk you from Portsmouth in just 15 minutes, so if you haven't been to the Isle of Wight since your school days, now is the time to go. Most people tend to think of the island as an old-fashioned childhood haunt or as a seafarers' haven – where owning a boat is almost mandatory. Of course it is all these things but somehow the island seems to have acquired a jauntier feel, with lots of young people bringing over their bikes or hiring bikes on the island, plus the windsurfing fraternity, and, of course, it's still a great place for kids, with lovely sandy beaches and lots of child-friendly hotels.

- **HOW TO GET THERE** *A hassle-free way to get to the island is to travel by train, hiring a car when you get there. Take South West Trains (☎ 0845 6000650) from Waterloo to Portsmouth: £21.70*

Network AwayBreak. It takes 1½ hours. Then take the fabulously modern and speedy Catamaran from Portsmouth Harbour to Ryde Pier, which costs £10.30 return for an adult (☎ Wightlink 0870 582 7744) and takes 15 minutes. Hire a car through Avis from £25 per day (☎ 01983 615522). Or go by car ferry with Wightlink, from Portsmouth to Fishbourne (☎ 0870 582 7744). It is best to book your return ferry well in advance

WHERE TO STAY

THE PRIORY BAY HOTEL

ADDRESS Priory Drive, Seaview, Isle of Wight PO34 5BU
☎ 01983 613146 **FAX** 01983 616539
A new hotel, owned by Andrew Palmer of the Covent Garden Soup Company fame, with a fabulous location perched on a cliff with marvellous views overlooking Priory Bay. Approached through a medieval stone arch, the rooms are attractively airy and furnished and decorated by designer Annabel Claridge. The main rooms are beautifully decorated and there are lots of areas for dining al fresco. The Captain's Room on the top floor, where we stayed, has a cool nautical theme and boasts a balcony with lovely views out to sea. The hotel has its own little path through a wooded area down to Priory Bay, where a seafood restaurant has also been created – ideal for lunch after a quick dip in the sea. Other facilities include tennis courts, swimming pool and nine-hole golf course. It is also possible to stay in self-catering cottages in the grounds (sleeps 4).
• **COST** *Double rooms from £52.50 per person per night, including continental breakfast, £67.50 half board. Cottages, three nights self catering from £250, depending on season*
• **HOW TO GET THERE** *From Ryde, take the B333. The hotel is between Nettlestone and St Helens*

THE NORTHBANK HOTEL

ADDRESS Seaview, Isle of Wight PO34 5ET
☎ 01983 612227
The Northbank is a smashed up, quirky but incredibly friendly hotel, with lawns running down to a small beach. There is a large, comfy residents' drawing room with copies of *Country Life* and squashy arm chairs, and a small bar, as well as the dining room, games room and television room. The great thing about the Northbank is that the atmosphere is so laid back you relax totally over your weekend. It's one of those strange places where nothing is absolutely right – there are no en-suite bathrooms, for instance – but everything is perfect all at the same time. There is children's high tea, served at about 6pm, of the chicken nuggets or macaroni cheese and jelly and ice cream variety, and no-one seems to mind too much about sand and odd things in buckets being traipsed

through. It is slightly 'Battersea on Sea' with lots of professional couples with small children, and most tables at dinner seem to be garnished with the obligatory baby-listening device, but there are also guests without families. There is lots to see and do on the Isle of Wight, even if you aren't a yachtie. Small children will love the proximity of the beach and can spend hours doing whatever it is small children do with a bucket of water and some sand, whilst you are only 30 seconds walk away from a cup of tea, some sandwiches and fruit cake or a drink. All in all, it is a lovely, unpretentious place, perfect for a relaxed weekend by the sea.

• **COST** *Bed and breakfast per person per night, £30 in low season, £35 in high season. Dinner, £15 per head. Children aged under 2 stay free and children aged between 2 and 12 are half price*

• **HOW TO GET THERE** *Seaview is a few minutes' taxi ride from Ryde, where the ferry and catamaran dock*

WHERE TO EAT

In either of the Priory Bay Hotel's two restaurants or the restaurant in the Northbank Hotel.

WHAT TO DO

OFFSHORE SPORTS
ADDRESS Orchardly Road, Shanklin PO37 7NP
☎ 01983 866269
The island has some lovely cycle rides (though around the Shanklin area there are lots of steep hills). Offshore also supply routes, from the simple to the more challenging. Our route took us through a camp site past the Isle of Wight aeroport onto the Alveston road. You follow an incredibly rural winding track and then come back along an old railway line.

• **COST** *From £5 for half a day and £9 for a day*

OSBORNE HOUSE
ADDRESS York Avenue, East Cowes PO32 6JY
☎ 01983 200022
The holiday home of Queen Victoria, this is a beautifully preserved house. You can see the bedroom where she died, which was kept as a shrine until it was reopened by George VI. There are paintings of the family, cribs where the grandchildren slept and even the Swiss cottage in the garden where the children played. Lots of history about the family to interest children, who are given a fact-finding form to fill in which had our bunch totally absorbed.

• **OPENING TIMES** *10.00–17.00 Daily, April to October 10.00–17.00; grounds open until 18.00*

- **COST** Adults £6.50, concessions £5.20, children 6–16 years £3.50. Family ticket (2 adults, 3 children) £17.30

CARISBROOKE CASTLE

ADDRESS Carisbrooke, Newport PO30 1XY
☎ 01983 522107
- **OPENING TIMES** Winter 10.00–16.00; summer 10.00–18.00
- **COST** Adults £4.50, concessions £3.40, children 5–16 years £2.30. Family ticket £11.30

BLACKGANG CHIME FANTASY THEME PARK

ADDRESS near Ventnor PO38 2HN
☎ 01983 730330
- **OPENING TIMES** Apr–Oct 10.00–17.00; some evenings it is floodlit and stays open until 22.00
- **COST** Adults £5.95, concessions £5.50, children 3–13 years £4.95. Family ticket (2 adults plus 2 children) £19.50. Free return visit within 4 days on all tickets

NEEDLES PLEASURE PARK

ADDRESS Alum Bay, Totland PO39 0JD
☎ 01983 752401
With chair lift to Alum Bay, Robin Hill Country Park, Shanklin Chine.
- **OPENING TIMES** Every day in summer, 10.00–17.00; Sat–Thurs in winter 10.00–16.45
- **COST** Entrance to the park is free but to park the car all day costs £3. Return trip on the chairlift: adult £2.60, children £1.90

RARE BREEDS AND WATER FOWL PARK

ADDRESS St Lawrence, Ventnor PO38 1OW
☎ 01983 854144
- **OPENING TIMES** Mar–Oct 10.00–17.30
- **COST** Adults £3.70, concessions £3.20, children £2.20. Family ticket (2 adults, 2 children) £10.50

ORFORD

Orford is a great place to go, whether it's in high summer or off season. A winding lane edged with pretty red brick houses and cottages leads down to the quay, where you can watch the boats go by or fish for crabs with a piece of string and a lump of bacon. Orford has a couple of small grocery stores for ice creams and essentials as well as a good basket shop selling huge log baskets and Jeremy-Fisher-style panniers. There is also a small antique shop, which sometimes has some pretty items.
- **HOW TO GET THERE** Follow the A12 to the B1084 and turn off at Orford. This road takes you directly to the village

WHERE TO STAY

THE FROIZE INN

ADDRESS The Street, Chillesford, near Woodbridge, Suffolk IP12 3PU
☎ 01394 450282

Although not in Orford itself, the Froize Inn is only 3 miles by road and about 40 minutes' walk from Orford and is on the site of a former friary, where friars walking between the priories at Orford and nearby Butley would stop for refreshment. (A 'froize' was a monastic dish, and was like a pancake stuffed with mushrooms, bacon and vegetables, which could be folded up and eaten 'on the hoof'.) The pub was 1998 Seafood Pub of the Year and 1999 Dining Pub of the Year and is famed for its seafood, prepared by chef-patron Alistair Shaw. The pub is painted inside in an attractive jade green colour, with lots of fishing paraphernalia hanging from walls and ceiling. The staff are friendly and helpful and there is an easy-going, relaxed atmosphere. Meat and vegetarian dishes are also always on the menu and they do a roast lunch on Sunday. Fresh fish dishes are, obviously, a speciality – we had the best haddock and chips for a long time at £7.95. The imaginative starters were delicious: we chose six oysters deep-fried in batter, served with a sweet chilli sauce, £7.95. Other appetisers include: home-made soup of the day, £4.15; chicken-liver and armagnac parfait with a grape chutney, £5.95; or seared squid on an apple and fennel salad, £7.25. Typical main courses are home-made 'fish pie de luxe' (fillets of fish and shellfish with a pastry topping), £10.95; 'seafood froize', filled with prawns, mussels, scallops and white fish in a crab sauce, £10.95; or sizzling fillet of beef, with water chestnuts and wild mushrooms, in a black bean sauce, served with potatoes and vegetables, £13.95. Nostalgic 'nursery puddings' – such as spotted dick and custard and chocolate bread and butter pudding – and unusual ice creams and sorbets are all £3.95. If you can't manage a full lunch, there is a good ploughman's for £5.50 and salads such as fresh dressed crab, £7.25, and filled rolls, from £3.35. Children are welcomed; there is a children's menu or the Froize will split adult portions (although they do not have any high chairs). There is a large garden and a climbing frame to keep children happy and no silly nonsense about their not being allowed to set foot in the bar. Stay in one of the two en-suite bedrooms and use the Froize as a base for visiting the wild and beautiful Suffolk coast. The pub also has caravan parking space and charges £5 per pitch per night for water only or £7 per pitch per night including electricity.

• **COST** *£50–£55 per room per night for bed and English breakfast*

• **HOW TO GET THERE** *Turn off the A12 towards Orford on to the B1084 and you will come to the village of Chillesford. The Froize Inn is on your right*

WHERE TO EAT

THE BUTLEY-ORFORD OYSTERAGE

ADDRESS Market Hill, Orford, Suffolk IP12 2LH
☎ 01394 450277   **FAX** 01394 450949

The Butley Oysterage has now achieved almost cult status from all the foodie journalists who have 'discovered' it. If you are a fan of oysters and seafood as well as home-smoked fish, then this is the place to go. Although it is now fiendishly popular (best to book in advance) it retains its simplicity and charm. The Oysterage has been going for more than 35 years, and has grown with its popularity. Be sure to visit their shop behind the restaurant and take home smoked fish and useful gadgets like oyster-opening knives.

• **COST** £15–£20 per head

• **HOW TO GET THERE** From the A12, take the B1084. This takes you into the market square and the Oysterage is on the square

THE OLD WAREHOUSE

ADDRESS The Quay, Orford, Suffolk IP12 2NU
☎ 01394 450210

A pleasant brasserie right on the quay that serves locally caught fish and chips, speciality seafoods as well as snacks and take-aways. Good for afternoon tea, when you can sit outside and enjoy the sea air whilst eating home-made cakes and scones.

• **OPENING TIMES** Summer, Tues–Sun, 10.00–17.00; winter, Thurs–Sun 10.00–17.00

• **COST** £4.95 for fish and chips, £5.95 for speciality foods

WHAT TO DO

LADY FLORENCE BOAT TRIPS

ADDRESS 33 Potkins Lane, Orford, Suffolk IP12 2SS
☎ 0831 698298

The best way to see the local coastline and wildlife is from a boat. Choose a 4-hour lunch, evening dinner or 2½-hour brunch cruise from Orford, passing Aldeburgh, Shingle Street, the RSPB's Havergate Island and the National Trust's Orford Ness. These cruises run all year round, regardless of the weather or tides and, in winter, there is a cosy coal fire. On board there is a full bar and the food is based on fresh local produce. The Lady Florence is an ex-Admiralty vessel taking 12 passengers.

• **OPENING TIMES** Brunch 9.00–11.30; Lunch 12.00–16.00; Dinner, Apr–Sept, times dependent on sunset

• **COST** 4-hour cruises, £10 per person. Main courses from £6.95; other courses, £2.50. 2½-hour brunch cruise (inclusive of three-course brunch), £18.25 per person. All prices plus 5% service charge

ORFORD CASTLE

ADDRESS Orford, Suffolk IP1Z 2ND

☎ 01394 450472

Although rather empty inside, this English Heritage-run castle is
well worth a visit, not least for the view over Orford Ness from the
top. Still in pretty good nick, and not just a ruin with a few walls
and stones to wander over, it gives an excellent impression of what
castles were like in medieval times.

- **OPENING TIMES** *1st Apr to 31st Oct, 10.00–18.00; (17.00 in Oct); Nov to 31st Mar, Wed–Sat, 10.00–16.00*
- **COST** *Adults £2.50, concessions £1.90, children £1.30*
- **HOW TO GET THERE** *Take the B1084 off the A12. The castle is plainly visible from Orford and is within walking distance of the market square, where you can park*

ORFORD NESS (NATIONAL TRUST)

ADDRESS Orford Quay, Orford, Woodbridge, Suffolk IP12 2NU

☎ 01394 450900

Wild and unspoilt Suffolk coastline that is the largest vegetated
shingle spit in Europe, with important plant communities and bird
colonies. The maximum stay is 3 hours during peak periods only.
There are 5 miles of walks as well as information and displays on
the flora and fauna.

- **OPENING TIMES** *Easter to end Oct, Thurs–Sat. Outward ferries from 10.00–14.00. Last ferry 17.00*
- **COST** *National Trust members £3.20; non-members £5.20; children half price, under-3's free. Admission includes price of ferry*
- **HOW TO GET THERE** *Access is by ferry from Orford Quay*

SOUTHWOLD

If you want to go on a nostalgia trip recreating your childhood
seaside holidays, then this is the place. The town itself does have
a sort of 1950s feel to it; you expect the gentlemen that pass you
on the pavement to doff their hats to you. The beach is long and
uncrowded and is fringed with much-photographed coloured
beach huts that now command quite a price. If Brighton is raffish
and sophisticated, Southwold is stylish in a 'bicycle clips, wicker
baskets and hot cocoa before bedtime' sort-of-way. General
enquiries and shops ☎ 01728 688303/5.

- **HOW TO GET THERE** *Take the M25 and then the A12. Turn off onto the A11095 to Southwold*

WHERE TO STAY

COTTAGES AND BEACH HUTS
☎ 01502 723292 H A Adams or ☎ 01502 722065 Jennie Jones
Rent a cottage or a beach hut from either of the above. Then take
the small ferry across the harbour entrance to Walberswick and
visit the Bell or the Anchor pubs.

THE CROWN HOTEL
ADDRESS High Street, Southwold, Suffolk IP18 6DP
☎ 01502 722275 **FAX** 01502 727263
Apart from the town's charm, one of the best reasons to visit
Southwold is the Crown Hotel. The buzz in the main bar of this
former coaching inn on a Friday night is palpable, as guests
arriving from London mix with the local crowd. The Crown
operates on a first-come-first-served basis, so tables in the bar are
often hard to come by, particularly in the summer months. It is not
unusual to spot a 'table sitter' queuing at opening time with a
rolled-up newspaper, ready to sit out the hour before the menus
are produced. Fortunately, the Crown's popularity is well founded:
delicious food, an excellent wine list and a relaxed atmosphere
make a perfect combination. For those who prefer to know that they
will be able to sit down to eat, tables in the restaurant and front room
parlour can be pre-booked. The bedrooms are comfortable and there
is a particularly good family room in the eaves of the hotel.
• **COST** *Bed and breakfast, £72 per night for a double room;
single rooms, £47. One family room, £98 per night*

NEWLANDS
ADDRESS Halesworth Road, Southwold, Suffolk IP18 6NL
☎ 01502 722762 **FAX** 01502 724696
If you want to stay in a traditional English seaside guest house,
then try Newlands. Run by the very friendly and helpful Penny Ball,
the great thing about Newlands is that Penny has just added a
purpose-built extension for disabled guests. It includes a wheelchair
ramp to a private lounge through to a double bedroom with an
en-suite shower room. Car parking is right next to the wheelchair
ramp and the French windows open from the bedroom to the
back garden. Penny will cook evening meals for guests by prior
arrangement, but don't turn up on her doorstep expecting dinner
without pre-booking or she won't be a happy bunny. Disabled
guests can eat in their own private sitting room or join other guests
in the dining room.
• **COST** *Small double room and en-suite bathroom, from £45 per
night per couple. Double/twin rooms with en-suite shower, from
£50 per night per couple. Ground-floor family suite with fully fitted
disabled en-suite, from £65 per night per couple. Three-course
evening meal with coffee and mints, £15 per head*

WHERE TO EAT

THE CROWN HOTEL

ADDRESS High Street, Southwold, Suffolk IP18 6DP

☎ 01502 722275   **FAX** 01502 727263

The hotel restaurant has lovely food; typical dishes include: fresh asparagus with quail's eggs and hollandaise sauce for starters; a superb Caesar salad; roast fillet of salmon with crushed potato, wilted spinach and tomato and pepper dressing; calves' liver with basil and olive oil mash. There is a choice of wines, white or rosé with the starter, red with the main course and then a pudding wine.

• **COST** *Dinner, £19.50 for two courses or £24.50 for three courses. There is also an excellent bar menu, with dishes from £4 to £10. Three glasses of wine for £8.75*

WHAT TO DO

RSPB NATURE RESERVE AT MINSMERE

ADDRESS Westleton, Saxmundham, Suffolk IP17 3BY

☎ 01728 648281   **FAX** 01728 648770

See many types of breeding birds such as the Avocet and Marsh Harrier. A large visitors' centre with a tea shop and a good shop selling a selection natural history books as well as outdoor clothing.

• **OPENING TIMES** *Winter 09.00–16.00; summer 09.00–dusk; (Closed Tues)*

• **COST** *Adults £5.00, concessions £3.00, children £1.50. Family ticket (2 adults plus any children) £10. RSPB members free*

THE OLD SAILORS' READING ROOM

ADDRESS East Cliff, Southwold, Suffolk IP18 6EL

☎ 01502 723782

This reading room on the seafront is still used by fishermen and packed with info on Southwold's marine history.

CONCERTS

ADDRESS Snape Maltings, Snape, Saxmundham, Suffolk IP17 1SP

☎ 01728 453543 Concert Hall Box Office

Particularly for the Easter Festival, Snape Proms in August, a Britten Festival in the autumn and seasonal concerts at Christmas. However, the main festival is in June and features contemporary music. Golf at Southwold's Golf Club (☎ 01502 723234). Riding at Grove View Stables in Wenhaston (☎ 01502 478275) costs £8.50 per ½ hour for private riding or £6 per ½ hour for hacking.

THORPENESS

Thorpeness is a one-off, really. Edwardian Suffolk landowner G Stuart Ogilvie decided to turn 6,000 acres of his family estate into a purpose-built holiday village aimed at families of the Raj and other colonial outposts who would appreciate a holiday away from the sticky heat, amongst the dunes and bracing winds of the East Coast. The original brochure said of Thorpeness 'It will attract those who have no desire for promenades and cinemas... those who can appreciate a beautiful little hamlet situated between sea and lake, and backed by the purple heather and golden gorse of the Suffolk woods' and not much has changed. The plans were originally outlined in 1908 and, by the 1930s, most of the major buildings were in place. The Tudorbethan houses were built round a man-made freshwater lake, The Meare, with a golf club and a country club.

• **HOW TO GET THERE** *A map in the original 1930s brochure actually shows the route from Hyde Park Corner! These days, it's a much easier journey. From the M11 and M25, take the A12 as far as the junction with the B1094, which is signposted to Thorpeness. By rail, take the train from Liverpool Street to Saxmundham, changing at Ipswich. The station is approximately 5 miles from Thorpeness. There is also a coach service from Victoria to Aldeburgh, 2 miles away*

WHERE TO STAY

THORPENESS COUNTRY CLUB

ADDRESS Benthill, Thorpeness, Suffolk IP16 4NU
☎ 01728 454704
The country club has now been turned into eleven fully-fitted two- or three-bedroom apartments, which can be rented on a weekly or weekend basis. All the apartments have a sea view and some have sun decks overlooking the tennis courts. All are newly decorated and have a fully equipped kitchen, en-suite bath/shower rooms, central heating, living areas and private parking. Guests staying in the apartments can use the seven tennis courts at reduced rates along with discounted golf-club fees.

• **COST** *From £200 to £800, depending on size and season, for a week's stay. Weekend breaks are subject to availability and are charged at a rate of around 75% of the weekly tariff*

THORPENESS HOTEL AND GOLF CLUB

ADDRESS Lakeside Avenue, Thorpeness, Aldeburgh, Suffolk IP16 4NH
☎ 01728 452176   **FAX** 01728 453866
If you don't want to cater for yourselves, this hotel has 30 en-suite bedrooms, a clubhouse, snooker room and restaurant.

• **COST** *Hotel breaks from £45 per person per night for Friday and Saturday with en-suite rooms and full English breakfast. Children*

aged 8–16 sharing their parents' room are charged at 50% of the adult rate. Children under 8 are charged on a meal-only basis

THE HOUSE IN THE CLOUDS

ADDRESS near Leiston, Thorpeness, Suffolk IP16 4NQ

☎ 0171 252 0743

When Thorpeness village was created, there was suddenly a need to supply sufficient water to the influx of holidaymakers. The problem was, how to do this without building an unsightly water tower that would spoil the skyline? It was eventually decided to disguise it as a cottage, albeit one 70 feet in the air. The tower part underneath was designed to provide further holiday accommodation. It was originally called The Gazebo but was christened The House in the Clouds by a children's-author friend of G Stuart Ogilvie. The water tank was removed in the 1970s and the building was completely refurbished in the 1980s. The self-catering property now has a fully fitted kitchen with all appliances including microwave, washing machine and dryer; a pretty drawing room, five bedrooms and three bathrooms, as well as a magnificent bedroom right at the tiddly top where the water tank used to be. The folly has an acre of private grounds, tennis and badminton courts as well as ping-pong kit and a snooker table. Generations of children on their way to Thorpeness for their holidays have used The House in the Clouds as a marker for how near they are to their destination as you can see it from quite a distance.

• **COST** *The House in the Clouds is only available for a full week's stay during the summer months but off season you can take it for a weekend break. Minimum booking two nights, between £263 and £374 per night January to mid-July. All charges include VAT, gas, electricity, linen and towels*

• **HOW TO GET THERE** *Take the M11, M25 and then A12 to the junction with the B1094 to Thorpeness. You will see The House in the Clouds as you approach the town*

WHERE TO EAT

In The Thorpeness Hotel and Golf Club or the restaurants in Aldeburgh (see p. 43).

WHAT TO DO

THE MEARE

Spending time around this beautiful freshwater lake is a wonderful way to lose a few hours. Equally appealing for children or adults are the small islands dotted around which you can 'conquer'; some have small buildings, such as Wendy's House, The Fort or The Pirate's Cave. Hire a rowing boat, punt or canoe and meander along the waterways watching coots, ducks and moorhens.

WHITSTABLE

The main reason to visit Whitstable must be its world-famous oysters, which can be sampled in several of the local pubs and restaurants. However, it is also a pretty little seaside town, with weatherboarded cottages and winding lanes and a rich maritime and fishing history. Whitstable makes a good base from which to explore East Kent and Canterbury, with its beautiful cathedral. Or you could take gentle stroll along the coast.

• **HOW TO GET THERE** *By car, take the A2, M2 and then the A299 and A290 to Whitstable. By rail, the train from Victoria to Whitstable takes around 80 minutes*

WHERE TO STAY

HOTEL CONTINENTAL

ADDRESS 29 Beach Walk, Whitstable, Kent CT5 2BP
☎ 01227 280280   **FAX** 01227 280257

The Hotel Continental is on the sea front at Whitstable and is run by the Whitstable Oyster Fishery Company, which also owns the famous Fish Restaurant and the Imperial Oyster Cinema. A million miles removed from the traditional image of the British Seaside Landlady, the Hotel Continental is a stylish place to stay, popular with both families and couples alike. A recent total refurbishment has provided twenty-two en-suite rooms decorated in Art Deco style with clean lines and clear bright colours, in keeping with the building, which opened in 1930. The rooms are simply furnished as the management feels that most of its guests are there only on a short-break basis and so they have put the emphasis on providing large, comfortable beds – it must be something to do with all those oysters. If you are taking your family with you, you might choose to book the hotel's 'flat', which has full cooking facilities, laundry room, en-suite bathroom, lounge and bedroom sleeping up to four people. Or, better still, book into one of their seafront Fisherman's Huts, staying in which is like sleeping in a grand and comfortable Wendy House. At night, all you can hear is the sound of the waves washing on to the shingle and in the morning you wake to the soulful cry of seagulls circling overhead.

The hotel restaurant serves a French-style menu at £9.50 for lunch, £12.50 for dinner. A typical menu would include dishes such as charcûterie, oysters, fish soup, fillet of haddock with parsley sauce or rib-eye steak with frites, followed by crème brûlée, pear tart or ice cream. Children's portions are available and there is an extensive bar menu from which children are also welcome to order.

• **COST** *A basic double room costs from £48 per night, rising to £100 for a room with a sea view and a balcony; a family room costs £84 per night. The family flat costs £102 per night at the*

weekend. The six Fisherman's Huts are all different but cost from £90 per night for double occupancy up to £120 per night for up to four people

WHAT TO DO

THE WHITSTABLE MUSEUM
ADDRESS 5 Oxford Street, Whitstable, Kent CT5 1DB
☎ 01227 276998
- **OPENING TIMES** *Daily except Wed & Sun 10.30–13.00, 14.00–16.00*
- **COST** *Free*

THE FISHERY AND OYSTER EXHIBITION
ADDRESS East Quay, Whitstable Harbour, Kent CT5 1AB
☎ 01227 280753
- **OPENING TIMES** *Daily, Easter–Oct 10.00–16.00; weekends only Nov–Christmas*
- **COST** *Adults £1.50, concessions and children £1, family ticket £3.50*

THEMED WEEKENDS

A weekend break is the ideal opportunity to learn a new activity, or to spend two days doing something that you already know you enjoy. You may have always wanted to throw a pot, learn how to 'horse whisper' or take up a new sport and, if you have a busy job or family commitments, fitting it in during the week can be a problem. On a weekend course, you can really concentrate on learning or just having an exhilarating time. For some, spending a weekend doing something is far more relaxing than lazing around doing nothing, and learning something creative can be great for combating stress.

However you want to spend your weekend, there are activities to fit – from gentle, creative courses to dare-devil all-action pursuits that are especially great for stag and hen weekends. You could easily choose to get together a group of friends and take over a course or get one of the specialist companies to plan a tailor-made weekend break.

Equally, if you want to go away on your own, courses can be a good way of doing it. Most of us don't want to sit on our own in a hotel eating dinner, so joining a group is ideal. Even if you have nothing obvious in common with the others, you will at least have a common objective, and you can become great mates with people you might not otherwise have met.

ACTIVITY CLUBS

GO FOR IT SATURDAY (GFI)
ADDRESS 3 Genoa Avenue, London SW15
☎ 0181 785 0786 **FAX** 0181 516 7670

GFI is an activity club that caters mostly for youngish Londoners who'd like to do something fun at the weekend. The range of days and weekends out is impressive. Activities can be anything from waterskiing, rollerhockey, sailing, gliding, rock climbing and paintball to days out at Alton Towers and weekends away doing watersports, skiing, diving or general activities.

The club costs very little per year – just £45 – but then activities cost on top. Again, costs are kept low and events can be as little as £5 up to a couple of hundred pounds for a weekend away. The people taking part are generally young professionals about mid-twenties to mid-thirties, with a liberal helping of Antipodeans and Europeans. They tend to be pleasant and friendly, not overbearing but not particularly shy either. It is definitely not a singles club although the majority of members happen to be single.

The great advantage of doing things with GFI is that all the hassle of organising an event for yourself is taken away and you have instant companions. The organisers, Chris and Elizabeth (childhood friends), run things in a low-key, laid-back manner that rubs off on participants and makes for a relaxing time.

The weekends away are very much geared towards activity junkies. In the summer, there are weekends at activity centres where you can windsurf, water-ski, canoe, climb, play golf and do archery, among other things. The club organises weekends for the hardy in spring and autumn, with white water rafting, climbing, 'coasteering' (a new craze, apparently) and pot-holing.

The club is very much open to suggestions from members and weekends can be set up specially if there is enough demand. So, if a group insists on a whole weekend surfing in Devon, that can be arranged.

• **COST** £45 annual membership. Costs for weekends depend on the activity involved. A recent Mountain Biking Weekend cost £145 for members or £165 for non-members

DINNER DATES
ADDRESS 8 Millers Court, Chiswick Mall, London W4 2PF
☎ 0181 741 1252 **FAX** 0181 741 9799

If you're currently single and don't really want to stay that way, maybe you should try a weekend with a purpose. Dinner Dates is a relaxed and friendly organisation – more like joining a club than an agency – which organises regular dinners and weekends away to sporting and cultural events. If you have ever been through a period in your life when you didn't have a partner – and that includes most of us – you'll know that it can be a depressing experience. It's so tempting not to go out and do anything, but lounge at home with a bottle of wine, a Sainsbury's ready-cooked meal and huge quantities of chocolate. Dinner Dates is a civilised way to get out and meet people without feeling 'predatory'. The dinners are arranged twice a week and each one comprises around 32 guests, usually divided between a number of small tables. Hillie Marshall, who runs Dinner Dates, makes sure that the men move around the table after the main course, so that everyone gets a chance to meet. There is no pressure to attend the dinners, which are held at venues such as the Ritz, the Lanesborough and Mosimann's and members go along as and when they feel like it. The average cost of an evening is £55, including pre-dinner drink, wine, food, service and VAT. You could join in for a Flotilla sailing weekend, ski-in, a guided walking holiday, a spring break in Bangkok or a week's summer holiday in Bodrum, Turkey. Dinner Dates also organises trips to many of the features of 'the season', such as Henley Royal Regatta, polo at Cowdray Park or racing at Royal Ascot, when many guests make a weekend of it by booking into local accommodation.

The venues reflect the sophisticated membership. Dinner Dates is a very civilised way to ensure that you don't miss out on having a good time, just because you aren't attached.

• **COST** *There is no annual fee for belonging to 'the club', only a one-off lifetime membership payment of £125. Dinner and weekend costs depend on the activities: flight simulators £165, treasure hunt £145, opera £70–£110, clay pigeon shooting £89, Vienna £515 including flights, Club Med to Tunisia £643*

COOKERY

THE ALDEBURGH COOKERY SCHOOL
ADDRESS 84 High Street, Aldeburgh, Suffolk IP15 5AB
☎ 01728 454039
Aldeburgh Cookery School is run by Thane Prince (ex-*Daily Telegraph*) and Sara Fox, who co-owns and runs The Lighthouse Restaurant (see Weekends by the Sea, page 44). It only opened in July 1999 to fill great local demand after the pair did a cookery demo to raise funds for the local lifeboat. The Consuming Passions long-weekend courses are a foodie's dream. The course starts on Friday morning at 11am, when you check into your accommodation, followed by a Champagne Reception at the school at midday. This is the chance to meet Sara and Thane and the 11 or so others on your course. After lunch at the Lighthouse, you repair to the school to cook dinner from 3pm. A sample menu might include: potted shrimps; rare fillet of organic beef with horseradish mash and roasted baby beets; and fresh cherry and almond cake, with crème fraîche and ice cream. At 6pm you change for dinner, followed by drinks at 7.30 and a candlelight dinner at the school.

On Saturday morning you visit the beach, buy lobster and fish and so on and then discuss the day's menu over coffee. At 11am you learn how to make risotto and fresh pasta and then eat lunch in the school from 12.30pm. After lunch you have some free time to explore Aldeburgh or just chill out on the beach until 4pm, when it's back to the school again to cook dinner. A typical menu for this would be: lobster ravioli, roast cod on puy lentils, rocket and parmesan salad; chocolate mascarpone cake with raspberry sorbet and red berries. Sunday morning and you'll be sweating over a hot stove again. At 10am you kick off with coffee and croissants, followed by cooking for the Champagne Brunch. From 10.30 until 1.30 when you get to eat, you'll be baking breads, muffins and waffles. A sample menu for brunch might be: kedgeree; steamed Thai coconut mussels; oysters Rockefeller; eggs Benedict; carpetbagger steaks and corned beef hash; exotic fruit soup. At 3.30pm there is coffee-tasting, plus tips on how to make the perfect cup, and then a talk through the recipes and a final cup of tea or glass of wine before you kiss everyone goodbye at 5pm.

The school also runs a selection of one-day courses, including subjects such as Men in the Kitchen, Shellfish Extravaganza and Glorious Game.

- **WHERE TO STAY** *The Wentworth Hotel, ☎ 01728 452312. Prices from £50 per person per night. £72 per person, for two nights' dinner, bed and breakfast. It is within walking distance of the school*

- **COST** *The costs for residential courses include a car service from the school to your accommodation, to alleviate any worries about drinking and driving. Local accommodation can be booked in local hotels or self-catering. Consuming Passions long weekend course, £350 per person; day courses, £75 per person*

- **HOW TO GET THERE** *To get to Aldeburgh, take the A12 exit from the M25 and turn off onto the A1094. By train, leave from Liverpool Street to Saxmundham, changing at Ipswich*

COUNTRY PURSUITS

FAIR GAME (COUNTRY PURSUITS) LTD

ADDRESS King Lane, Over Wallop, Stockbridge, Hants SO20 8JQ
☎ 01264 889884

John and Anthea Russell run Fair Game from their home in Over Wallop. If you hanker after a weekend of country pursuits, this is a pleasant and personal way to experience just that. Fair Game is, first and foremost, an attractively decorated private home. Anthea has an eye for beautiful things, and has an impressive collection, artistically and interestingly displayed. Nothing is so staggeringly valuable that it makes you feel nervous, but the overall impression is stylish as well as welcoming. The weekend starts with supper on Friday night. The hospitality is impressive, not least because of

John's past experience in the fine-wine business and Anthea's skills as a cook. Expect exceptionally good food and wine, coupled with a friendly, informal atmosphere. The couple's in-depth knowledge of the local area and its sporting attractions also sets the scene for the day's activities to come. The tailor-made weekend fishing breaks include chalkstream fishing, with a ghillie and tackle if required. Alternatively, you could get a party of friends together and plump for a day's clay-pigeon shooting at the Apsley Shooting School near Andover. Here, they cater for parties of 10-20 for a full day of traditional sporting clays, orchestrated by David Olive, one of the best instructors in the country. A typical day starts with coffee, a general welcome and talk about the day. At this stage, they create the teams for the day and assess the shooting skills of each member of the party. Lunch and drinks are at about 1pm followed by further shooting. The day ends with a finale shoot from the high tower, which is always the highlight of the day. You can choose to use this as a friendly competition and give out prizes. The other option is to go for a simulated driven shoot. This form of clay shooting has all the outdoor pleasure of a driven day on an estate that has a serious pheasant and partridge shoot during the season. The optimum number for this day is 16 people and instructor and loaders can be provided. Choose either a buffet lunch or a cooked lunch. The farm's manor house provides a perfect setting for lunch, with drinks in the garden first.

Anthea also organises days out sightseeing and shopping for non-participants. Normally, this involves something formal in the morning, such as visiting a country house, followed by lunch and then antique hunting or shopping in the afternoon.

- **WHERE TO STAY** *If you don't want to stay at Fair Game House, you could choose to stay at the Grosvenor House Hotel, High Street, Stockbridge, ☎ 01264 810606 (£82 per night for a double room), or Carberry Guest House, High Street, Stockbridge, ☎ 01264 810771 (£53 per night for a double room)*
- **COST** *Prices depend on the activities you choose. Two nights with dinner, bed and breakfast staying at Fair Game House cost £160 per person. The guided tours exploring local houses and shopping cost from £100 per day for up to four people. Two days trout fishing, together with the catering and the services of a ghillie, start at £450 per person. Simulated driven shooting costs from £190 per head for food and beverages, clays and guns, but excluding accommodation and cartridges, whilst the cost of a day's clay shooting at Apsley Shooting School is £125 per person, including all food and drink, clays, cartridges and guns, if needed, but excluding accommodation*
- **HOW TO GET THERE** *Take the M3 and then the A303 at Junction 8, after Basingstoke. Take a left along the A343 just after Andover. By train, go to Andover from Waterloo. Fair Game House is a 7-mile taxi journey from the station*

CYCLING

ALTERNATIVE TRAVEL GROUP

ADDRESS 69–71 Banbury Road, Oxford, Oxon OX2 6PE
☎ 01865 315678   **FAX** 01865 315697

If you want a weekend combining exercise, fabulous scenery and wonderful meals, then you should book up a weekend of cycling through Alternative Travel's Footloose Programme. Even with the best of bicycles, however, you might very well end up just a little saddle sore, but it's definitely worth the pain. If you are coming by train, Alternative Travel will be happy to arrange transportation from the station, to take you to your hotel or B&B and provide you with detailed maps of your selected routes. An Alternative Travel Group Representative will go through your itinerary with you and answer any questions you may have. These maps are easy to follow, pointing out areas of interest and giving you the opportunity to explore the Oxfordshire countryside. We started in Oxford and cycled out of the town through lovely, quiet country roads that stretched across gently undulating farmland, and we arrived in Woodstock that afternoon. The Blenheim guest house we stayed in was simple and sweet and situated right next to the entrance of Blenheim Palace, in whose grounds we wandered for a small fee. Dinner at the Bear was a gastronomic feast. Starters consisted of wild mushrooms, smoky bacon and baked parmesan cheese millefeuille with tomato essence, £8.00, or flash-fried smoked salmon with marinated cucumber, char-grilled lemon and basil bread, £9.50. Main courses were braised beef in beer, with parsnip and grain-mustard mash, £16.00, and spicy pork fillet with mint and garlic spinach, £18.00. Puddings were blackberry sponge and lemon custard and sticky toffee pudding with clotted cream. The next day we cycled from Woodstock up to Charlbury, encountering a few more hills than we had the day before but the countryside made up for any discomfort as we wove our way through beautiful little villages.

• **COST** *This suggested itinerary would cost £87 per person, including cycle hire, accommodation in the same guest house and breakfast*

• **HOW TO GET THERE** *Take a train from Paddington on Thameslink to Oxford, £23.10 cheap day return. By road take the M40 to Oxford*

DECORATIVE PAINTING

KIM SISSONS, FRIEND OR FAUX

ADDRESS 28 Earsham Street, Bungay, Suffolk NR35 1AQ
☎ 01986 896170

A small town in north Suffolk is the last place that you would expect to find a shop as stylish as Friend or Faux. Kim Sissons and her interior-designer mother Jane co-run this cross between style emporium and antique shop, which is crammed with exquisite items that you just have to have once you've seen them. Kim and Jane only buy things that they themselves really love and like things to go to 'good homes'. The two tiny rooms are beautifully decorated and show off the stock to best advantage. Friend or Faux's speciality is 'decorative salvage' – they are brilliant at 'recycling' little pieces of ormolu or bits of gilding and giving them new life. Small bits such as the decorative handles off furniture or gilt serving dishes are turned into paper weights, and old crystal drops from 'dead' chandeliers are hung on sumptuous ribbons for Christmas decorations.

Kim runs the painting courses in the 'atelier' two doors away from the shop, where she and her mother lovingly restore some of their finds. She is currently offering two courses, but will tailor something to your exact requirements if there are four of you who want to do a course together.

• *Paint class weekend* – a two-day class, starting with basics but slanted towards painting furniture and doors. Students learn how to prepare a surface, cover it with different effects, and finish with details such as lines, flowers and so on, with the aim of giving things a period feel – 'painted yesteryear not yesterday'.

• *Cheat's gilding* – a course on how to repair gilded frames, mirrors, lampbases and the like. Students learn to take moulds from good parts to replace lost ones. The course covers gessoing and gold leaf but, as most gilding is worn with age, the idea is to learn to match the existing gold leaf.

• **WHERE TO EAT** *Kim prepares lunch for you, which you eat in her own living quarters above the shop. Expect dishes such as pasta with fennel and salami (from Thomas's the Grocer, the very good deli across the road), or roast chicken and tomato salad, with fresh bread with some good cheese or fruit to follow*

• **WHERE TO STAY** *Although Friend or Faux has no accommodation on site, Kim will be happy to recommend local bed and breakfasts or pubs where you can stay. The Fox and Goose at Fressingfield is worth a visit for dinner. (See Gourmet Weekends, page 154)*

• **WHAT TO DO** *While you are in Bungay, it's worth having a stroll around to look at the 18th-century house fronts and the site of Bigod's 11th-century castle. Nature lovers might also like to stop off at the nearby Otter Trust. Worth a visit are Black Dog Antiques on the other side of the road from Friend or Faux, which is the retail outlet for a group of eight antique dealers. Past finds have included beautiful Victorian parasols, shoes and clothing, old decorative kitchen utensils, leather gun cases and pretty cups and plates for a few pounds each. Further up Earsham Street in the opposite direction is Cork Brick Antiques, which sells pretty French antique furniture and accessories with the odd bit of old textile for cushion covers and curtains*

• **COST** *Two-day painting course, including lunch and as much tea and coffee as you have time for, £125 per person, excluding*

accommodation. B&B costs about £35 per person per night
- **HOW TO GET THERE** *Take the M11, A14 and A143 to Bungay; alternatively take the M25, A12, A14 and A143*

ANNIE SLOAN
ADDRESS 21 Iffley Road, Oxford OX4 1EA
☎ 0870 601 0082

Annie Sloan is probably one of the best-known exponents of paint effects and her dozen or so books on the subject include *The Complete Book of Decorative Paint Techniques, Simple Painted Furniture*, and her latest, *The Painted Furniture Sourcebook*. Annie now concentrates on running courses and writing as well as undertaking the odd mural or decorative commission and launching her own range of paints. Knowing all that, you can be sure that you are booking onto a course with someone who really knows what they are talking about, and not just anybody who thinks that they can run a course and bungs an ad in the back of an interiors magazine. Annie runs three different one-day courses, which start at 10.15am and finish at 4.15pm. There is a maximum of 12 students on each course, plus the course tutors and Annie herself and an assistant, so there is plenty of opportunity for individual attention. The Decorative Gilding course covers bronze-powder work, applying metal leaf and many other techniques explained in her book on the subject. The Decorative Furniture Painting course teaches several useful techniques, such as ageing, découpage and stencilling. The aim of the course is to provide you with the skills to transform bits of old junk furniture into something that you would want to give house room to. The third course is the Colourwashing course, which Annie reckons to be the definitive class on the 12 effects used by interior designers. Find out how colour works with different water-based glazes to make subtle and pale or strong and bold effects. Try frottaging, stippling, several ragging techniques, combing and mutton cloth, as well as combination techniques.

- **WHERE TO STAY** *There is no accommodation on site, but Annie will be pleased to recommend local B&Bs or hotels. As the courses are only for one day, you could book into somewhere either in Bladon, or in one of the great places to stay in Woodstock and use the other day for sightseeing locally and in Oxford (see Cultural Weekends, page 175)*
- **WHERE TO EAT** *There are plenty of local wine bars for dinner*
- **COST** *One-day Decorative Gilding course, one-day Decorative Furniture Painting course, one-day Colourwashing course, each £85 per person, including a light lunch. Annie Sloan's paints and books are available at the course. B&B costs around £40 per person per night*
- **HOW TO GET THERE** *By car; take the M40 to Oxford and then, from the ringroad, take the A44 towards Evesham (also marked Woodstock and Blenheim Palace). After several roundabouts the*

road meets the A4095 at a roundabout just before Woodstock. Take the left exit along the A4095 in the direction of Witney and you will arrive in Bladon. There are two pubs in the village and Knutsford House is after the White House and before the Lamb. By rail there is a direct train from Paddington, leaving at 08.45, which arrives at Hanborough Station, half a mile from Knutsford House, at 10.04. Transport from Hanborough Station is provided free

ELGAR APPRECIATION

ACORN ACTIVITIES
ADDRESS PO Box 120, Hereford HR4 8YB
☎ 01432 830083   **FAX** 01432 830110

Actually doing something strenuous, or even applying your brain to learning a new skill, may sound all too much like hard work. It may be that what you're really after is a couple of days when you don't have to make decisions for yourself, just relaxing and going with the flow, but, at the same time, come away feeling virtuous because you have been doing something constructive. Acorn Activities Elgar Appreciation weekend could be the ideal solution.

'When I die, if I go to heaven, that is what it will be like', people have said. The weekend starts with dinner on Friday evening – a chance to meet your guide and the other guests on the trip. In this case, the guide was Cara Weaver, who really knows her Elgar and was witty, charming and friendly. Saturday is spent visiting various locations with Elgar connections, including some of his former homes, his grave, and Hereford Cathedral. The journeys between the locations are made more interesting with anecdotes from Cara and relevant Elgar compositions.

After dinner, take the opportunity to stroll on the beautiful Malvern hills, and sample Malvern's famous mineral water. If you're there at the right time of the year, you may be lucky enough to hear the nightingales sing in the woods – a hidden extra added to the schedule by the thoughtful Cara.

Sunday morning takes you off to Broadheath, Elgar's birthplace and a museum housing Elgar memorabilia. The curator played 'Salut d'amour' on the composer's own wind-up gramophone. From there, you travel to Worcester for a picnic lunch by the river and a guided tour that ends up at the Cathedral. Back to the hotel for tea and cakes before saying goodbye to Cara and checking out.

The weekend is intelligently planned and extremely well organised. The guide clearly knew what she was talking about, and the talks and trips were pitched at a level that would appeal to both Elgar enthusiasts with an existing knowledge of the composer, and those who could write what they know about him on the back of a postage stamp.

- **WHERE TO STAY** *Our accommodation was in a charming local hotel – very comfortable and with good facilities. The food was plentiful and delicious and the proprietors welcoming and hospitable. Acorn Activities have a range of styles and prices of accommodation on offer, from bed and breakfast to smart country-house hotels, so you can choose which grade will suit you best*
- **COST** *Two nights, dinner, bed and breakfast, with lunch en route on both days, £175 per person*
- **HOW TO GET THERE** *Take the M41 and then the A40, M40, M42, M5, A44, A442 and A49 to Malvern. Detailed instructions to your chosen accommodation are provided on booking*

EXTREME SPORTS

EXHILARATION EXTREME SPORTS (UK) LTD

ADDRESS Liscombe Park, Sudbury, Bucks LU7 0JL
☎ 01296 689099   **FAX** 01296 689097
WEB www.exhilaration.co.uk

James Bond wannabes can sign up for a variety of extreme sporting activities, from yachting in Essex or Dorset, through multi-activity weekends to Extreme Caving. Accommodation on the yachting weekends is on board and Exhilaration reckon that they have chosen the best locations in the country for beginning to learn high-speed water sport. The courses begin on Friday night and are designed to provide a 'taster' of yachting. You can become as involved as you want in the actual sailing as you will be taught the correct techniques and given a chance to take part in all aspects of sailing, or you can just sit back and watch the waves rush by. The organisers will send you details of what you need to take with you, and recommend that you take sea-sickness tablets along just in case. The multi-activity weekends take place in Powys and normally include a selection of climbing and abseiling, canoeing, gorge-walking, scrambling, orienteering, archery, quad biking and clay-pigeon shooting. The Extreme Caving weekends sound like hell on earth, but if that's what you dream of doing then this is a good way of doing it with qualified people. This is definitely not for claustrophobics as you are taken through passages too narrow to turn round in and tiny crevices that you have to squeeze through.

Exhilaration also organises a range of day courses, such as a racing-driver's trial, tank-driving and classic-car driving – bound to leave you shaken but not stirred – in a MKII Jaguar, Aston Martin DB5 and E-Type Jag. The Classic car experience ends with a white-knuckle drive in the Lola T74, with a professional driver at the wheel.

- **COST** *The yacht-sailing weekend costs £159, including accommodation on board, fuel, gas, safety equipment, soft drinks, breakfast, lunch and tea. Multi-activity weekends cost £179,* *including two nights' bed and breakfast accommodation, and the extreme caving course costs £199 including two nights' bed and breakfast*

FLY FISHING

THE ARUNDEL ARMS

ADDRESS Lifton, Devon PL16 0AA

☎ 01566 784666   **FAX** 01566 784494

A weekend learning to fish, or just getting on and doing it, staying in a lovely pub in beautiful countryside, will get a lot of hearts racing. The Arundel Arms is situated on the edge of Dartmoor National Park and is one of the UK's most famous fishing hotels. With access to fishing on over 20 miles of rivers such as the Tamar, the Lyd, the Ottery, and the Thrushell, for salmon, sea trout and wild brown trout, the Arundel Arms offers great variety for both experienced and 'virgin' fishermen alike. The hotel has its own team of award-winning fishing instructors, who will teach the novice and, for someone wishing to take up the sport, the Arundel Arms is one of the most enjoyable and comfortable places to do it. In the winter when the fly fishing season is closed, the hotel also arranges regular weekend driven shoots for both snipe and pheasant.

The hotel itself is based around an 18th-century coaching inn. Guests stay either in the main building itself or in a converted stable block. The hotel restaurant is regarded as one of the best in Devon and specialises in first-class local produce. Devon-reared lamb and beef, local cheeses and Plymouth-landed seafood all feature on the menu. So, even if you don't manage to catch a single thing, you can console yourself with a slap-up meal.

Fishermen gather in the bar in the evenings to discuss the day's sport and, after dinner, the conversation moves into the lounge in front of large open fires, surrounded by a unique collection of antique fly-fishing tackle. The relaxed friendliness of the hotel makes it a popular spot with those whose partners don't share their passion for fish and who, consequently, come on their own. Non-fishing partners could note, however, that even if you have absolutely no inclination to learn to fish, the Arundel Arms is a fab place to stay for a weekend. Just lap up the fantastic scenery and enjoy the superb food.

• **COST** *Dinner, bed and breakfast costs around £88 per person for a two-night stay, on a single-occupancy basis, or £78 per person for a two-night stay for two sharing a double room. Rates do vary depending on the season, and cheaper rooms are available in the annexe. A two-day beginner's fishing course costs £170 per person, including tuition, but excluding accommodation and meals. The hotel also runs Spring Trout fishing weekends during the season, which cost approximately £150 per person for two days' fishing, dinner, bed and breakfast*

- **HOW TO GET THERE** *By car, take the M4, then the M5 and then the A30. Lifton is 1½ miles from the A30. By rail, take the train from Paddington to Exeter. It's then a 45-minute taxi journey to the hotel*

GARDEN DESIGN

ACORN ACTIVITIES

ADDRESS PO Box 120, Hereford HR4 8YB

☎ 01432 830083   **FAX** 01432 830110

For gardeners, there can be nothing more pleasurable than to switch off from everything and think only about gardens for two whole days. Tuition is from 10am-5pm, in the grounds of Burford House. The gardens are home to the largest collection of clematis in the UK and the beautiful 18th-century house is covered with roses intermingling with wisteria and jasmine.

This course will suit even the most inexperienced, who will be able to get to grips with the fundamentals of opening a pair of secateurs. Beginning with the basics of garden design and how to measure the garden and prepare a ground plan, the course takes you through the successes and pitfalls of structuring a garden. As with all things, the more time that you take on the planning, the better, no matter how keen you are to get your hands dirty. There is ample opportunity to discuss your personal horticultural problems – rather like a personal 'Gardener's Question Time' – and the course tutor really did seem to know her onions. If your garden shed needs to be in a better position or you can't think what would look best on your pergola, or you've simply lost the plot completely, then this is the course you should go on before you even think about doing any digging. Even those who don't have gardens of their own but are keen on gardening might find it interesting to create their 'fantasy' garden. The informal, relaxed atmosphere allows everyone to contribute and swap gardening tips and old-wives tales. A more experienced gardener might prefer a more demanding course, but they will still relish the stunning grounds of Burford House.

This is one of Acorn Activities' most popular courses and attracts a wide range of age groups. Most students come away full of inspiration to start tackling new projects.

Be sure to take a note pad and pen and stout shoes and a waterproof with you. There's a coffee shop on site, where you can buy lunch and a garden centre only 100 yards from the course.

- **WHERE TO STAY** *Accommodation for one or two nights can be arranged for you by Acorn Activities*
- **WHERE TO EAT** *In the local hotels. Those staying on a bed and breakfast basis can also book on a half-board basis if wished*
- **COST** *£100 for two days' garden design*
- **HOW TO GET THERE** *Acorn Activities provide full directions on booking*

HORSE WHISPERING

KELLY MARKS INTELLIGENT HORSEMANSHIP

ADDRESS Lethornes, Lambourn, Hungerford, Berks RG17 8QS
☎ 01488 71300 **FAX** 01488 73783

If you wept buckets at Kristin Scott Thomas and Robert Redford in the film of *The Horse Whisperer*, if you're a horsy person or even if you're a stressed-out City executive, you may have a hankering to try your hand at horse-whispering. The concept actually dates back to the 17th-century, when the term was used to refer to people who had a special way with breaking in wild or young horses. Monty Roberts is the most famous current exponent of the skill of 'joining up', a term he has patented, and it was he who inspired Nicholas Evans to write the novel that was later filmed. Kelly Marks, who runs the weekend courses, is Roberts' UK Agent, the only qualified female teacher and a holder of his Advanced Professional Certificate. The two-day 'Starting the Young Horse with Kelly Marks' weekend clinic covers the Monty Roberts concept, the essential horse psychology, achieving 'join up' and follow up, common mistakes to avoid, safety considerations, long lining, how your body language affects the horse, early riding, leading and handling a young horse and the principles of mouthing. The courses are limited to ten participating students and their horses and each one has the opportunity to go into the pen at least twice and practice 'join up' with a young horse.

Monty's methods are based on learning the horse language Equus which he observed from watching wild mustangs as a teenager in his native California. It relies strongly on a horse's body language, and he has astounded audiences by saddling up and riding a previously untamed horse within 20 minutes.

A weekend with Kelly Marks is as positive an experience for the humans as it is for the horses, dealing as it does with learning how to meet and bond with a horse. In fact, some large business organisations have now asked Marks to teach Equus to their executives, as part of their corporate training programmes.

● **WHERE TO STAY** *Accommodation can be arranged with local bed and breakfasts, some within walking distance of Willow Farm, where the courses take place*

● **WHERE TO EAT** *Bring a packed lunch; tea and coffee are included in the price. There is a good choice of places for dinner in Witney*

● **COST** *Two days' 'Starting the Young Horse with Kelly Marks', £299, including stabling and a pre-course tuition manual for home study in advance of the course. Non 'hands-on' (just observing) students, £30 per day. Bed and breakfast from £15 to £25 per person per night*

● **HOW TO GET THERE** *From the A40, take the first exit to Witney, on the B4022. Go along this road for about a mile, until you reach a pair of mini-roundabouts. Go left at the first and directly to the right*

*at the second, keeping the Court Inn on your left. Continue along
the B4022 and you will reach yet another mini-roundabout.
Willow Farm is the first set of grey buildings on your left*

LEARNING TO DRIVE

ACORN ACTIVITIES
ADDRESS PO Box 120, Hereford HR4 8YB
☎ 01432 830083   **FAX** 01432 830110
Some people can't wait to get behind the wheel on their
seventeenth birthday; for others, learning to drive is something that
is put off almost indefinitely. If you are one of those who have just
never got round to learning, don't have time to fit in the lessons
or are too embarrassed to admit that you can't drive already, a
residential weekend could be the answer. Not only will you be
given expert tuition but you will also be able to sit your test at the
end of it. What you get is five and a half hours of driving lessons,
enough for most people to reach the required standard to pass
the practical test. All the instructors are Ministry of Transport-
approved and the dual control vehicles include Ford Escorts,
Renaults and Fiats.

Many people who attend this course are nervous of driving or
discouraged by repeated test failures. Acorn are very sensitive
to matching personalities of instructors to pupils and they have
found, in particular, that women pupils respond better to women
instructors. 'We try to love our guests to bits, as we recognise
that many are nervous. We certainly feel that they will get more
nurturing and understanding with us than they might from their
local driving instructor.'

Booking this kind of weekend does require a bit of forward
planning. For a start, you will need to book between four and six
weeks in advance, to allow the organisers to arrange for your
driving test. In addition, you are now required by law to pass a
theory test as well as the practical. It is suggested that you buy
the book *Complete Theory Test* by the Driving Standard Agency
and take your Theory Test locally before you book your driving
weekend. You will also need to be in possession of a provisional
driving licence and supply the number with your booking form.

- **WHERE TO STAY** *Accommodation for one or two nights can be
arranged for you by Acorn Activities*
- **COST** *£250 for a weekend course*
- **HOW TO GET THERE** *Directions given on booking*

NATIONAL TRUST WORKING WEEKENDS

NATIONAL TRUST

ADDRESS PO Box 84, Cirencester, Glos GL7 1ZP
☎ 01285 644727 **FAX** 01285 657935

If you want to do something worthwhile with your weekends or want to get out of London for a break and are very strapped for cash, you could consider a Working Weekend with the National Trust. Their vast network of properties and sites of natural beauty need constant maintenance and attention and, as a charity, they are crying out for extra pairs of hands. You could find yourself rebuilding dry-stone walls, repairing eroded paths or helping map out local flora and fauna. No previous experience or skill is necessary as every site has a Trust Warden to explain how and why a job needs doing. You don't even need any special clothing, although taking a stout pair of walking boots is recommended. Most breaks are made up of a dozen or so other participants and you do need to be reasonably fit and prepared to do your share.

The accommodation will be in a Trust basecamp – more often than not a farmhouse, cottage or stable block that has been specially converted. Most are very well equipped, with kitchen, hot showers, and bunk beds in small dormitories. Everyone takes a turn at cooking and general cleaning but you are left to your own devices in the evenings. The Trust Warden will be able to direct you to the nearest pub or give you suggestions of local attractions.

As the work that needs doing varies greatly, you will need to contact the National Trust to find out what is happening on a given weekend, but they do produce an annual brochure with details of all sites and dates for projects. There is loads of choice both in terms of the work involved and the locations – work on the magnificent Cliveden estate clearing woodland and planting trees or help with hay-baling, fencing, clearing ornamental water gardens or footpath maintenance at Fountains Abbey.

Short breaks start at 6pm on the first day and finish at 4pm on the last day.

Your travel is not included in the price, but you will be collected from the designated rail/bus station. On booking, you receive a full Confirmation Pack, which will tell you all the details and let you know what you need to take with you – sleeping bag, gardening gloves and so on.

• **COST** *Really fantastic value at £23 including VAT for board and lodging but excluding travel. You may catch the bug and want to book onto one of their week-long breaks, which start at £45 for a whole week's accommodation and food as well as a National Trust admission card, valid for one year, which gives free entrance to all National Trust Properties*

PORCELAIN RESTORATION/ CHINA MENDING

THE MOWBRAY SCHOOL OF PORCELAIN RESTORATION

ADDRESS Flint Barn, West End Lane, Essendon, Hatfield, Herts AL9 5RQ
☎ 01707 270158

The aftermath of a really good party, having had a pack of Greek friends to stay or simply an all-out, no-holds-barred row with your partner might mean that you need to book yourself on to a porcelain restoration course pronto. Maureen Aldridge, who runs the Mowbray School, is herself a professional restorer and has converted the Flint Barn into a dedicated teaching school. The weekend basic china mending course is aimed at the absolute beginner and students learn how to dismantle badly repaired china and about cleaning and stain removal, bonding together simple breaks, filling chips, replacing missing sections, press moulding and painting and retouching. You will need plenty of patience and an eye for detail but you do not need to be particularly creative. As you are trying to repair something as faithfully as possible, you do need to be able to copy the original work. The tuition starts at 6.30 on Friday evening, going on until 8.30pm. It recommences at 10am on Saturday, going on to 5pm and runs from 9.30am to 4.30pm on Sunday. Usefully, a help line is available for those students who encounter unexpected difficulties when they go back and try this at home.

• **WHERE TO STAY** *There is no accommodation on site. Maureen will point you towards small local hotels and B&Bs. The latter are host families within the village who offer this accommodation exclusively to students attending the Mowbray School courses. All the B&Bs have private bathrooms and are in beautiful and tranquil settings, and you can have dinner with the family if you like*

• **COST** *The course costs £165 per person, including all materials used throughout, all protective clothing, a set of course notes for use at home, coffee and tea and light lunches. You can purchase specialists materials to take home with you at the end of the course*

• **HOW TO GET THERE** *From the M25, take the A1000 to its junction with the A414 towards Hertford. Turn right onto the B1455 and then right again before the village of Essendon. Go past the Salisbury Crest pub and turn right to the Flint Barn just before the Candlestick Pub*

POTTERY

DEBORAH BAYNE'S POTTERY STUDIO

ADDRESS Nether Hall, Shotley, Ipswich, Suffolk IP9 1PW

☎ 01473 787055 or 01473 788300

Combine staying in a beautiful house dating back to 1600, on the Shotley peninsular outside Ipswich, with learning how to throw a pot. Deborah Baynes first set up her pottery in 1971 and is a founder member of the East Anglian Potters Association. In 1993, Deborah's daughter calculated that they had taught over 2,800 students, many of whom come back time and time again.

The course starts with dinner on the first night – Deborah feels that the combination of good food and good wine soon produces a relaxed atmosphere and helps her guests to get to know one another before they start work the next day. Each course consists of around six or eight students of all standards, from complete beginners to seasoned throwers. Some come as a group who already know each other but many come individually.

Breakfast is served at about 9am. Stoke up for the day with free-range eggs (from Deborah's own hens), bacon, toast and home-made jams and marmalades. However, Deborah says that if you can't face all this first thing in the morning she'll just thrust a cup of tea or coffee into your hand.

Teaching starts in earnest at 10am, and Deborah's years of experience mean that even the complete beginner will soon be able to make mugs, jugs, jars, casseroles and even teapots. Classes break for coffee and biscuits mid-morning and mid-afternoon.

Lunch is a focal point of one of Deborah's courses. 'I usually serve three courses and try to fit the menu to the weather, eating in the garden when it is pleasant' she says. Expect dishes such as home-made quiches, pies, casseroles or pasta, with fresh local fruit and cheese to follow.

Classes stop at 4pm but many students choose to carry on working if they're fired with enthusiasm.

Use the evenings (in the summer) to explore the local countryside. The River Orwell is only 600 yards from the house and the River Stour is about twice that distance in the opposite direction. Deborah can direct you to good local pubs – the nearest is within 10 minutes walk – or try the Butt and Oyster at Pin Mill, a delightful riverside pub only a short drive away.

If your partner wants to come too, but has no wish to 'pot', Deborah is happy to accommodate them on a bed and breakfast basis as long as they are sharing a room with a potter. Amazingly, children are welcome on the course, presumably as long as they behave, and Deborah stresses that they are firmly the responsibility of the accompanying adult.

• **COST** *Weekend courses, including accommodation, food, teas, coffees, soft drinks, all materials and equipment: residential, £145, non-residential, £120. Bed and breakfast only for non-potting* *companions, £16 per night, plus dinner on the first night £15 and £10 for lunches when required. Deborah runs week-long courses which start from £310 and Bank Holiday weekends at £215*

● **HOW TO GET THERE** *From the M25, take the A12 towards Ipswich. Take the A14 out of Ipswich and then turn onto the B1456 to Shotley*

PSYCHIC HEALING/ FLOWER ARRANGING

VICTORIA MITCHELL ACADEMY OF DESIGN

ADDRESS Crowsheath Farm, Hawkswood Road, Downham, Billericay, Essex CM11 1JT

☎ 01268 711707

Victoria Mitchell is a psychic healer who conducts her therapy through flowers. Book yourself on to a course and bingo – learn to arrange flowers and cure your sciatica at the same time. This may sound eccentric but it must be said that Victoria is a very charismatic person and has complete faith in her work – and she does seem to have had some fantastic results. Victoria started off as a designer and wholesaler of artificial flowers and florists' requisites and then, through a series of disasters in her personal life, developed her healing powers; she now uses flower design as a medium for therapy. Her courses are based on the premise that you can use a hobby or any creative activity to lead to deeper spiritual awareness, and that the cause of much people's pain and of many of the problems in their lives is frustration at having no channel for their creativity.

Whilst teaching flower arranging, Victoria picks up on her students' pain psychically and helps them to relieve their bodies of pain. A weekend course might include flower arranging on the first day, with, perhaps, psychic development in the evening, and then a 'Well Woman' Day – with a holistic approach to health, using personal consultations or psychic healing sessions.

The house itself is both rambling and cramped at the same time and seems to be stuffed with people, flowers and cats.

It has a slightly shambolic feel but is not in the least 'spooky' or really quite what you would expect from a psychic healer. Victoria is assisted by the redoubtable Bronwyn, whom she has cured and who now can walk unaided instead of in pain and with the aid of sticks. Bronwyn is fiercely protective of Victoria and comes across as 'the W.I. does psychic'. They also have a 'psychic pussycat'.

Take the weekend on whatever level you fancy – go just for the chance to learn how to arrange flowers and create something beautiful, or throw yourself into the whole spirit of the place and get in touch with your spiritual side.

● **WHERE TO STAY** *Accommodation is either in the house (four guest bedrooms) or in a bungalow in the grounds. Alternatively, they can book you into a local bed and breakfast*

- **WHERE TO EAT** *Victoria runs a small restaurant at the Academy for students and outside visitors, which is situated in a pretty conservatory next to her studio. The dishes are all completely home-cooked and freshly made and are absolutely delicious. A bowl of home-made wild mushroom soup came with an enormous garnish of all sorts of delicious vegetables and salad, and fresh home-made bread, all beautifully arranged. A baked potato with chilli was similarly presented. The puddings are equally tempting – don't miss the chocolate-dipped fruit with milk and dark chocolate poured rather than drizzled over a very stylish glass platter, covered with bananas, strawberries, grapes and so on*
- **COST** Design on Life Creative Healing Weekend Luxury Break, £595 per person. This includes: full board, including late supper; accommodation in en-suite room, with TV and tea-making facilities; all floral materials and mechanics, use of equipment, professional glue guns and aprons; private and group tuition in flower design, professional reflexology; private healing; private body audit; use of library and use of gardens and grounds for meditation
- **HOW TO GET THERE** *Take the M25 and A12 to the Billericay turn (B1007). After the roundabouts, follow this road until you reach Downham Road and turn left. Follow this road to Hawkswood Road and turn left again. The Academy is on your right, before you reach the reservoir*

RE-ENACTMENT

CALL TO ARMS

ADDRESS 1 Lying Lane, North Lopham, Norfolk IP22 2HR
☎ 01953 681676

If you really want to get away, not just from London, but from your entire life, a weekend 're-enacting' could be for you. Whilst you need to be part of a society to do this on a regular basis, many societies are happy for you to join in for a weekend's trial to see if you like it. You will need a tent, or some sort of a vehicle in which to camp, a strong constitution and, I suspect, a sense of irony. The basic idea is that you spend a weekend living as someone from history – you could be re-enacting a battle, or you could simply be swapping your 20th-century lifestyle for something a bit less high tech. The first stop is to get hold of a copy of *Call To Arms*, which is the main publication for re-enactors. This will give you a list of all the different societies and their contact numbers. At this juncture you need to decide what period in history you want to belong to. You may decide that fighting is the most appealing, or it may be the costumes that attract you. There does seem to be plenty of choice, from Celts and Romans, through Tudors, Roundheads and Cavaliers to the Napoleonic Wars. If you have any specific queries, the *eminence grise* of the re-enacting seems to be Duke Henry Plantagenet (yes, he really is called that) who is contactable at Call to Arms.

Whilst this might, at first sight, seem to be an activity for bearded weirdies, and one imagines that the quantities of real ale, or more probably mead, drunk at these events is fairly prodigious, it does appear to attract a real cross-section of people.

There are endless quantities of clothes, equipment – in fact everything that you need to live life as it was – that you can buy, many of them made using authentic materials and methods; however, some societies have 'starter packs' that you can borrow for a trial weekend.

If you want to do something totally different and, some might say, completely off the wall, then do go for a weekend's re-enacting.

• **COST** *Dependent on the event in question. Current and complete directory available for £6 from the above address which lists all events. This also includes a brief guide to living history and events can be booked using the directory*

SHOPPING

BICESTER VILLAGE

ADDRESS 50 Pingle Drive, Bicester, Oxon OX6 7WD

☎ 01869 323200 Information Line

For some, shopping is something that you just can't have too much of. If you are the kind of person who can easily fill a weekend with 'retail therapy' then take a break near Bicester Village. This purpose-built shopping centre opened in 1995 and is an upmarket fashion village. The buildings have a New England look about them and the area is attractively landscaped to make it a pleasant place to shop. Free car parking means that you can offload all those carrier bags as you shop, and you will find many of the retailers here that you would find in Bond Street – without the hassle of having to walk miles along crowded streets. As part of their lease agreements, the stores here must be offering goods at least 25 per cent cheaper. And these are not cheap, shoddy goods either. The 57 big-name shops here include Polo Ralph Lauren, Cerruti, Benetton, Monsoon, OshKosh, Nicole Farhi, Christian Lacroix, Reebok, Villeroy and Boch and Price's Candles. Outdoor play areas mean that you can let the children have a run around when they get fed up with shopping till they drop, and there is a dedicated baby-changing and feeding area, where fathers as well as mothers can perform nappy changes. And the shops are open on Sunday so you can spend all weekend shopping. Otherwise, you can rest on Sunday and take a day to go sightseeing in nearby Oxford (see Cultural Weekends, page 175).

• **WHERE TO STAY** *Stay in a local B&B in Bicester or Oxford*
• **WHERE TO EAT** *When you need food, the Brioche Dorée is a self-service restaurant and coffee shop, whilst the Café du Jour serves French, brasserie-style food*

- **OPENING TIMES** *Daily 10.00–18.00; including Sundays and Bank Holidays. The café is open from 09.30*
- **HOW TO GET THERE** *By road, take the M40 to Junction 9. Follow the A41 for 2 miles towards Bicester. At the first roundabout, follow the signs into the Village Retail Park. By rail, the village is a 5-minute taxi ride from both Bicester North and South stations. For train information, contact British Rail on 0345 484950*

CLARKS VILLAGE

ADDRESS Farm Road, Street, Somerset BA16 0BB
☎ 01458 447384 Visitor Information Centre or
☎ 01458 840064 Information Line

A purpose-built shopping village with good facilities and 59 high-street retailers. Big names to look out for include Aquascutum, Benetton, Monsoon, Warehouse, Laura Ashley, Warner's Lingerie, Hallmark Cards, Jaeger, Royal Worcester and Next, all offering goods straight from the factory at great discounts. As well as shops there is an outdoor children's adventure playground, indoor soft-play area and an open-air swimming pool less than 100 yards away. At the weekend, there is entertainment such as street theatre, Punch and Judy shows and jazz quartets and a Village Pottery, where you can watch demonstrations and have a go at throwing a pot yourself, or paint onto china. In the Clarks Shoes Museum, you can trace the history of shoes and shoemaking with exhibits from all over the world. Committed shoppers will not be surprised to learn that Clarks Village is now the number one free tourist attraction in the West Country, with over 2.8 million visitors.

- **WHAT ELSE TO DO** *There are plenty of other interesting things to do in the area, such as: Glastonbury, Cheddar Gorge, Wookey Hole Caves, Wells, the Fleet Air Arm Museum at Yeovilton, Stourhead, Bath and Longleat*
- **WHERE TO STAY** *You can stay on site in the Bear Inn, located opposite the Clarks Village. This is an old country inn that has been in the Clark family for over 100 years and is very reasonably priced. Alternatively, you can ring the Information Centre, which runs a full accommodation service. The Bear Inn costs from £58 per room per night (for up to four people)*
- **WHERE TO EAT** *Breakfast costs from £4.75 for continental or £6.95 for full English. The bistro-style restaurant has a complete range, from bistro to full à la carte. They have a children's menu and high chairs*
- **COST** *Entry to the village is free*
- **HOW TO GET THERE** *Take the M4 and then M5 as far as Junction 23. Turn onto the A39 towards Street and Glastonbury. The Village is well signposted and there is ample parking. By rail, take the train from Paddington to Castle Cary. A taxi from Castle Cary to Clarks Village will take approximately 20 minutes*

STAG AND HEN WEEKENDS/ ACTION WEEKENDS

FREEDOM

ADDRESS 39 Naylor Road, London N20 0HN

☎ 0181 446 2425

freedom is a company devoted to organising stag and hen weekends and they will tailor a weekend to your specific requirements. They organise everything – events, accommodation, meals and transport – all to suit your budget, so that the only thing you and your friends need to do is turn up and enjoy yourselves. They even take the aggro out of making sure that your guests know where and when they are supposed to turn up. The company was started because one of the founders was a best man and had to organise just such a weekend. Finding the right place to stay, which will normally be in unfamiliar territory, and locating the right place to do the activities if you don't already know is not easy. And, on top of all that, you have to cater for differing tastes, budgets and locations.

Most of *freedom's* customers are in their late 20s or early 30s and many travel from completely different directions but, as the company has 15 sites across the UK, there should be one to suit. A typical weekend begins on Friday evening with all the guests arriving. Saturday kicks off with a big breakfast at around 9.30 and then on to one of the activities. Lunch is followed by a further activity, such as tank-driving or jet skiing. Saturday night is the high point of the weekend and *freedom* can lay on a wide variety of entertainment. Wine-tasting sessions, medieval banquets or 70s evenings are all very popular. At about 11pm the entertainment ends, and guests tend to head off to clubs or discos, or back to the hotel bar. A late breakfast on Sunday is followed by a 'Recovery Period', which might including lounging by the pool, a sauna and massage or the sort of activity that helps get rid of hangovers, such as white-water rafting.

The list of options is impressive, from abseiling and assault courses, beauty treatments, glass blowing, horse racing, laser games, land yachting, photography, raft building and river cruises. Evening entertainment could be a beach party, a murder mystery, sumo wrestling or a brewery tour.

freedom also organises weekends for groups of people who are not necessarily on a stag or hen weekend but want to rent a cottage for 16 people for a break. They will also organise activities in the same way that they do for the hen and stag weekends. To keep up to date with all that they have on offer, it's worth checking their website: stag&hen@freedomltd.net

freedom are confident that, not only do they take all of the hassle out of arranging this sort of weekend, but you also end up paying less than if you tried to organise it yourself.

• **WHERE TO STAY** *Bed and breakfasts, country-club hotels, four star hotels, or even a canal barge, depending on your guests' budget. All arranged by* freedom

• **COST** *The beauty of this is that you tell them what your budget is each, and they tell you what they can arrange.* freedom *weekends range from £89-£199 per person and this can include two activities, evening meal and entertainment, one or two nights' accommodation, 'big-boy' breakfast and Recovery Period. A 'for instance' weekend of 'Pure Indulgence' would be in an Edwardian mansion near Bath, with pool, spa, sauna and gym, and would include manicure, skin revitalisation, facial, scalp massage, murder mystery dinner, a late brunch and a make-up technique instruction, for £150 per person for one night. A boys' weekend of assault course and Gladiators, a brewery tour, barbecue, comedian five-a-side football and entrance to an aquapark would cost £129 per person for one night*

ANGLIAN ACTIVITY BREAKS

ADDRESS 29 Yarmouth Road, Norwich, Norfolk NR7 0ED

☎ 01603 700770

Another company specialising in hen and stag weekends, or just breaks for groups of friends who want to do something together rather than loafing around. They have over 100 activities on their books and take care of everything, including bookings, insurance, helping collect payment, arranging accommodation, meals, night-club entry and evening entertainment. Choose from a day's paintballing, archery, go-karting, military circuit training, or driving. The 'Marines' package includes commando-style pistol and rifle shooting, an army-style workout, assault course, raft-building and racing session while the 'Brass Monkeys' package includes special skills in shooting, abseiling, unarmed combat, fitness, personal shelter, navigation, and escape and evasion techniques, with instructors who are former paras and marines. Less testosterone-laden are line-dancing, ceroc, real tennis, mosaics, and an 'Absolutely Fabulous' package. But there is tons of choice for all tastes.

Accommodation is to suit all budgets, from Swedish-style cabins at £20 per night to Super Luxury hotels at £60 per night, and all the activity sites are within easy reach of London.

• **COST** *Entirely dependent on the activities and accommodation that you choose. Archery costs £22 per person, plus between £22 and £36 for accommodation. The 'Marines' package costs £78 per person, including a two-course evening meal, dormitory accommodation and full English breakfast; the 'Brass Monkeys' costs £113 for 24 hours, the 'Luxury Pampering' weekend costs between £76 and £114*

STAINED GLASS MAKING

HALF A SIXPENCE

ADDRESS The Art, Craft & Home Interiors Gallery, Evergate Art & Craft Centre, Station Road, Smeeth, near Ashford, Kent TN25 6SX
☎ 01303 814221

Half a Sixpence runs a selection of craft-related courses in their Kentish granary and oast-house. Each course has a maximum of six students, to ensure that you get individual attention and actually come away having achieved something. Stained glass making is their newest course and is much easier that you would think: you will be taught techniques such as making straight cuts on glass, using copper foil to join pieces together and basic soldering. By the end of the day, you might not have produced a Tiffany lampshade but you will have completed a project that you can take home. Half a Sixpence supplies a range of designs for you to work from, or you can bring along your own creations.

If stained glass doesn't appeal you might like to book onto another of Half a Sixpence's courses, such as Stencilling, Paint Finishes or Painted Furniture. If you fancy a day doing what most toddlers seem to spend their time doing at playgroup – cutting and sticking – then go for an introduction to découpage and revamp a tray or small box. Otherwise plump for gilding and verdigris, the mosaic workshop, the beginner's watercolour course or painting *trompe l'oeil* and skies. The courses start at 10am and the afternoon session finishes at between 4.30 and 5pm.

- **WHERE TO STAY** *There is no accommodation on site, but Half a Sixpence are happy to recommend reasonably priced B&Bs nearby*
- **WHERE TO EAT** *Have dinner in Dr Watson's Wine Bar, which is directly below the studio*
- **COST** *Stencilling, Paint Finishes, Painted Furniture, Découpage, Glass Painting, Patchwork and Beginner's Watercolours courses all cost £45, including refreshments, lunch and all materials. The Gilding and Verdigris, Mosaic and Stained Glass courses cost £55, due to the higher cost of materials. B&B costs from £30 per person per night*
- **HOW TO GET THERE** *Take the M25 and then the M20 as far as Junction 10. Turn onto the A20 and follow signposts to Sellinge. At the Smeeth crossroads turn right and you will find the Evergate Art and Craft Centre on your left*

TENNIS

WINDMILL HILL PLACE TENNIS ACADEMY

ADDRESS Windmill Hill, East Sussex BN27 4RZ
☎ 01323 832552

If you want to improve your tennis in a really lovely country location then Windmill Hill is the place. 'It's very countrified, with friendly coaches and a holiday atmosphere', says Director of Tennis, John Mills. Everyone arrives for their tennis weekend at 5.30 for drinks and dinner. It's almost impossible not to get chatting over dinner as you all know you will have at least tennis in common and maybe more. Saturday morning begins with a backhand and forehand session. Our coach, Dan, was possibly the best coach I have ever encountered. Not only was he friendly and nice but incredibly positive and encouraging. There's nothing worse than having your game taken to pieces and feeling there's no hope for you, but watching the videos of our individual performances over coffee turned out not to be the trauma I thought it might be, largely because Dan always seemed to find something encouraging to say to make me feel that I really wanted to improve. There's a break for lunch and in the afternoon you practise your serve. It's quite wearying but incredibly helpful. You then play a few games mixed and matched with others, so you soon get to know everyone and there's just a little bit of healthy competition too. After all that, if you feel you have the stamina, there's free play so you can set up your own game with the people you have met. In the evening there's a disco at the poolside bar, which is a lot of fun, followed by more tennis the next day. The morning sessions are on volleying and smash and a second session on doubles tactics, followed by lunch and a social tournament with prize-giving at the end. A lot of people had been on the course before and I would definitely go again. It makes a big difference to most people's game and you can feel yourself improve through the weekend. You also might come back, as I did, having made some really nice friends. Open all year round.

• **WHERE TO STAY** *You can stay in a cottage or a room with a shower or bath or an executive room*

• **COST** *From £140 per person for the weekend, including all coaching and meals, depending on season and accommodation*

• **HOW TO GET THERE** *From the M25, take the A22. Turn off onto the A271, towards Battle, and you will reach Windmill Hill. By rail, take the Eastbourne train from Victoria or London Bridge and get off at Polegate. The centre is a 10-minute taxi ride from the station*

WALKING

BUSHWAKKERS ACTIVITY WEEKENDS
ADDRESS 15 Chartwell Court, 145 Church Road, Hayes, Middlesex UB3 2LP
☎ 0181 573 3330

If it's adventure and thrills you are seeking, then sign up for a Bushwakkers Activity Weekend. They take parties of people – some stressed-out execs, some Aussie and South Africans and some who just want to escape the rigours of urban life – for camping activity holidays in the Brecon Beacons. Everyone meets at Ealing Common station at 6.30pm on a Friday night and you are transported by bus to the Beacons. Any singing of Kumbaya or Ging Gang Goolie Goolie is discouraged, although spontaneous sing-songs sometimes ensue. The average age of participants is 27–44 but all ages are welcome 'so long as they have the right attitude. Train-spotters and anoraks are not encouraged', says Tony Young. Co-ordinator Young is a trained chef, so can create some wonderful campside confections on the trip. On the hill-walking trip you walk up the Beacons in the morning and ride in the afternoon – even novice riders are catered for here. On the canoeing trip, you go down river and set up camp along the way. Accommodation is in decent tents and there are plans to include cottages for the winter months, when tents can be a bit chilly. Lunch is taken in a good, pre-selected pub. Or if you are walking the organisers build in a visit to a local baker where you can buy a roll and a bun for a packed lunch.

• **COST** *You pay £98 for a weekend of hill-walking and riding and £110 for the canoeing trip. Breakfast and dinner are included, as is all the equipment. All you need is a pair of walking boots, a sleeping bag and a spirit of adventure*

WATERSPORTS

BRAY WATERSPORTS

ADDRESS Bray Lake, Monkey Island Lane, Windsor Road, Maidenhead, Berks SL6 2EB

☎ 01628 638860   **FAX** 01628 771441

Bray Lake is an attractive, 40-acre lake surrounded by woodland – the ideal spot to perfect your windsurfing skills in time for that holiday in Corsica. They have been teaching at Bray for 17 years and offer a RYA Learn-to-Windsurf course over a weekend. The introductory course takes place over two four-hour sessions on consecutive days. You are taught the theory, how to sail the board, turn it around, control the board and safety aspects and, by the end of the two days, you should be able to sail the board around a small triangular course and return to where you started out. If you achieve this then you are presented with the RYA Level One Windsurfing Certificate. This entitles you to hire equipment and sail out in moderate weather conditions at any RYA centre with limited supervision. If you don't make the grade, and very few people don't, the school will coach you free of charge until you do. The school also has its own club house and watersports shop. Dinghy-sailing courses are also run here, as well as RYA powerboat courses and canoeing courses. The school is also a club so, if you really get hooked, you can join up and try one of the windsurfing holidays – they have recently been to Wales, Yarmouth, Poole and on a trip to Ireland. 'We often find that the ones who find it most difficult in the beginning learning stages turn out to be the most enthusiastic', says director Simon Frost, who maintains anyone can learn to windsurf. 'We even teach people in their 80s.'

• **WHERE TO STAY** *Stay near the school at the Brayfield Arms Hotel, Windsor Road, ☎ 01628 620004, on the A308 between Maidenhead and Windsor. Prices start at £70 for a double room, including breakfast. Four-poster rooms, £80*

• **WHERE TO EAT** *At the Brayfield Arms Hotel*

• **COST** *A full beginner's course is £89 plus two hours extra tuition that you can take at a later date*

• **HOW TO GET THERE** *Take the M4, exit at the Slough turning and follow signs to Bray*

WEEKENDS
WITH CHILDREN

Much of the tourist or travel industry still has to wake up to the fact that bearing children does not automatically mean that you a) no longer want to go away for weekends or b) have had a complete taste bypass in all senses and so are happy to eat chicken nuggets or burgers literally *ad nauseam*.

A successful weekend away with children is a tricky beast, needing as it does to fulfil the wishes and requirements of a group of people with wildly different expectations. Parents probably want to eat good food, stay in relatively civilised surroundings, enjoy a bit of peace and quiet and throw in a bit of sightseeing or shopping. Children, on the other hand, could often happily eat wall to wall McDonalds and want to make as much noise as it is possible for a small human to make. Taking children round museums, art galleries or stately homes can be a nerve-wracking experience as you constantly rack up the cost of potential insurance claims and, at the end of the day, most members of the family go home feeling dissatisfied. The solution is to find venues that do not expect parents to have to put up with tasteless surroundings and to plan activities that will keep everyone happy. Almost anything outdoors is normally a winner but then you are dependent on good weather. Some enlightened museums and attractions, however, do manage to pull off the double whammy of entertaining children whilst making their parents feel that they are adding to their little monsters' education.

BERKSHIRE

WHAT TO DO

LEGOLAND WINDSOR

ADDRESS Windsor, Berkshire SL4 4AY

☎ 0990 040404

Legoland Windsor has to be one of the best theme parks around for smaller children. As well as endless piles of Lego for them to play with, there are loads of rides suitable even for quite small kids. Our favourite bit is the 'model Europe' made entirely from – guess what? – which has working models of Europe's capital cities and major features. Don't miss the live shows, which are just the right length to keep the attention of little children and are very professionally performed. Food within the park is not cheap, but of a much better standard than is normally found in theme parks. The restaurant has delicious freshly cooked pasta dishes and lots of nutritious but still child-appealing food. Parents will want to avoid the many retail outlets, unless they are feeling particularly flush, as there will be heavy pressure to buy cartloads of Lego.

- **COST** *1-day tickets: adults £17, children 3–15 £14, concessions £11; 2-day tickets: adults £19.50, children 3–15 £16.50, concessions £13.50*
- **OPENING TIMES** *Daily 10.00–18.00; check for opening times over the Christmas season*
- **HOW TO GET THERE** *Legoland is 2 miles from Windsor and is well signposted from the M25, M3 (Junction 3) and M4 (Junction 6)*

WHERE TO STAY

THE POSTHOUSE

ADDRESS 500 Basingstoke Road, Reading, Berkshire RG2 0SL

☎ 0870 400 9067 Enquiries, 0345 404040 Bookings

The Posthouse, Reading is within easy reach of the park and offers a special Legoland Wicked Weekend. The hotel has a health club with a pool and is very child-friendly, with special children's welcome packs, children's menus, play areas and entertainment. The food was also surprisingly good, and the whole weekend break very good value.

- **COST** *Wicked Weekend Breaks cost £98 per adult, which includes two nights' dinner, bed and breakfast and entrance to Legoland. Children under 13 cost £15 per night if they share their parents' room*
- **HOW TO GET THERE** *Take the M4 to Junction 11. Follow the A33 towards Reading to the 2nd roundabout. The Posthouse is on the left on Imperial Way*

GLOUCESTERSHIRE

THE TALLET HOLIDAY COTTAGE

ADDRESS Calmsden, Cirencester, Gloucestershire GL7 5ET

☎ 01285 831437

Renting a self-catering cottage if you have children can be a hit or miss affair. It either works brilliantly or is a disaster because the cottage you have taken is unsuitable and ill-equipped to meet children's very specific needs. What you don't want to find, even on a weekend break, is that you are doing all the boring jobs that you have to do at home, but in someone else's kitchen with less kit than you have at home. The Tallet Holiday Cottage falls into the brilliant category. Deep in the Cotswolds, with rolling countryside and loads of woolly baas, this cottage combines stylish interiors with a child-friendly atmosphere. Indeed, owner Vanessa Arbuthnott and her husband have four children themselves, who eagerly await the arrival of the 'Wingers' as they call the paying guests. There is a garden with a sandpit, a rough football pitch in the goat's paddock for family footie, and, in the summer, they have a large above-ground swimming pool. Loads of animals wander around – currently, ten whippet puppies, ducks, chicken and geese – and the grounds are a children's paradise – lots of lawns and woodland paths to explore (very Famous Five). You can either choose to have cooked food supplied in your fridge – pies and such like – or you can ship in staff who will cook, serve and wash up a three-course meal.

- **WHAT TO DO** *Cotswold Farm Park and Butts Farm are good places to go with children. Also of interest are the Roman Baths at Bath (see Cultural Weekends, page 160), the Wildfowl Trust at Slimbridge and Sudeley and Berkeley castles*
- **WHERE TO EAT** *Local pubs include the Hare and Hounds at Foss Cross, which does excellent food, and the Village Pub in Barnsley. Consider also the Polo Canteen in Cirencester, a bistro-style restaurant at about £15–£20 per head (☎ 01285 650977)*
- **COST** *From £442 for three nights' accommodation (Friday to Sunday) for up to 12 people*
- **HOW TO GET THERE** *Take the M4 to Junction 15 (Swindon) and then the A419 to Cirencester. Come off at the exit signposted Cirencester Town Centre, Burford, Stow-on-the-Wold. At a roundabout turn right onto the B4425, signposted for Burford. Take the first left, after about ½ mile, which is the A429, to Stow-on-the-Wold. After 3 miles, take a left turn to Calmsden. Go right at the crossroads, then it's the first house on the right, after ¾ mile*

HAMPSHIRE

WHAT TO DO

You will find loads to amuse the children in Portsmouth, particularly boys. The seafront has an amusement park, or you could visit one of the ships in the harbour – HMS Victory, HMS Warrior, or the Mary Rose. If you want to venture further afield, you could try a day trip to the Isle of Wight (see pages 54, 148).

D-DAY MUSEUM

ADDRESS Clarence Esplanade, Southsea PO5 3NT
☎ 02392 296905
- **OPENING TIMES** *Nov–Mar, Mon 13.00–16.00; Tues–Sat 10.00–16.00; Apr–Oct, Tues–Sat 10.00–17.30; closed Sun–Mon*
- **COST** *Adults £4.75; Children or Students £2.85; OAPs £3.60; Monday afternoon admission free*

SEA LIFE CENTRE

ADDRESS Clarence Esplanade, Southsea PO5 3PB
☎ 02392 734461
- **OPENING TIMES** *Mon–Fri 10,00–15.00; Sat–Sun 10.00–16.00*
- **COST** *Adults £5.50; Children £3.50; OAPs £4.50*

WHERE TO STAY

FORTE POSTHOUSE

ADDRESS Pembroke Road, Portsmouth, Hants PO1 2TA
☎ 01705 827651 general enquiries and reservations or
0845 603 6000 Liberty Breaks
A good-value weekend break, particularly for single parents. The exterior of the hotel is not very impressive, but it is lively once you're inside. The staff are great with children at check-in. Each child is given a welcome pack and a dinner invitation confirming the reservation. The bedrooms are pleasant and designed to induce a peaceful rest – earth-tone colours, medium to soft mattresses and a leaflet on the bed about how to get a good night's sleep.

The staff are extremely welcoming, and there is a happy, relaxed atmosphere. Face painting and other children's activities are laid on and there is an attractive swimming pool, sauna and steam room, beauty treatments and a gym. The children felt comfortable and, if the facilities are unpretentious and not over-smart, this is more than made up for by the atmosphere and service.

There are three children's menus, one for baby food, one for under-6s, and one for older children.

- **COST** *A two-night Liberty Break, with dinner, bed and breakfast, costs £96.90 per person. Children under 16 stay and eat free, which represents tremendous value when you consider how much most teenage boys can cram away*
- **HOW TO GET THERE** *By road, take the M3 as far as Junction 5 and then the M27 to Portsmouth. By rail, take the train to Portsmouth from Waterloo. An adult return costs £21.70 and the journey takes 1 hour and 25 minutes*

NORFOLK

POTTERS LEISURE RESORT

ADDRESS Coast Road, Hopton-on-Sea, Norfolk NR31 9BX
☎ 01502 730345   **FAX** 01502 731970

A traditional 'holiday village' set on the Norfolk coast that provides great-value weekends for families. There are activities to appeal to everyone, with a high level of guest participation and a huge element of fun. Each weekend has a different theme – we went for the International Cabaret Weekend, which features the Illegal Eagles. The staff at check-in are extremely helpful and friendly and provided a full activity list, which created excitement at the thought of non-stop activities and night life. Our rather world-weary American pre-teen tester had a fabulous time and was asking to return even before the Sunday evening departure. He disappeared for much of the weekend, occasionally resurfacing on the way to another activity to 'airkiss' his mother. She lost him completely on Saturday evening and finally found him in the disco, doing a John Travolta impression and pointing out potential dance partners for her. This is obviously a great place to go if you are a single parent, as there is plenty for children to do in safe environments. The activities and facilities on offer include a swimming pool, sauna, gym, beauty clinic, golf, mini-golf, tennis, bowling, archery, shooting, aerobics, bingo, squash, badminton, line dancing, snooker, cricket, children's and teen activities (this doesn't mean nipping round the back of the bike sheds for a snog and a crafty fag), nightly entertainment and disco.

Potters won't appeal to everyone, particularly those who like to keep themselves to themselves, but for all-round good value and tremendous fun it's well worth a visit.

- **WHERE TO STAY** *The resort provides onsite accommodation*
- **WHERE TO EAT** *The food in the holiday village isn't marvellous but is made to feel more special with a nicely presented menu. Meals include soup or a starter, choice of two main courses or buffet. Wine costs extra, but you can save unfinished bottles from one meal for another*
- **COST** *A two-night stay (Friday and Saturday) costs £149 per adult, £89 for children aged 9–16, £69 for children aged 2–9 and £15 for under-2s. This includes all meals and accommodation and use*

*of the facilities. You have to pay extra for wines and spirits, which
are very reasonably priced*

• **HOW TO GET THERE** *Take the A12 through Lowestoft and look for
the signposted turning for Hopton-on-Sea*

NOTTINGHAMSHIRE

CENTER PARCS
ADDRESS c/o Kirklington Road, Eakring, Newark, Notts NG22 0DZ
☎ 08705 200300
See main entry under Suffolk (page 100).

OXFORDSHIRE

BRUERN STABLE COTTAGES
ADDRESS Redbrick House, Bruern, Chipping Norton, Oxon OX7 6PY
☎ 01993 830415
See main entry in Romantic Weekends (page 18). Beautifully
furnished cottages with all sorts of facilities to keep children happy
– swimming pool, walled garden with playhouse, swings and
slides with a tractor, a games room for bad weather with a
dressing-up box, tennis court. At the back of the walled garden
there is croquet, cricket and football. There are eight cottages,
seven of which are suitable for families; they sleep from two adults
plus a cot to six plus a cot.

• **WHAT TO DO** *There is lots to see and do locally; local riding
stables, pretty Cotswold villages to wander around, boating at
Lechlade and an 18-hole golf course within 10 minutes*

• **COST** *From £252 for three nights*

• **HOW TO GET THERE** *From the M40, take Junction 8 and then go
west on the A40 to Oxford. Continue on the A40, following signs
for Cheltenham and Witney. Where the A40 crosses the A361
at Burford, turn right at the roundabout. Travel down the High
Street to where the road crosses a single-lane bridge controlled by
traffic lights. Just over the bridge, turn left at a mini-roundabout,
following the signs for Stowe and the A424. After 3 miles, at a
sign marked Bruern, turn right. The single-track road descends
into the Evenload valley; after ⅓ mile, turn right at a broken
crossroads and immediately left. Continue for 2 miles and see
Bruern Abbey on your right and the stable cottages on the left.
By train, from Paddington to Kingham takes 1½ hours. Then it's a
5-minute taxi ride to the cottages*

SUFFOLK

CENTER PARCS AT ELVEDEN FOREST

ADDRESS c/o Kirklington Road, Eakring, Newark, Notts NG22 0DZ
☎ 08705 200300

If you have just-pre-teenage and teenage children, a visit to Center Parcs provides a welcome break from the stress of bringing them up. Center Parcs are purpose-built holiday villages, with self-catering villas set in forested areas and undercover, controlled-temperature areas such as the Sub Tropical Swimming Paradise. There is an impressive list of facilities and activities for both children and adults. Center Parcs purport to have a country-club atmosphere and it is true that there is plenty to keep children occupied, so you won't hear the dreaded 'I'm bored'. Not only that, but the parks provide a safe environment and professional sports instruction, so that you can relax without worrying about supervising the children all the time. The parcs are car-free, so children can safely cycle about. Activities include: pool, art classes, basketball, badminton, kite-making, line dancing, yoga, short tennis, roller skating, squash, clay-pigeon shooting, golf, archery, canoeing, pedaloes, windsurfing and many more. While the kids are wearing themselves out, you can unwind in the spa, sauna and Turkish bath or have treatments such as aromatherapy massage, reflexology or thalassotherapy at the Aqua Sauna.

It's true to say that Center Parcs are not everyone's cup of tea, and we have reports that some of the restaurants are on the pricey side and that, on some weekends, the parcs are very crowded, particularly in the pool. However, for a weekend that will please all of the family and won't involve driving to twenty different locations, they're hard to beat. There are also Center Parcs in the Sherwood Forest, Nottinghamshire (see page 99) and in Longleat Forest in Wiltshire (see page 109).

• **WHERE TO STAY** *Center Parcs provide two-, three- and four-bedroom villas*
• **WHERE TO EAT** *All of the Center Parcs have a wide range of restaurants and cafés to suit all tastes*
• **COST** *The typical price for a four-bedroom villa for a weekend (Friday to Monday nights) based on eight people sharing is £48.75 each. For a two-bedroom villa for a weekend, based on four people sharing, £72.50 each. For a three-bedroom villa for a weekend, based on six people sharing, £44.67 each. Prices vary depending on season and location*
• **HOW TO GET THERE** *Elveden: take the M25 and then the M11. Come off at Junction 9 (A14) and then take the A11 to Elveden. Sherwood: take the M1 to Junction 27 with the A611. Then get onto the A614 to Rufford Abbey. Longleat: take the M4 out of London and come off at Junction 18, towards Warminster*

WHAT TO DO

CHRISTCHURCH MANSION

ADDRESS Christchurch Park, Ipswich, Suffolk IP4 2BE

☎ 01473 253246

Set in the middle of the 65-acre Christchurch Park in the centre of town, Christchurch Mansion is a good example of Elizabethan domestic architecture. The interior is laid out as it would originally have been and is relatively child-friendly. The large Tudor kitchen seems always to appeal, as does the ducking stool and the Tudor bedrooms with four-poster beds. It also has the most important collection of works by Thomas Gainsborough and John Constable outside London. The separate Wolsey Art Gallery houses temporary and touring art exhibitions.

There is plenty of room for children to run wild in the park, including the obligatory duck pond and playground.

- **COST** *Admission free*
- **OPENING TIMES** *Tues–Sat, plus Bank Holiday Mondays, 10.00–17.00; Sun 14.30–16.30*

TOLLY COBBOLD BREWERY

ADDRESS Cliff Road, Ipswich, Suffolk IP3 0AZ

☎ 01473 231723

This is a visit guaranteed to please parents as well as children. Fully guided tours take you through the brewing process in one of the finest examples of a Victorian brewery in the country. End your visit with a stop at the adjacent Brewery Tap pub for Tolly Cobbold beer straight from the brewery.

- **COST** *£3.90 per person, including a sample of beer. Under-14s free*
- **OPENING TIMES** *One tour a day at midday, every day including weekends*

EASTON FARM PARK

ADDRESS Easton, Woodbridge, Suffolk IP13 0EQ

☎ 01728 746475

If your city-bred children need to see farm animals, then go to Easton Farm Park. A 19th-century 'model farm', it is set out just like a toy farmyard, with pretty red-brick stables and farm buildings and a delightful dairy decorated with Victorian encaustic tiles. There are lots of interactive things for the children, including feeding lambs and calves (when possible), pony rides and watching the cows being milked. The farm has various animals, including rare breeds such as Longhorn and Red Poll cattle, Gloucester Old Spot pigs and Suffolk Punches (heavy horses). There is a tea-room that is open from 11am-5pm and which sells teas, coffees, cakes, sandwiches and light lunches. A slice of home-made cake costs from 60p while hot meals are from £3.10 for adults or £2 for children.

- **COST** *Adults £4.50, children 3–16 £3, concessions £4*
- **OPENING TIMES** *Daily 10.30–18.00, from the end of Mar to end of Sept*
- **HOW TO GET THERE** *Take the A12 out of Ipswich towards Woodbridge. Easton Farm Park is signposted off the A12*

FRAMLINGHAM CASTLE

ADDRESS Framlingham, Woodbridge, Suffolk IP13 9BP
☎ 01728 724189

Framlingham is a small, typical, Suffolk market town that is attractive rather than stunning. Its major feature is the very well preserved castle which is both educational and great for make-believe games. You could easily visit Framlingham before or after a stop off at Easton Farm Park (above).

- **COST** *Adults £3.10; children £1.60; concessions £2.30; under-5s free*
- **OPENING TIMES** *1 Apr to 31 Oct, 10.00–18.00; 1 Nov to 31 Mar, 10.00–16.00*
- **HOW TO GET THERE** *From the A12, take the turning for Wickham Market and Framlingham and follow signs to the castle*

TANNINGTON HALL HORSE AND CARRIAGE RIDES

ADDRESS Tannington, near Framlingham, Woodbridge, Suffolk IP13 7NH
☎ 01728 628226

If you want a leisurely look at the Suffolk countryside, an unusual way to get it is to hire a carriage for the afternoon or evening, and relax while your coachman does the work. You can arrange to stop for a pub lunch at the King's Head in Laxfield, either a snack or a proper meal. Or you can book a trip that includes lunch or dinner back at Tannington Hall and then wander round the gardens and stables. The King's Head (☎ 01986 798395) is an old-fashioned inn, little changed since Victorian times. There is no bar, and customers are served at their tables from the Tap Room, whilst sitting on the original high-backed settles round open fires. There is a large family room in which children are welcome.

Alternatively, take your children for a gypsy picnic. Arrive at the hall with your picnic in tow, and be driven off in a real gypsy caravan to a quiet spot in a woodland clearing. Your kids can pretend to be real Romanies, collecting sticks for a campfire and then cooking sausages over it. The caravan takes 8–12 children with two adults or 6–8 adults and is hired for up to 5 hours. We strongly advise that you book in advance if you fancy one of these drives, as the gypsy caravan, in particular, is much in demand for local children's parties, especially on Saturday. However, Tannington Hall will take spur-of-the-moment bookings if they have the transport available.

- **COST** *Carriage rides from £15 per head for 2–2½ hours. Children under 10, half price. Three-course lunch or dinner at Tannington Hall, from £15 per person. Gypsy caravan, £80 for up to 5 hours*
- **OPENING TIMES** *Rides and caravan hire by arrangement*
- **HOW TO GET THERE** *From the A12, take the B1116 to Framlingham and then the B1119 to Saxstead Green. Turn briefly onto the A1120 and look for the turning to Saxstead and Tannington. Tannington Hall is signposted from here*

KENTWELL HALL

ADDRESS Long Melford, Suffolk CO10 9BA
☎ 01787 310207   **FAX** 01787 379318

Long Melford was so called because it had the longest village street in medieval England. Formerly one of the rich Suffolk wool towns, it is now much frequented by antique-hunters, who stroll in and out of the hundreds of shops that line the streets. The town in the TV series Lovejoy was reputedly based on Long Melford. At the far end of the village is a beautiful Tudor house, Kentwell Hall, which featured as Toad Hall in the last film of The Wind in the Willows. Kentwell has made a name for itself by staging re-enactments of Tudor life, complete with a cast of hundreds of costumed participants speaking 'Tudorese'. There is something slightly giggle-making about grown adults in costumes talking what sounds like an amalgamation of Hollywood's best and Ye Olde Englishe, and it is surprisingly catching. Heavily pregnant on a recent visit, I was approached by Ye Olde Midwife, who asked 'When ist thy baby due, Mistress?' to which I found myself replying 'On the morrow'. Kentwell is a great day out, particularly on a sunny day when it looks at its best. Children will either be fascinated or as terrified as some of ours were when smaller.

- **WHERE TO EAT** *There is a small café/restaurant on site where you can eat lunch or just have a cup of tea*
- **COST** *Prices vary according to the event. Re-creations from £7.75 per adult and £5.20 per child. Family tickets available – pay for two adults and two children and third child goes in free. Under-5s, free*
- **OPENING TIMES** *The hall is privately owned and open on Sundays, in summer only. Great Annual Re-creation of Tudor Life: mid-June to mid-July every day, 11.00–17.00. Smaller re-creations at Bank Holidays and other selected weekends. Ring for details. House, garden and farm open from end of July to beginning of September, 12.00–17.00*
- **HOW TO GET THERE** *Off the A134 between Sudbury and Bury St Edmunds*

WHERE TO STAY

MOCKBEGGARS HALL
ADDRESS Claydon, Ipswich, Suffolk IP6 0AH
☎ 01473 830239

Mockbeggars Hall is a stunning listed Jacobean manor in its own grounds. Priscilla Gibson will happily cook you dinner if you book in advance at £7.50 per person, and says that she is very child friendly. The house has two double rooms and a family room that can sleep up to four as well as a separate flat that can also be taken as self-catering accommodation.

• **COST** *Bed and breakfast, £50 per double room, per night; £38 per single room. Family room £65 for three, £70 for four. Costs for self-catering breaks on application*

• **HOW TO GET THERE** *Take the A14 and, 4 miles north of Ipswich, take the turning to Claydon. The Hall is ½ mile down the road*

COLSTON HALL
ADDRESS Badingham, near Framlingham, Woodbridge, Suffolk IP13 8LB
☎ 01728 638375

Colston Hall is a 500-year-old Suffolk farmhouse tucked away in the peace and quiet of pretty, undulating countryside. Liz Bellefontaine is charming and friendly and is well geared up for families – both children and elderly or disabled family members. The farm really is a working farm, not just one that says it is, and children can help bottle-feed the lambs or fish for carp in one of the two well-stocked lakes. Obviously, you have to go at the right time of year to see little baa-lambs frisking in the fields, but the surrounding farmland is attractive in any season. There are three bedrooms in the farmhouse itself, with another three in a converted stable block. The self-catering cottage on the farm sleeps five to six and also has a downstairs bedroom – great if you want to take along a doddery Granny as well. Liz doesn't do supper but there is plenty of choice locally in the way of pubs serving good-quality food, and nearby Framlingham has a selection of restaurants, including Indian and Italian. Bowling fans might like to note that one of the old barns has been converted into a full-scale bowling rink, for lawn bowls, with a proper floor.

• **COST** *£25 per person per night bed and full English breakfast; children half price if sharing their parents' room. The self-catering cottage costs between £200 and £425, depending on occupancy and time of year. Off season, Liz is happy to rent the cottage for two or three nights on a pro-rata basis*

• **HOW TO GET THERE** *Take the A14 round Ipswich and then the A12 towards Southwold. At Yoxford, turn left onto the A1120. At Badingham, the third village along, the hall is signposted from the main road*

TANNINGTON HALL

ADDRESS Tannington, near Framlingham, Woodbridge,
Suffolk IP13 7NH

☎ 01728 628226

Tannington Hall has three double-bedded rooms available on a
bed and breakfast basis.

• **COST** *£25 per head per night. £12.50 for set supper*

WHERE TO EAT

BAIPO THAI

ADDRESS 63 Upper Orwell Street, Ipswich IP4 1HP

☎ 01473 218402

This may not be an obvious choice, but some children – ours
included – love spicy food. Small but good Thai restaurant.
Convenient for the Gaumont theatre and Odeon cinema complex.

• **COST** *Set menu at £17.95 per head*
• **OPENING TIMES** *Mon–Sat 18.00–22.00; Tues–Sat 12.00–14.00*

THE GALLEY RESTAURANT

ADDRESS 25 St Nicholas Street, Ipswich IP1 1TW

☎ 01473 281131

Housed in a 16th-century building with exposed oak beams and
an open plan kitchen, this is a fantastically friendly restaurant
serving international cuisine. The owner uses only fresh ingredients
and everything is home made – apart from the filo pastry. He even
butchers and hangs his own meat for the sausages and cures his
own salmon. There is a charming terrace for outdoor eating in fine
weather and an extensive menu.

A typical menu might include home-cured fresh salmon with
beetroot and star anise, Feta cheese filo parcel with sundried
tomato, braised English lamb with date and wholegrain mustard
sauce, breast of chicken with pistacchio sauce, braised rice and
currants, coconut rice pudding with home made apricot jam.

In the right season, expect to find lobster on the menu – very
reasonably priced at £12.95 for an entire 1½ lb lobster, cooked in
a choice of 7 different ways. There is no specific children's menu,
but they are at pains to provide whatever your children would like
– chicken or fish and home made chips or pasta made on site if
there is nothing on the menu that they want.

• **COST** A la carte *menu around £19 per head for 3 courses*
• **OPENING TIMES** *Mon–Sat 12.00–14.00, 19.00–22.00*

THE GALLEY ET PAPILLON

ADDRESS Clarice House, Bramford Road, Ipswich IP8 4AZ

☎ 01473 464888

An Art Deco-style restaurant within the area's smartest health club.
The menu is different from the Galley, but the service and welcome

are the same. Choose from dishes such as Orford smoked duck breasts with pear chutney, autumn mushrooms with lemon and garlic gratin, salmon with home made pasta with a white wine and vanilla bean sauce, chargrilled loin of Bungay pork with sage and onion.

- **COST** A la carte *around £19 per head for 3 courses*
- **OPENING TIMES** *Sun–Fri 12.00–14.00; Wed–Sat 19.00–21.30*

MORTIMER'S SEAFOOD RESTAURANT
ADDRESS Wherry Quay, Ipswich IP4 1AS
☎ 01473 230225
A simple, friendly restaurant serving fresh fish. Oilcloths on the tables, a glass ceiling and lots of plants add a 'greenhouse' feel. The first floor, which seats 25, is available for private parties.

- **COST** *Starters from £2.50 to £7.50; main courses from £5.95 to £16.50*
- **OPENING TIMES** *Mon–Fri 12.00–14.00; Mon–Sat 18.15–21.15*

IL PUNTO
ADDRESS Neptune Quay, Ipswich, Suffolk IP4 1AX
☎ 01473 289748
Run by M. and Mme. Crépy, who own The Great House in Lavenham, Il Punto is a floating French brasserie in the historic old docks. Nearby is the pretty Georgian customs house and the one-way system takes you past Wolsey's Gate – all that remains of a college commissioned by Ipswich's most famous son. The barge, which was first launched in 1899, is stylishly decorated and provides an unusual venue for lunch – particularly appealing to children. The Great House won Family Restaurant of the Year in 1997, and the Crépys' restaurants do pride themselves on being child-friendly.

- **COST** *The three-course set dinner menu at £17.95 includes dishes such as mussel and haddock cooked in a light curry sauce, served in a puff-pastry case and pan-fried marinated lamb steak with a mushroom and rosemary sauce. The extensive à la carte menu contains dishes such as: deep-fried tiger prawns wrapped in filo pastry with tomato chutney and teriyaki dipping sauce, £5.15; crawfish and courgette ravioli served with a dill and tomato sauce, £4.80; confit of pork belly, roasted and served on a bed of cabbage and a Dijon mustard sauce, £9.50; poached monkfish tail with a rich banyuis and vanilla sauce, £10.95; and a daily selection of vegetarian dishes at £6.95. Alternatively, there is also an Upper Deck Wine Bar menu, with all dishes at £3.95. The children's menu is priced at £4.95, which includes a choice of ice cream and a lemonade.*
- **OPENING TIMES** *Mon–Fri 12.00–15.00; Mon–Sat 19.00–21.30*

WILTSHIRE

WOOLLEY GRANGE HOTEL

ADDRESS Bradford-on-Avon, Wiltshire BA15 1TX
☎ 01225 864705 **FAX** 01225 864059

Probably the best-known decent hotel that caters for young children, Woolley Grange provides the perfect hotel environment for children whilst at the same time recognising that their parents want something a little more glamorous than chicken nuggets and colouring sheets. The staff are brilliant with small children. The waitresses must be recruited from Olympic gymnastic teams for their abilities to side-step crawling babies, even when carrying plates of hot food. The bedrooms in the main house are quirky but well furnished and there are roaring log fires and fantastic English breakfasts. The Woolley Bear's Den in the Victorian Coast House is staffed with full-time nannies and a games room with pool table and videos cater for older children. Ask for a bottle of baby milk at 2am and a jug of warm milk is delivered to the room within 2 minutes! The hotel has a large supply of bicycles for their guests, including tricycles and even a penny-farthing.

Children's lunch and tea are laid on each day, providing the kind of food that children like.

Woolley Grange is particularly good as a break for new parents who need to recharge their batteries and remember what life could be like pre-children – in other words, civilised, peaceful and involving decent food.

The hotel itself is housed in a stone Jacobean manor house, built from mellow Bath stone and furnished with 'friendly antiques'

• **COST** *From £105 for a small double room per night, including breakfast. Children stay free if sharing their parents' room and are charged for their meals. Three-course menu with coffee and canapés, £34.50 per head*

• **HOW TO GET THERE** *By train, from Paddington to Chippenham takes about 1½ hours. Then it's a 20-minute taxi ride to the hotel. By car, take the M4 and come off at Junction 17 (A350). Continue to the A4 in the direction of Bath. Then take the B3109 to Bradford-on-Avon. Follow the road through Bradford Leigh and at the crossroads turn left to Woolley Green. Woolley Grange is on the right-hand side*

THE OLD BELL

ADDRESS Abbey Row, Malmesbury, Wiltshire SN16 0AG
☎ 01666 822344 **FAX** 01666 825145

The Old Bell is England's oldest hotel, catering to England's youngest guests. The hotel was founded in 1220 by Abbot Walter Loring, as an inn for visitors to Malmesbury Abbey, and was built on the site of a Norman castle. Some of the castle's stone walls can be seen in the terraces below the gardens at the back of the hotel and there are plans to restore those walls and lower terraces – currently a jumble of wildflowers and nettles – for use by hotel guests. The entire building has been in continuous use as an inn since its founding.

Each room has been individually decorated and there is one suite on the second floor. The refurbished Coach House, reached via an enclosed walkway, has 15 family rooms, suites and interconnecting rooms decorated completely differently in calm and soothing Far-Eastern style. The names reflect the décor; Kazuko, Hokusei, Kodomo. Some are fairly small but the layout is intelligent and the rooms don't feel cramped.

Two types of Hildon water are provided in the rooms, with a pot to make tea or instant coffee, as well as several types of biscuit and a lollipop.

The staff are helpful and have a relaxed attitude to children. Our toddler was still bright-eyed and bushy-tailed at 10pm on Friday evening, and, although last orders for dinner are at 9.30pm, the staff suggested that he was brought into the dining room in his jimjams as well. For fear of disturbing other diners, this offer was declined and, without any fuss, dinner was served in an empty reception room while a wide-awake William chased the cat. A potentially stressful situation was thus turned into a pleasant one.

- **WHERE TO EAT** *The food at the hotel was superb throughout. The hotel offers a choice of two menus at dinner, one at £19.75 and the other at £26 for three courses, coffee and petits fours. For a surcharge, you can pick and choose between the two. Lunch is served in the bar or the Great Hall and features 'snackier' dishes such as salade Niçoise with poached egg, or hamburgers with red-onion marmalade and chips. The atmosphere is rambling and informal and the hotel provides an excellent combination of child-friendliness with grown-up food and relaxed service*

- **WHAT TO DO** *There is a 'cyber-room', with Nintendo machines for older children. Places to visit nearby include Bowood, a great adventure playground in Calne; Cotswold Water Park, near Cirencester; and Westonbut Arboretum, a wonderful world of trees*

- **COST** *Single rooms from £75; small doubles, £95; standard doubles, £110; superior doubles, £130; deluxe doubles, £150. The price includes bed, continental or full English breakfast, early-morning tea or coffee, and newspaper*

- **HOW TO GET THERE** *By car, follow the M4 out of London to Junction 17. Go north towards Cirencester and, at the first roundabout, take the first left towards Malmesbury. Follow signs to the town centre and turn left again where the High Street forms a T-junction. The Old Bell is just past the Abbey on the right. There is 2-hour parking in front of the hotel, which is useful for unloading, and the hotel has a private car park to the rear. By train leave from Paddington to Remble (15 minutes by taxi) or Swindon (30 minutes by taxi)*

CENTER PARCS AT LONGLEAT FOREST

ADDRESS c/o Kirklington Road, Eakring, Newark, Notts NG22 0DZ

☎ 08705 200300

See main entry under Suffolk (page 100).

BIRMINGHAM

WHAT TO DO

TAMWORTH CASTLE

ADDRESS The Holloway, Tamworth, Staffs B79 7LR

If you're making a weekend of it in Birmingham and you can prise your children away from the hotel, then Tamworth Castle, 15 miles outside Birmingham, is worth a visit. A proper motte and bailey castle, its curtain wall and keep date back to the late 12th century. Tudor and Jacobean buildings are housed inside the medieval walls and you can get a good idea of what life would have been like. The castle has two 'Living Images' exhibitions – figures that talk. In the Norman Exhibition, a Baron tells of medieval castle life, whilst in the Tamworth Story, a 19th-century prisoner traces the history of the town. The attractive grounds have an adventure playground and there are special events during the year, particularly at Bank Holidays, as well as children's workshops during most school holidays. There are even the requisite couple of ghosts to look out for.

- **WHERE TO EAT** *Tamworth has a good selection of pubs, cafés and restaurants, including McDonalds and Pizza Hut*
- **COST** *Adults £4; children £2; senior citizens £3; family ticket £11; under-5s free*
- **OPENING TIMES** *Mon–Sat 10.00–5.30; Sun 14.00–17.30*
- **HOW TO GET THERE** *Take the M40 and M42, coming off at Junction 10 (A5), and take the A5 towards Tamworth. Follow signs to the castle*

CADBURY WORLD

ADDRESS Bourneville, Birmingham B30 2LD

☎ 0121 451 4159

Real chocoholics who want to justify their lust for chocolate by putting it on the same rather lofty plateau as wine appreciation will be pleased to know that they can spend a whole day learning about the history and production of their favourite scoff. A well-planned, informative and interesting display tells of the Aztecs and how they sacrificed chocolate-spotted dogs to appease the gods and ensure a good crop, as well as the history of chocolate in this country and the social reforms undertaken by the Cadbury family in the nineteenth century for their workforce. You will be pleased to know that there are also opportunities to taste as well as 'chocolate-themed' rides for children.

- **COST** Adults £6.50, children (4–15) £4.75, under-4s free. Family ticket £23.50.
- **OPENING TIMES** Mon–Fri 10.00–15.00; weekends 10.00–16.00. Winter times: Tues–Thurs, Sat–Sun 10.00–16.00
- **HOW TO GET THERE** Take the M40 and the M42. Come off at Junction 2 onto the A441 and you will then see signs for Cadbury World

WHERE TO STAY

FORTE POSTHOUSE, GREAT BARR

ADDRESS Chapel Lane, Great Barr, Birmingham B43 7BG
☎ 0870 400 9009   **FAX** 0121 357 7503

If you're going to Cadbury World (see page 110), stay at the Forte Posthouse on a Wicked Weekend Break, which includes the cost of entrance to Cadbury World. Each child receives a welcome pack and there are dedicated play areas within the hotel. The staff are friendly and welcoming and really make children feel like welcome guests rather than nuisances. Our six-year-old 'researcher' had an unfortunate nose bleed at 3am and the staff didn't bat an eyelid, or make anyone feel uncomfortable.

- **WHERE TO EAT** The Trader's Bar restaurant at the hotel or the Harvester pub just across the road
- **COST** Wicked Weekend Breaks cost from £94 per adult for two nights' dinner, bed and breakfast, including entrance to Cadbury World. Children pay £3.50 for entrance. Children under 13 sharing a room stay and eat free
- **HOW TO GET THERE** Take the M1 and M6 and come off at Junction 7. Continue along the A34 to Walsall and the hotel is on the left

BRISTOL

Bristol has lots to offer families as well as grown ups, who will enjoy the shops and architecture in Clifton. As with most university towns, it is much quieter when the students aren't about. Famous as England's wine port (hence Harvey's Bristol Cream), and as a centre of the slave trade, there's lots to see and do. Although much of the floating harbour was bombed during the Second World War, and rebuilt with an abomination of a shopping centre known as Broadmead, a lot of the old city remains. The expression 'cash on the nail', comes from the Bristol corn exchange, where large, nail-shaped bollards were used by the corn dealers, and the old centre was used to represent London in the TV series *House of Elliott*. Brunel's famous suspension bridge and Gothic castellated Temple Meads station are worth a look. Although it is built on hills, it's very easy to get around the attractive bits of Bristol on foot, and it's a pleasant place to wander about.

• **HOW TO GET THERE** *Head straight down the M4 or take a train from Paddington Station*

WHAT TO DO

There is certainly a lot to entertain families in the city and one of the best ways to get around is the Open-Top Guided Bus Tour, which costs £6 for an all-day ticket for adults or £5 for children (5–15), students and OAPs. Children under 5 travel free. The great advantage of these tours is that you can hop on and off at will, and you also get discount vouchers for some of the attractions. You will also be able to concentrate on seeing Bristol, and not have to worry about parking. You can visit Bristol Zoo, Clifton village, with its attractive Georgian terraces, Clifton Suspension Bridge, SS Great Britain and the Industrial Museum, all by hopping on and off the bus. You can use the bus and the Ferry Boat Company to do a round trip of the attractions below, or just visit the ones that appeal individually to you.

BRISTOL ZOOLOGICAL GARDENS

ADDRESS Clifton, Bristol BS8 3HA
☎ 0117 973 8951
Bristol Zoo is perhaps most famous for its gorilla-breeding programme, but it has loads of other animals – in fact, over 300 species. A new Seal and Penguin Enclosure opened in 1999, and the zoo runs lots of special events throughout the year, such as Teddy Bears' Picnics and Easter Bunny Egg Hunts.
• **COST** *Adults £7.95, children 3–13 £4.50, children 14–18 and concessions £6.95*

CLIFTON SUSPENSION BRIDGE VISITOR CENTRE

ADDRESS Bridge House, Sion Place, Clifton, Bristol BS8 4AP
☎ 0117 974 4664
The famous suspension bridge has become the symbol of Bristol, since it was completed in 1864. Its dramatic setting spanning the Avon Gorge makes it a favourite jumping spot for the terminally disaffected and looking down from it into the water is not for the vertigo sufferer. The Visitor Centre is on the Clifton side, about 200 metres from the bridge itself, and is housed in a Victorian hotel.
• **COST** *Adults £1.20; concessions £1; children under 16 £0.80. Family tickets £3.50*

SS GREAT BRITAIN

ADDRESS Great Western Docks, Gas Ferry Road, Bristol BS1 6TY
☎ 0117 929 1843
The precursor of the modern ocean-going liner, the *SS Great Britain* was an amazing feat of Victorian engineering by Brunel.

The restoration of this mould-breaking ship is now almost complete, and you can walk round the promenade deck, the first class cabins, the grand First Class Dining Saloon, and the Ladies' Boudoir, which have all been restored with careful attention to period detail.

• **COST** *Adults £6; senior citizens £5; children £3.50; family ticket £16*

BRISTOL INDUSTRIAL MUSEUM

ADDRESS Princes Wharf, Wapping Road, Bristol BS1 4RN
☎ 0117 825 1470

Attractions here include steam trains; a steam crane; the Mayflower (which is the oldest steam tug in the world); and the pyronaut, a fire boat from the 1930s. Check which exhibits will be operational before your visit.

• **COST** *Free*

BRISTOL FERRY BOAT CO.

ADDRESS Motor Barge Tempora, Welshback, Bristol BS1 4SP
☎ 0117 927 3416

Landing stages at Hotwells Pump House, Baltic Wharf, Mardyke Steps, Pooles Wharf, *SS Great Britain*, Prince St. Bridge and City Centre. Back to the *SS Great Britain* and it's time to head off on the waterborne leg of your round trip. Ferries run back to the city centre, where you started, or you might choose to take a round trip, which will give you a different perspective of Bristol. A boat trip will really give you a sense of Bristol's maritime history and is a pleasant way of getting back to your starting point.

• **COST** *Prices vary depending on where you are going but are roughly in the region of adults from £2.50 and children from £1.50*

• **OPERATING TIMES** *From around 11.00–18.00. A morning commuter service operates between Hotwells and Temple Meads and vice versa from around 08.00–09.20 and costs a flat rate of £1 one way*

@BRISTOL

ADDRESS Deanery Road, Harbourside, Bristol BS1 5DB
☎ 0117 909 2000

This very latest attraction that will appeal to young visitors is due to open in spring 2000 and promises, if it lives up to the hype, to be fantastic. 'A brilliant, waterfront destination built round the most imaginative mix of science, nature and art. An environment in which visitors can stretch their minds, and where fun and entertainment are created through discovery and participation' is what the pre-launch blurb says. @Bristol is a £97 million Landmark Millennium Project and covers 11 acres of Bristol harbourside. There are to be three main elements to @Bristol:

• *Explore@Bristol* This aims to be a 21st-century version of the Science Museum, with lots of interactive, hands-on and multimedia displays that will encourage visitors to learn about scientific discovery. Visitors will be able to take part in experiments, often with other people in other parts of the work, via the Internet, and we are told that it will be 'one of the places to explore information technology and the digital revolution'.

• *Wildscreen@Bristol* Apparently, over 95 per cent of the earth's animal species are smaller than a hen's egg – don't you learn something new every day! Wildscreen aims to teach us all about these tiny creatures, which will be the stars of the show in 'a completely new concept in wildlife centres'. Live exhibits, state-of-the-art technology and superb educational resources will help visitors to get the most out of their visit. A botanical house and giant screen IMAX cinema will bring the whole experience to life.

• *Open Spaces@Bristol* The two attractions of Explore@Bristol and Wildscreen@Bristol will be linked to each other and to the Harbourside by tree-lined spaces, squares, promenades and open spaces, which will feature public works of art including a water feature and a light feature. New World Square is 6500 square metres of open space that will hold open-air events, street theatre, and include pleasant places to walk and sit and cafés.

• **COST** *Entrance costs are around the £6 mark*

WHERE TO STAY

Bristol has masses of big hotels, which provide all the facilities that you might need for a weekend. The Tourist Board has a very sensible tip: as Bristol is a large commercial centre and their hotels are booked up mainly during the week, they say you can get excellent rates at weekends. For the very best deals, book your accommodation through the Tourist Information Centre (☎ 0117 926 0767 for general enquiries) who will be able to help you choose something suitable and will also be able to get you the best price for your stay.

THE GRAND THISTLE HOTEL
ADDRESS Broad Street, Bristol BS1 2EL
☎ 0117 929 1645 **FAX** 0117 922 7619
• **COST** *Bed and breakfast costs £45 per person per night including full English breakfast or £57 per person per night including dinner as well*

JARVIS INTERNATIONAL BRISTOL
ADDRESS Redcliffe Way, Bristol BS1 6NJ
☎ 0117 926 0041 **FAX** 0117 923 0089
• **COST** *Bed and breakfast from £43 per person per night*

SWALLOW ROYAL HOTEL

ADDRESS College Green, Bristol BS1 5TA

☎ 0117 925 5200   **FAX** 0117 925 1515

• **COST** *Bed and breakfast from £88 to £145 for a single room or £120 to £165 for a double room per night*

AVON GORGE HOTEL

ADDRESS Sion Hill, Bristol BS8 4LD

☎ 0117 973 8955   **FAX** 0117 923 8125

• **COST** *Bed and breakfast costs £99 for a single room, £109 for a double or twin room. Suites cost from £125 per night*

THE BERKELEY SQUARE HOTEL

ADDRESS Berkeley Square, Clifton, Bristol BS8 1HB

☎ 0117 925 4000   **FAX** 0117 925 2970

• **COST** *Bed and breakfast costs £49 for a single room or £80 for a double or twin room per night*

JURY'S BRISTOL HOTEL

ADDRESS Prince Street, Bristol BS1 4QR

☎ 0117 923 0333   **FAX** 0117 923 0300

• **COST** *Bed and breakfast costs £69 per night per room whether double or single*

GOLDENEY HALL

ADDRESS Lower Clifton Hill, Bristol BS8 1BH

☎ 0117 903 4873 (Business Secretary)

FAX 0117 903 4877

Goldeney Hall was once the residence of a wealthy Bristol merchant, and is now one of the University Halls of Residence. During the summer vacation, the self-catering flats can be booked by the week, or for weekend breaks. The flats are set in 10 acres of formal gardens that include five follies – an ornamental canal, gothic tower, gazebo, mock bastion and shell-lined grotto. The flats have recently been refurbished and upgraded. They are self-contained, one per floor and are fully equipped. Each flat comprises six or eight bedrooms, all with washbasins, two showers, a bath, three WCs, a large kitchen/dining room, cooking facilities and colour TV. If you have a large family, or want to go away with friends, these flats offer fantastic value and are brilliantly situated for visiting the shops, restaurants and attractions of Clifton village. On-site facilities include: coin-operated launderette; tennis and squash courts; games room; babysitters by arrangement; cots and high chairs on request. Bear in mind that these flats are very popular during the summer, so you do need to book early.

• **COST** *£330 per flat per weekend (Friday and Saturday night). A week's let would cost £490 for an eight-person flat or £430 for a six-person flat, either from Saturday to Saturday or Wednesday to Wednesday*

WHERE TO EAT

THE RIVER STATION
ADDRESS The Grove, Bristol BS1 4RB
☎ 0117 914 4434
A child-friendly restaurant serving modern, British-style food in a very elegant, stylish building. They have high chairs and a children's menu.
• **COST** *Expect to pay around £20 per head per adult for* à la carte. *The two-course set menu at lunch costs £10.75*

OVER THE MOON
ADDRESS 117 St Georges Road, College Green, Bristol BS1 5UW
☎ 0117 927 2653
Very busy and buzzy, with lots of families having lunch on Sunday. Relatively child-friendly although no high chairs. Unusual as well as traditional food.
• **COST** *Warm cherry tomato tartlet with mozzarella and garlic, £3.95; flash-fried tiger prawns, £3.75; smoked haddock and potato soup, £3.85; smashed kidney beans, mint and herb butter filo pastry tartlets, £7.95*

SAN CARLO
ADDRESS 44 Corn Street, Bristol BS1 1HQ
☎ 0117 922 6586
A traditional Italian restaurant with a lively atmosphere. They don't have high chairs, but, in typical Italian fashion, are keen on kids and will do small portions of the adult menu.
• **COST** *Expect to pay around £22 per adult*

THE CAMBRIDGE ARMS
ADDRESS Coldharbour Road, Bristol BS6 7JS
☎ 0117 973 5754
The usual pub food, such as sandwiches and fish and chips in a relaxed atmosphere, with a large garden with slides for children.
• **COST** *An average meal will cost around £4.25 to £5.50 per head*

THE FARM PUBLIC HOUSE
ADDRESS Hopetown Road, St Werburgs, Bristol BS8 2LY
☎ 0117 924 3622
To the north of the centre, this pub is next door to one of the city farms. Their menu is mostly vegetarian, with interesting and creative dishes cooked with fresh, healthy ingredients. A fun, pleasant atmosphere with a large play area next door for children and a large garden.
• **COST** *An average meal costs £4.25*

HENRY AFRICA'S HOTHOUSE

ADDRESS 65 Whiteladies Road, Bristol BS8 2LY

☎ 0117 923 8300

A small restaurant on trendy Whiteladies Road which provides balloons, high chairs and a specific children's menu. The food is a mix of 'global' and Tex/Mex.

- **COST** *An average two-course meal costs between £15 and £20 per adult. The fixed menu costs £8.95 for two courses and £10.95 for three*

COLCHESTER

For spending an appealing weekend, Essex may not immediately spring to mind, but Colchester has lots to recommend it as a destination for a short break with kids. Firstly, and if your children are young this will be very appealing, Colchester is an easy drive from London, and a doddle by train, so you won't have to put up with too much 'Are we there yet?'. Secondly, the surrounding countryside is very pretty and the town is an ideal base for touring round the area.

- **HOW TO GET THERE** *Take the M11, M25 (Eastbound) and then the A12 to Colchester. Or take a train from Liverpool Street to Colchester*

WHAT TO DO

COLCHESTER CASTLE

ADDRESS Castle Park, High Street, Colchester, Essex CO1 1YG

☎ 01206 282939

As England's oldest recorded town, Colchester has a tremendous heritage including a very fine castle. Child-friendly exhibits make this a great place to go on a wet day and, during the school holidays, there are very often activities for children, such as painting, or Roman cooking. Children can try on Norman armour or dress up in a Roman toga or medieval headgear. Lots of the displays are designed to be touched so there is no problem with inquisitive little fingers.

- **COST** *Adults £3.70; children 5–15 £2.40; under-5s free*
- **OPENING TIMES** *Mon–Sat 10.00–17.00 (last admission, 16.30)*

FLATFORD MILL

ADDRESS National Trust, Bridge Cottage, East Bergholt, Colchester, Essex CO7 6UL

☎ 01206 298298

Owned by the National Trust, Flatford Mill is the scene of Constable's most famous painting The Haywain.

- **COST** *Free entry to Bridge Cottage*
- **OPENING TIMES** *10.30–17.30*
- **HOW TO GET THERE** *Take the A12 towards Ipswich, pass the*

*Colchester turnoffs and take the B1070 to Hadleigh and East
Bergholt. Stay on the road to East Bergholt, passing the High
School. Eventually you will see a sign on the right for Flatford:
turn right and follow the signs for the Field Centre*

BOAT HIRE

ADDRESS The Granary, Flatford, East Bergholt, Essex CO7 6UL
☎ 01206 298111

More fun by far than the Mill for children is to hire a rowing boat
and take a gentle trip down the River Stour. Small children are
provided with their own small oars and decoy ducks on strings.
Take stale bread for the millions of real ducks and a picnic to
eat on the very beautiful riverbank, and glide gently through
Constable country. Very good-value entertainment and the decoy
ducks are, surprisingly, a tremendous hit with small children.
Teenage kids could be let loose with their own boat.

- **COST** *£10 deposit, £3 for half an hour, £5 per hour*
- **OPENING TIMES** *Spring to Autumn*

DEDHAM FAMILY FARM

ADDRESS Mill Lane, Dedham, Colchester, Essex
☎ 01206 323111

Dedham village is very pretty with some slightly twee shops. It gets
extremely busy in the summer and parking can be difficult, but it
is certainly worth driving through. The farm has lots of animals
such as sheep, goats, cattle and chickens, a pet's paddock, where
children can feed and stroke the animals, as well as a playground,
picnic area and gift shop.

- **COST** *Adults £4, children 3–16 £3, under-3s, free*
- **OPENING TIMES** *Mar–Sept 10.30–17.30*

HEDINGHAM CASTLE

ADDRESS Castle Hedingham, Essex C09 3DJ
☎ 01787 460261

A complete Norman castle built by the Earls of Oxford, perfect
for would-be knights in shining armour or damsels in distress. You
get a fantastic feel for Norman England and can really imagine
what it would have been like to live in a castle, although it is only
sparsely furnished. There's a good gift shop selling wooden swords
and shields and other knightly paraphernalia. Lots of space for
children to run around or to have a picnic. Castle Hedingham
village is also pretty and worth a visit.

- **COST** *Adults £3.50, children £2.50. Family ticket £10.50*
- **OPENING TIMES** *Daily 10.00–17.00 from late Mar–Oct*
- **HOW TO GET THERE** *Take the A604 from Colchester through
Halstead. Castle Hedingham is on the B1058*

LAYER MARNEY TOWER AND HOME FARM

ADDRESS Layer Marney, near Colchester, Essex CO5 9US

☎ 01206 330784

Layer Marney Tower was built as the gatehouse to what was intended to be an extravagant Tudor mansion in the style of Hampton Court – unfortunately, the house was never built. The tower, which is several storeys high, is now lived in as a family home, but visitors can see the public rooms, the gardens and the home farm, which houses over 350 animals. At the right time of year, children can bottle-feed lambs and goats, as well as cuddle rabbits and feed the other livestock with bags of food available from the shop. There is a good tea shop in the courtyard, which sells a selection of rolls, bowls of Covent Garden soups, cakes and biscuits as well as hot and cold drinks. Don't leave Layer Marney without some of their excellent home-made sausages or some venison, lamb or beef from the farm. The pork chops taste like pork chops always used to (instead of tasting like the polystyrene they are packed in).

- **COST** *Adults £3.50, children £2. Family ticket (2 adults, 2 children) £10*
- **OPENING TIMES** *Every day except Saturday, from 1 April to beginning October, 12.00–17.00. Bank holidays 11.00–18.00*
- **HOW TO GET THERE** *Take the B1022 towards Maldon from Colchester. Layer Marney is signposted to your left*

SEASIDES AND BEACHES NEAR COLCHESTER

If the weather's good then head down to the coast. Choose genteel Frinton which has a fabulous sandy beach or more robust Clacton or Walton-on-the-Naze. Both Clacton and Frinton feel like the sort of traditional British resorts celebrated on seaside postcards. Frinton has a fabulous beach that is washed clean by the tide, and lovely soft sand. Clacton has a pier and amusement arcades and is altogether more 'Kiss Me Quick'.

- **HOW TO GET THERE** *Take the A120 out of Colchester towards Harwich and turn off onto the B1033 for Frinton or the A133 for Clacton*

COLCHESTER ZOO

ADDRESS Maldon Road, Colchester CO3 5SL

☎ 01206 331292

One of the best zoos in the country, well laid out and not too large and daunting for smaller children. Take a picnic or eat in one of the zoo's own restaurants, which tend to be of the 'chicken nuggets and chips or burger and chips' variety. An indoor play area with ball pond and climbing frames will keep the children amused when the thrill of looking at the monkeys and tigers palls. There is a large brand-new elephant enclosure as well as a small animals' 'petting' area, and a large and very good gift shop, with lots of the sort of complete rubbish that children like at reasonable prices.

- **COST** Adults £8.25, concessions and children aged 3–13 £5.25, under-3s free. Winter charges offer a discount of 10% on summer prices
- **OPENING TIMES** Every day except Christmas Day from 09.30. Closing times vary, depending on season
- **HOW TO GET THERE** Take the A604 exit from the A12 and follow the elephant signs

FINGRINGHOE WICK NATURE RESERVE AND CONSERVATION CENTRE

ADDRESS South Green Road, Fingringhoe, Colchester, Essex CO5 7DN
☎ 01206 729678

Just because you've got the children with you for a weekend away doesn't mean that you can't have some time to yourself to do what you want to do, whether it's lingering over a pub lunch or going antique hunting. The days run at Fingringhoe Nature Reserve are a heaven-sent opportunity to build some grown-up time into a weekend break. What is even better is that you can have a guilt-free day, as the children absolutely adore their day's activity. Children over eight only need to be provided with a packed lunch and left at the visitor centre at around 10.30am and collected again at 4pm. The cost per child is fantastically good value at £3.50. Courses range from pond-dipping and mini-beast hunts to monster-building, crafty creations, cave-painting and orienteering. The courses are run by enthusiastic, capable Group Leaders and are very well organised. There is a café in the visitor centre as well as a good shop selling nature-related gifts and books as well as sweets and lollies.

If you are planning a weekend in this area and think that your child would enjoy a day out at the Nature Reserve, then it is best to ring and check what exactly is going on. It is also advisable to reserve your child a place, as these courses are very popular locally.

- **COST** Suggested donation, £3.50
- **OPENING TIMES** Daily 09.00–17.00
- **HOW TO GET THERE** Take the B1025 out of Colchester towards Mersea, and follow signs for Fingringhoe. When you reach a crossroads in the village centre, with the Whalebone pub on your right and the church on your left, go straight across and the Nature Reserve is signposted

WHERE TO STAY

THE POSTHOUSE HOTEL

ADDRESS Abbotts Lane, Eight Ash Green, Colchester, Essex CO6 3QL
☎ 01206 767740   **FAX** 01206 766577

Part of the Posthouse chain and not in a particularly scenic location, this is nevertheless great for access to the area, as it is relatively close to the A12. The hotel has a Health Club and swimming pool as well as good children's facilities. The Posthouse chain run 'Liberty Breaks' designed for families, which represent very good value. The price includes full traditional breakfast, three course evening meal with coffee, with up to two children under 16 staying and eating for free, providing they share their parents' room.

- **COST** *Two nights' dinner, bed and breakfast 'Liberty Break' is £99 per person. Children under 16 sharing their parents' room stay and eat for free*
- **HOW TO GET THERE** *Take the A12 past Chelmsford to Colchester West. Take the A604 exit towards Eight Ash Green. The hotel is on the 2nd roundabout*

THE BUTTERFLY HOTEL
ADDRESS A12/A120 Ardleigh Junction, Colchester, Essex CO7 7QY
☎ 01206 230900   **FAX** 01206 231095

Part of a chain of four hotels across East Anglia. Although not exactly on the main road it is pretty close, which does mean that it's easy to get to other places, and, with children, one tends not to spend too much time just loafing around in a hotel.

- **COST** *Room only £52.50 per adult, per night; dinner, bed and breakfast, £75*
- **HOW TO GET THERE** *From the A12, take the Colchester North turn-off and then the next left, signposted Ardleigh. Go straight on at the roundabout and turn left to the hotel entrance*

GLADWIN'S FARM
ADDRESS Harper's Hill, Nayland, Suffolk CO6 4NU
☎ 01206 262261

Gladwin's Farm is a working farm just outside the pretty village of Nayland. Either stay in the farmhouse itself for bed and a home-cooked breakfast using fresh local produce, or rent one of the self-catering cottages, which might be a more relaxing choice if you have small children. The cottages are in the Tudor barn and stables, which have been attractively converted to provide open-plan, beamed sitting/dining areas, modern fitted kitchens and pretty bedrooms; they sleep from two to six people. All five cottages are equipped with remote-control TV, heating and comfortable seating; three of them have wood-burning stoves for chilly autumn evenings, and the Gainsborough cottage has been adapted for disabled visitors. Unusually, the farm also has an indoor heated swimming pool, a trout lake, children's play area, hard tennis court and croquet lawn.

- **COST** *£56 per night per double room for bed and breakfast. Self-catering cottages, for weekend lets from November to March, £55–£95 per night*
- **HOW TO GET THERE** *From Colchester, take the A134 towards Sudbury for about 6 miles. Continue past the right-hand turning to Nayland, up a hill. Gladwin's Farm is on the crest of the hill, on the left-hand side*

THE OLD VICARAGE

ADDRESS Higham, near Colchester, Essex CO7 6JY

☎ 01206 337248

Meg Parker has been offering bed and breakfast in her pretty Old Vicarage for some time now, and is an old hand at it. She doesn't provide dinner, but there are plenty of good pubs locally and she can direct you to something suitable. Having had children of her own, and now grandchildren, she is very child-friendly and is well supplied with cot, high chair, rocking horse and a climbing frame in the garden. She also has two punts on the river at the bottom of the garden, which she is happy for guests to use – the pub at Stratford, the next village, is easily within punting distance

• **COST** *£56 per en-suite room for bed and breakfast, £10 for a child sharing with its parents in the family room*

• **HOW TO GET THERE** *Take the A12 out of Colchester towards Ipswich. Turn left off the A12 towards Stoke-by-Nayland, along the B1068. At the triangle of grass in Higham village, turn left and the Old Vicarage is a pink house on your right*

WHERE TO EAT

THE RED ONION

ADDRESS 57 Ballingdon Street, Sudbury, Suffolk CO10 6DA

☎ 01787 376777

If you are in a car and are planning on visiting Sudbury or the surrounding area from Colchester, then the Red Onion is a good bet. In an old converted chapel it serves good-value French-style home-cooked food, such as sage and chicken casserole and mixed-fish goujons. High chairs are available and there is a small outdoor terrace where you can eat when the weather is warm. There is no specific children's menu, but there are normally a couple of 'child-friendly' dishes and they will serve smaller portions.

• **COST** *Set lunch, £6.25 for two courses, £8.25 for three courses*

• **OPENING TIMES** *Mon–Sat 12.00–14.00, 18.30–21.30 (last orders)*

• **HOW TO GET THERE** *From Colchester, take the A134 towards Sudbury. When you reach the market square in the town centre, keep left down Friar Street. Keep going until you reach a T-junction, at which turn left. The Red Onion is on the right-hand side, just before a junction. There is ample parking space to the rear*

THE WHITE HART INN

ADDRESS 11 High Street, Nayland, Suffolk CO6 4JF

☎ 01206 263382

Co-owned by Michel Roux, this erstwhile pub serves bistro-style food. Although it looks very 'foodie', they do provide high chairs and are very accommodating to small children. If there is nothing on the menu that the children fancy, they will cook up an omelette or suggest something that children might find appealing.

- **COST** *Typical dishes might be: mussels served on sautéed spinach, gratinated with Roquefort cheese, £5.70; navarin of lamb with root vegetables, £12.70; and chocolate crème brûlée with fresh raspberries, £5.70. The White Hart makes its own pasta, always a hit with kids, as well as their own delicious ice creams and sorbets*
- **OPENING TIMES** *12.00–14.45, 18.30–21.15*
- **HOW TO GET THERE** *Take the A134 out of Colchester towards Sudbury. Take the first turning to Nayland and follow the road into the village. The White Hart is on the left-hand side*

THE COMPANY SHED

ADDRESS West Mersea, Essex CA5 9PA

☎ 01206 382700

A delightful place for lunch on a warm day, this is really a wet-fish shop with a few tables. Take your own wine, bread and butter and so on and stuff yourself on fresh-cooked crabs, lobster, prawns, smoked salmon, smoked salmon pâté and native oysters in season for virtually nothing. The children can run around outside on the small quay once they've finished eating. Very basic but tremendous value. Get there early to be sure of a table, as it is very popular.

- **COST** *Seafood platters, including freshly boiled crab, prawns and cockles £7; pot of prawns, always a popular choice, even with kids, £2*
- **OPENING TIMES** *As this is primarily a shop, it operates shop hours*
- **HOW TO GET THERE** *Take the Mersea Road out of Colchester, over the causeway on to Mersea Island and keep going through the village of West Mersea and along the waterfront. The Company Shed, which is literally that, is on your left after the Victory pub and the Yacht Club*

THE BELL PUBLIC HOUSE

ADDRESS 10 St James Street, Castle Hedingham, Near Halstead, Essex CO9 3EJ

☎ 01787 460350

Large, sympathetically decorated pub with a large garden and swings. A high chair is available and it serves reasonably priced bar meals.

- **COST** *£2.20–£8.00*
- **OPENING TIMES** *Mon–Sat 11.30–15.00, 18.00–23.00; Sun 12.00–15.00, 19.00–22.30*
- **HOW TO GET THERE** *Take the A604 from Colchester through Halstead*

MAGNOLIA TEA ROOMS

ADDRESS St James Street, Castle Hedingham, near Halstead, Essex CO9 3EJ

☎ 01787 460197

Old-fashioned tea rooms serving home-cooked food made from fresh ingredients. A high chair is available and lunches include dishes such as broccoli and chicken lasagne and home-made sausage and mash.

- **COST** *Lunches are in the £4–£5 range and cream teas are £2.50*
- **OPENING TIMES** *09.00–17.00. Closed on Monday*

WILKINS & SONS LTD

ADDRESS Tiptree, Essex CO5 0RF

☎ 01621 815407

A factory making the world-famous Wilkin's Jam with a small museum (entrance free), a gift shop and a tea room where you can gorge yourself on home-made scones, cream and of course jam, cakes and sandwiches. Tiptree does not have an awful lot else to recommend it, but the tea is good.

- **COST** *Admission free*
- **OPENING TIMES** *Mon–Sat 10.00–17.00; Sun, Jun–Aug only, 12.00–17.00*
- **HOW TO GET THERE** *From Colchester, take the B1022 towards Maldon. When you get to Tiptree, turn left into the town just past a Shell petrol station. Continue along the main street and you will find the factory on the right-hand side*

THE WHALEBONE PUB

ADDRESS Chapel Road, Fingringhoe, Colchester, Essex CO5 7BG

☎ 01206 729307

If you've dropped the kids at the Nature Reserve, head for lunch at the Whalebone. What was a rather grotty village pub has been completely refurbished and, although it is now rather more like a wine bar than a pub, the food is very good and the atmosphere welcoming. Sit in the cosy bar with an open fire and pretty décor if it's cold, or take your pint and lunch in the garden overlooking fields full of sheep. The food is slightly more sophisticated than it is in a lot of pubs but good value. Service is sometimes a little slow if they're busy. Sample dishes include: herring roes on toast; home-smoked oysters and bacon salad; Mediterranean roasted vegetable soup; seared tuna on a garlic mash with balsamic roasted tomatoes; rump of lamb on noodles with bay sauce; seasonal vegetables in Stilton sauce en croûte; sticky orange pudding with caramelised oranges; Jamaican banana and rum puffs with crème anglaise; home-potted cheese.

- **COST** *Main courses range from £5–£11.95. Desserts cost about £3.95*
- **OPENING TIMES** *Mon–Sat 11.00–15.00, 17.30–23.00; Sun 12.00–15.00, 19.00–22.30*

PARIS

DISNEYLAND PARIS

ADDRESS BP100, Marne-la-Vallée, Cedex 4 France

☎ 0990 030303

WEB www.disney.co.uk

Now that Eurostar runs direct trains to Disneyland Paris, it is more than possible to nip across for the weekend. From Waterloo, the train journey is not too painful and at least you can wander up and down the train. The on-board catering is not the most inspiring, so it's probably best to take your own picnic to eat.

Most children dream of a visit to Disneyland, saturated as their little lives are with Disney's output, and to be fair, Disneyland Paris is magical. It's hard not to get caught up in the squeaky-clean 'it's a small, small world' of it all, and even quite cynical grown-ups may experience a twinge of excitement on entering the sugar-pink gates. It is the most unbelievably clean and wholesome park and the staff or 'cast members' are helpful and polite. It pays to get there early and to head for the more popular rides first, to ensure that you don't spend the entire morning in queues.

- **WHERE TO STAY** *Most children will want to stay at one of the themed hotels on the site, with easy access to the park. These range from the top-of-the-market Disneyland Paris Hotel to the Camp Davey Crockett, which is self-catering chalets. These are extremely well equipped and good news if you have a large family or have imported others for the trip. However, if you are on a budget, there are several reasonably priced hotels close by, such as the Hôtel du Moulin de Paris, Magny-le-Hongre (book through Eurodisney)*

- **WHERE TO EAT** *There are loads of restaurants and eating areas in the park but they do tend to be on the pricey side. Unfortunately, you cannot take a picnic into the park but have to return to your car if you want to eat your own food. It will also be difficult to convince your kids that a nice ham sandwich is a better option than eating inside one of the themed restaurants. It's probably best to go with the flow and view the whole experience as an expensive treat. If you're going for a birthday visit, you can choose to have a character breakfast in the Disneyland Hotel, which includes a cake brought to your table by Disney characters singing Happy Birthday. This will either thrill, terrify or embarrass your child, depending on his or her age and personality*

- **COST** *Prices for two adults and two children sharing a family room at the Newport Bay Club, for two nights and three days, including travel on Eurostar, theme-park passes and continental breakfast start at £184 per person. The same package travelling with le Shuttle or P&O Stena Line ferries starts at £112 per person. If staying in the Hotel Santa Fé instead, prices are £162 and £90 respectively. The Hôtel du Moulin de Paris costs £104 for a similar package*

- **OPENING TIMES** *Mon–Fri 08.00–18.00; Sat 09.00–18.00; Sun 09.00–17.00*

- **HOW TO GET THERE** *From Calais, take the A26 E15 and then join the A1, heading south and following signs for Paris. After Roissy/Charles de Gaulle airport, take the A104, following signs for Marne-la-Vallée. After about 27 km, turn left on to the A4, heading east towards Metz and Nancy. Then take Junction 13, Provins/Serris, for Davy Crockett Ranch or Junction 14, Val d'Europe, Parc Disneyland, for the hotels and theme park. Alternatively, take the Eurostar from Waterloo direct to the theme park.*

HEALTH & BEAUTY WEEKENDS

Everyone needs to escape from the strains of urban living from time to time, whether it's to lose weight, recover from a broken love affair, de-stress or simply chill out with the girls. You may have an important life decision that has to be made or you may just want to completely disappear from the world for the weekend.

What you don't want is to book yourself into that country-house hotel that everyone else is talking about. The last thing you need at times like these is to bump into an old friend, James from accounts or a chatty neighbour from down the road. What you need is somewhere you can unwind and de-stress, and, if you have a problem to deal with, someone you can talk to or somewhere you can go to be totally alone, to wander lonely as a cloud while you mend your broken heart or grab some time to think.

The great thing is that there is now an enormous choice of places you can go for a bit of R&R, so you can tailor your weekend specifically to your needs. If you want to lose weight, choose a serious health spa like Shrublands, where there will not be a preponderance of Kate Moss lookalikes with size-8 figures to make you feel like a beached whale. Or you may want a weekend of pampering with the girls, in which case, choose a luxury spa like Chewton Glen or the new hip Cowshed at Babbington House: if you are feeling at all sad, just the mere mention of their potions and lotions – Sad Cow, Stressed-out Cow or Happy Cow – should have you giggling again in no time. If money is no object or a special treat is the order of the day, then a trip to Les Thermes Marins in Monte Carlo is every girl's dream spa – just a short flight to Nice and a quick heli trip into Monte Carlo could be the answer. Or if you are one of the broken-hearted, or are deciding whether to take the plunge with a new job, or to emigrate to New Zealand, then why not consider visiting a retreat or a healing centre? Here you can talk to someone who might be able to offer a new perspective on the problem or you can decide to have a silent weekend, locked away with your thoughts.

Whichever option you go for, you are bound to come back feeling refreshed and better able to deal with whatever problems beset you. A bit of time out, even a quick weekend, can work wonders for your body and spirit. So, whether you take a lover, your best friend, a good book or just yourself, you are sure to feel the benefits for a long while to come.

WHAT TO TAKE FOR A HEALTH AND BEAUTY WEEKEND
A comfortable track suit
A pair of trainers
A box of tissues, if tears are part of the healing process
A 'sex and shopping' blockbuster
Glamorous underwear – you don't want to be caught out in grey
    knickers in the changing room

WHAT NOT TO TAKE
A hip flask
A large bar of Galaxy
An escape route to the nearest pub
A very slim friend
20 Silk Cut

BEDFORDSHIRE

YOGA FOR HEALTH FOUNDATION
ADDRESS Ickwell Bury, Biggleswade, Beds SG18 9EF
☎ 01767 627271   **FAX** 01767 627266
Enter a new and calmer world when you walk into the Yoga for Health Foundation. It's an excellent place to come for peace and tranquillity – you are actively discouraged from keeping abreast of world issues so newspapers and television are discouraged too. Yoga classes take place in the large, beautiful hall, with the first session starting at 7am. Other sessions take place throughout the day. Massage, reflexology and other complementary therapies are also available. Vegetarian food is the order of the day and special dietary requirements can be catered for. The accommodation is for 2–4 people sharing. The atmosphere is very calm and laid-back, with a very professional staff, including a registered nurse and counsellor. You can learn meditation and visualisation to reduce stress and help with sleeping. Regular anti-stress weekends are organised and are especially suitable for people with asthma or ME. Guests include pop stars, housewives and hippies.
• **COST** *£15 for annual membership of the foundation and then £95*

*for a weekend; includes all the yoga tuition, accommodation and
food, but not the other therapies. Single occupancy supplement, £14*
- **HOW TO GET THERE** *Take the A1M and A1 to Biggleswade.
Look for signs to Old Warden (B658) at the roundabout (first exit).
At the next roundabout follow signs for Ickwell Green*

BERKSHIRE

LIFESTYLE WEEKEND AT THE SWAN DIPLOMAT HOTEL

ADDRESS Streatley-on-Thames, Berks RG8 9HR
☎ 01491 878800   **FAX** 01491 872554

This is a weekend designed for you to reassess your lifestyle. When
you arrive, you are presented with a goodie bag containing full-
size Molton Brown products, a jogging suit, a fitness pack and –
just so you don't feel too deprived – a half-bottle of champagne.
Then there is a champagne reception, where you meet other
guests and instructors, followed by a delicious low-fat dinner.
Saturday morning kicks off with a power walk through pretty
countryside, which turns into a sort of property viewing, with
the instructor pointing out all the celebrity homes. After a buffet
breakfast, there's aqua aerobics, with lots of advice on exercise
and diet and beauty treatments, followed by another low-cal
dinner. Sunday begins with another power walk up a steep hill.
The agony was worth it for the view. Next was a mountain bike
ride, followed by a trip on the hotel's battery-powered boat up the
Thames to do more property viewing. The weekend finished off
with a low-calorie, beautifully presented lunch, including pudding
– three fruit sorbets served in shot glasses, accompanied by a
biscuit in the shape of a chef. The whole weekend was happy,
relaxed and fun, mostly because the staff were so good.
- **COST** *Two nights' accommodation for a Lifestyle Weekend
including breakfast, lunch and dinner, all treatments and activities,
plus a half-bottle of Jacquart champagne costs £210 per person*
- **HOW TO GET THERE** *Take the M4 to Junction 12 (A4 Theale) and
turn right onto the A340. Go through Pangbourne and then on the
A329 to Streatley*

BUCKINGHAMSHIRE

TYRINGHAM NATUROPATHIC CLINIC

ADDRESS Newport Pagnell, Milton Keynes, Bucks MK16 9ER
☎ 01908 610450   **FAX** 01908 207689

Tyringham is not a glitzy health spa but a serious health clinic,
offering a complete programme of holistic treatments aimed at
restoring well-being and preventing future health problems. The
aim is to stimulate the body to function at full capacity; if functioning

correctly, the clinic believes, the body has the ability to heal itself.
It is a testament to Tyringham that 87 per cent of people return –
so there must be a lot of satisfied customers. The clinic opened in
1967 under the direction of Sidney Rose-Neil, an osteopath and
naturopath; he had a passionate belief that people could learn
how to heal themselves. Patients would normally come for a week
in order to incorporate the full aspects of the treatment. However,
Tyringham does offer a weekend break as a taster of what you
might expect from a longer break. For instance, you could arrive at
your hotel on Saturday night for dinner (the clinic doesn't have its
own accommodation) and then arrive at the Tyringham at 8.45
am. The treatments include: a 15-minute introductory assessment
and short medical questionnaire; a half-hour massage; a yoga
session; a therapeutic bath, e.g. an Austrian moor and mud bath
or seaweed bath; a hot pack filled with peat to ease muscle tension;
an indoor pool session; finishing with sauna or jacuzzi. You would
also have a paraffin-wax treatment – warm wax on your hands or
feet. This eases joint pain and stiffness and increases circulation to
joint tissues. The package also includes drinks and a wholefood
vegetarian lunch.

• **COST** *Total package, to include a night's stay and dinner (at the
Swan Revived, High Street, Newport Pagnall, ☎ 01908 610565)
and treatments at Tyringham Clinic, £100. If you want to stay an
extra night in the hotel, that costs £57 per person*

• **HOW TO GET THERE** *About 5 minutes from Junction 14 on the M1.
Follow signs to Newport Pagnell and head into the town centre
over the bridge. At the mini-roundabout in the town centre, turn
right and follow the B256 towards Northampton. You will pass
the Swan Revived hotel on your right; carry on for about 2 miles
and then take the right-hand turn into the clinic. Go through the
gate-house, over the Soane Bridge and see the clinic straight
ahead. Or by train, travel from Euston to Milton Keynes Central
station and take a 20-minute taxi ride*

DORSET

MIDDLE PICCADILLY
ADDRESS Holwell, Sherborne, Dorset DT9 5LW
☎ 01963 23468   **FAX** 01963 23764
If you feel completely stressed out and want to get away from it all,
to reflect on the important issues in your life, and to be nurtured
rather than pampered, then Middle Piccadilly is the place for
you. It has a holistic approach and the therapists and treatments
complement each other. You may come out having decided to
rethink your life completely. First, having filled out quite a detailed
questionnaire, you are interviewed by Dominique Harvey. Most
guests find they end up telling her all their secrets, which, of course,
is the object of the exercise and from her initial discussions with

you she can decide which treatments will be most appropriate. Each therapist studies your profile before she treats you, then adds comments which are passed to the next therapist. No part of you is left unhealed, because the treatments work on a deeper level than most body treatments in spas and have been selected especially to suit you. The type of treatments used are aromatherapy with Collette, acupressure with Claire, alignment therapy, reflexology and LaStone therapy – which is massage with heated stones. Each therapy lasts approximately an hour and afterwards you are required to rest. The amazing thing is that you sleep so much, perhaps more than you have ever done before. Dominique says this is because you have been taken out of your normal, hectic lifestyle, as well as being due to the treatments themselves and the Dorset air. This is definitely not the sort of place for people who crave luxury but if you need a three-day session to look closely at the path you are following and to decide whether it is the right one, then this is the place for you.

If you do ever wake up from your slumbers you can take a walk round the lovely grounds or read one of the self-help books available. You may only need to look at the cover of *Feel the Fear and Do It Anyway* to feel braver when you face the world again. If you are a 'mobile phonaholic', or can't face life without the landline, you will find it a refreshing change that there are no phones at Middle Piccadilly. Not only that, but smoking is not allowed, there is no alcohol, and only the most delicious vegetarian food, cooked with great care by Michele. If you really love the weekend, which, incidentally, most people do, you may feel compelled to attend another weekend of de-stressing by attending one of Aliana's workshops, which include shamanic healing. Some people come back again and again.

• **COST** *From £218 for the two-night package*
• **HOW TO GET THERE** *The best way is by train, because it is not recommended to drive back after these sort of treatments. From Waterloo to Sherborne takes 2¼ hours. Middle Piccadilly will arrange for a taxi to collect you from the station*

ESSEX

VIVERANO SPA AT FIVE LAKES HOTEL, GOLF AND COUNTRY CLUB

ADDRESS Colchester Road, Tolleshunt Knights, Maldon, Essex CM9 8HX

☎ 01621 862324/868888   **FAX** 01621 869696

A reasonably priced spa hotel within easy reach of London, Five Lakes is set in 320 acres of Essex countryside and is surrounded by two 18-hole golf courses. It is a modern, purpose-built hotel, with a whole raft of leisure, health, beauty and sporting activities on site. The bedrooms are comfortable and well-fitted out although erring slightly towards the shiny chintz, 'knicker-blind' style. There is a dining room, brasserie and five bars. The great thing about this hotel is that you could take along your children, because there is a crèche and children's menus in the brasserie. So while they play, you can take a break with a few treatments. Choose from Clarins facials, ESPA facials, various massages, hydrotherapy, body wraps, aromatherapy, reflexology, Indian head massage, manicures and pedicures, professional make up, hair removal, shaping and tinting, tanning, an anti-stress facial for men, lifestyle evaluation, nutritional analysis and dietary control and stress monitoring.

• **COST** *The Pamper Time package is £99 per person per night, for a minimum two-night stay, which includes dinner, bed and breakfast and three half-hour treatments per person (for instance, back, neck and shoulder massage, mini facial and a mini manicure). Other treatments cost from £18 upwards. You also get free access to the pool, sauna, steam room and gym and guest rates for the tennis, badminton, squash and golf. Children sharing their parents' room are charged £7.50 per night, plus meals as taken. The crèche must be prebooked for up to 2 hours each morning. Under-2s £3.50 per hour. Over-2s £3 per hour. Children staying in their own connecting room pay 50% of the adult price*

• **HOW TO GET THERE** *From the M25, get onto the A12 and come off at the Kelvedon exit. Take the B1023 through Tiptree and follow signposts to Tolleshunt Knights. Five Lakes is signposted from there*

HERTFORDSHIRE

CHAMPNEYS AT TRING

ADDRESS Wiggington, Tring, Herts HP23 6HY
☎ 01442 291111 **FAX** 01442 291112

Sweep up the drive to Champneys – a grand country-house-style spa set in 170 acres of Hertfordshire parkland. As you arrive, an immediate sense of peace descends on you, as you are led to your room by rather oddly dressed men in beige suits. The emphasis at Champneys is on luxury and health, in glamorous surroundings and without deprivation. The food is like a three-course gourmet meal every night – the trick is that it tastes as though it is laden with calories but it actually isn't. After an initial check-up with a nurse – to check out blood pressure and heart problems – you are left to your own devices to choose one of almost 400 options. You could opt for the Decleor self-tanning treatment, which exfoliates the body and tans it almost immediately so that people will think you've spent two weeks in the sun. Or you could go for the Cleopatra Dry Flotation Bath, £39.50. All the dead skin is removed and you are given a moisturising aromatherapy massage. Then, swaddled in thermal blankets, you are lowered into a tank of warm water. All very relaxing and soothing. Alternatively, you could choose a

Himalayan rejuvenation programme, to revive your flagging spirits, or a Thai massage, which is a combination of yoga-style stretching and quick muscular massage movements. Other great treatments include: head massage and sinus inhalation; Japanese massage chair; and lots of treatments for men including the Thalgo men's-only salt rub, with seaweed for aches and pains; marine hydro experience; and sports manicure. Nice, friendly atmosphere – almost impossible not to make a friend if you are on your own – and a lovely pool and outdoor tub, open till late. Other options include painting in the art room or a pre-breakfast power walk around the lovely grounds. There are also aerobics classes and meditation suites. Nothing spartan about the rooms, which have every little luxury but best of all are the superb menus. A typical menu might include: goujons of skate wing with avocado mousse and tomato salsa, roast breast of organic partridge, steamed orchard fruit pudding with berries.

- **COST** *A two-night weekend escape costs £400 per person including heat treatment. Two-night 'discovery' package which includes facial and body treatments plus two massages costs £445 per person. Costs are full board and include exercise classes*
- **HOW TO GET THERE** *Take the M25 and come off at Junction 20 (A41), heading towards Aylesbury. Leave the A41 at the B4635 Tring exit, take the 1st left until you reach a crossroads signed Wiggington. Turn right onto Chesham Road. The Champneys gates are 1½ miles on the left. By train, go from Euston to Berkhamstead; a taxi to meet you can be arranged*

KENT

THE LUTEPLAYER CENTRE FOR WELLBEING
ADDRESS Heath Farm, Watering Road, East Malling, Kent ME19 6JH
☎ 01622 817300

An ideal spa for Londoners who want to do a quick disappearing act to rural Kent – it takes just an hour to get there from central London, even in heavy traffic – and when you do, it's well worth the effort. Get hip among the hops at this holistic spa, set in its own grounds with lots of wildlife: burrowing rabbits, fields of St John's Wort and woodland – it feels very countrified. The minute you walk in, the smell of incense hits you and has an immediate calming effect. This beautifully restored oast-house has only 12 rooms, so if it's peace and quiet you are in need of, this is ideal. Very minimalist with lots of cream walls and natural wood, there is none of the chintzy luxury you would normally associate with health farms: if you are looking for out-and-out luxury, this is not the place for you. There is a TV in every room and lots of Aveda products. Treatments include: revitalising customised facials; acne treatment package; Indian head massage; colonic hydrotherapy; iridology; reflexology; lots of aromatheraphy; yoga; Pilates muscle-strengthening techniques and Aveda beauty treatments. The staff were very helpful and friendly and the atmosphere calming. There are also the usual facilities – indoor swimming pool, jacuzzi and steam rooms, together with tennis court and library. Horse-riding and mountain-biking can also be arranged. The organic restaurant has a pleasant if not adventurous menu. All in all, we found a visit to the Luteplayer immensely calming and soothing – unfussy and informal.

• **COST** *1 day's full use of facilities including complimentary massage, plus breakfast (up to 9.30 am), buffet lunch, afternoon tea, £85. You have up until 6pm*

• **HOW TO GET THERE** *Take the M25 to Dartford Crossing, M20 to Dover. Take the A228 to the A20 roundabout and take the exit signposted East Malling. As you come into East Malling, you come to a bend with a pub. Go straight up the hill and you will see the Luteplayer on the right-hand side, after Heaths Lane*

ROWHILL GRANGE AND SPA

ADDRESS Rowhill Grange, Wilmington, Dartford, Kent DA2 7QH
☎ 01322 615136   **FAX** 01322 615137

Very luxurious, the bedrooms here are very attractively decorated, with lots of four-poster beds. The spa itself is decorated like a Roman bath, with pillars and mirrors everywhere. There's a lovely swimming pool and Turkish bath with Japanese showers and a jacuzzi. Treatments are brilliant, with very friendly and accommodating staff, and include aromatherm, which involves being wrapped in cold eucalyptus lotion and then in a hot blanket, to get all the toxins out of your body. The dining room was very nice and the restaurant food was delicious. There's an informal brasserie and a more formal dining room, all with sensible but delicious fare beautifully presented. The atmosphere is homely and you feel quite happy to be on your own.

• **COST** *Mini-Relaxation Break, including bed and breakfast, light lunch and dinner, introductory tour of spa, 1-hour facial, head massage and manicure, £179 per person*

• **HOW TO GET THERE** *Take the M25 to Junction 3 (B2173 Swanley). At Swanley, follow signs for Hextable B258. After ½ mile, you will see the entrance to Rowhill Grange*

LEICESTERSHIRE

THE PRACTICE

ADDRESS The Manor House, Gaulby Road, Kings Norton, Leicestershire LE7 9BA
☎ 0116 259 6633

The Practice is an alternative health centre. 'People come to detox, rest and, when life is a little jagged, to reassess things' says owner/practitioner Jo Pickering. There are two detoxification treatments, both of them ayurvedic, consisting of two therapists working sychronously with special oils, depending on your body type. Your body type could be one of three. Type one is *vata* – airy and spacy – usually people who are slim and wispy, 'light as a kite', Jo puts it. Their bodies usually show signs of being out of kilter when they become quick-tempered and fiery. The second type is *pitta* – fire and water. These type of people are easily fired up. They get into heated discussions and need cooling down. The third type is *kapha* – governed by water and earth. When these types are out of sorts they become lethargic and heavy, they put on weight and suffer from water retention. All these body types are treated specifically for their needs and clients are given advice on how to recognise when their body is out of balance. People often ring up after the course and say how they have recognised body types among family and friends or even people standing at the bus stop. 'Once you are aware of when things are going wrong, with the tools we offer, they find they are able to put things right.' There are plenty of treatments to choose from – one-to-one yoga, ayurvedic doctor, Indian head massage and so on.

- **COST** *For a weekend, £525 for members, £550 for non-members*
- **HOW TO GET THERE** *Take the M1 and leave at Junction 21. Follow signs for Oadby. At the Oadby roundabout, take the A6 to Great Glen. At Great Glen, turn left following signs to Kings Norton and then to Gaulby*

NORFOLK

ALL HALLOWS
ADDRESS Rouen Road, Norwich, Norfolk NR1 1QT
☎ 01603 624738

If you want to retreat from the world for a while, then All Hallows is the perfect place. The charming Anglican sisters greet visitors like long-lost relatives and everyone is instantly put at ease. People come from all over the world, from as far afield as Australia to the tiny house in the middle of Norwich. Next door is St Julian's Church, built on the site of the cell of a fourteenth-century mystic, Lady Julian of Norwich. It is not necessary to be at all religious and you will find the sisters themselves very broadminded. They are happy to talk to you about your problems but some people come here to be completely silent and, if that is the case, then they are left to their own devices. Sister Philippa is a wonderful listener and, no matter what you tell her, she will not be shocked. Lots of quite deep discussions go on over bowls of cereal and visitors find these spontaneous discussions can be enormously helpful. Facilities include a small library, which has a well-thumbed copy of Julian's *Revelations of Divine Love*, and a television for those who need to be reminded a little of the world outside. The rooms are terribly simple, with a small hand basin, and there are only communal shower facilities. Expect

to meet anyone from a student to a world-weary professional.
- **COST** *A donation of whatever you feel is appropriate*
- **HOW TO GET THERE** *Take the M11 and A11 to Norwich. From the station, cross the railway bridge and go straight up Prince of Wales Road. Just before the Anglia Television building, turn left down King Street. Go straight across at the traffic lights, pass the derelict church of St Peter's, staying in the right-hand lane. There is a small alley on the right and a sign for St Julian's; the church is on the left and the Convent of All Hallows behind, at the junction with Rouen Road*

SOMERSET

THE COWSHED AT BABINGTON HOUSE
ADDRESS Kilmersdon, near Frome, Somerset BA11 3RW
☎ 01373 812266

Yes it really used to be a cowshed but now has been transformed, like the rest of Babington House, into a hip hideaway and spa. Lots of minimalist décor – suede and leather blocks to sit on and a super juice bar serving, predictably, cowjuice – a mix of carrot, apple and orange. Although hip and fun, we found all the staff friendly and nice. The outdoor pool was one of the nicest we have come across. It's an infinity pool, so doors open between indoors and outdoors at ground level; it's heated to 85°F and surrounded by woodland. At the weekend there are as many men as women there having treatments as well as lazing by the pool. A massage with muscle-bound Roger provided lots of laughs, when we had to choose from the array of Babington's home-made aromatherapy oils. You can choose Knackered Cow, Stressed-out Cow, Stroppy Cow, Pasteurised Cow or Laughing Cow, depending on your mood. You can have facials, which, rather oddly, also include a foot massage, and therapeutic manicures and pedicures. There is a sauna, steam room and indoor pool. The Cowshed also offer one-to-one Pilates and yoga and you can also have a fitness assessment. All the products are made locally or are made from infusions from Babington's gardens. And when you go home you can buy some of these really gorgeous bottles. Choose bathcuds – a sedative bath foam made from ylang-ylang and camomile and, if you are giving it as a present to a friend, you can have their name printed on it. If this all proves too much for you, you can always repair to the Cowshed's cinema, to watch an arthouse or pre-released film to take your mind off everything. See the main entry for Babington House in Romantic Weekends, page 20.
- **COST** *See Babington House main entry in Romantic Weekends, page 20*
- **HOW TO GET THERE** *Take the M4 and leave at Junction 17 (A350 Chippenham and Trowbridge). At the A361 roundabout, turn right on to the A361 towards Trowbridge. Go through the town and*

*carry on on the A361 till you reach the A36. Turn left towards
Frome. Then take the B3090 and carry on to the junction with
the A362. Turn right and carry on following signs for Kilmersdon.
Bear right to Mells, passing a pub, carry on towards Vobster and,
at the T-junction, turn right. Babington House is on the left*

SUFFOLK

SHRUBLAND HALL HEALTH CLINIC
ADDRESS Coddenham, Suffolk IP6 9QH
☎ 01473 830404 **FAX** 01473 832641

The *grande dame* of health clinics, Shrubland Hall is set in extensive
grounds, including a beautiful Italianate garden landscaped by
Barry, the architect of the present Houses of Parliament. Unlike
some of its glitzier and slightly *parvenu* cousins, Shrubland Hall
has strong emphasis on the 'clinic' element. It's definitely not the
sort of place that you would want to visit for a hen weekend, but
it's perfect for those who want to lose weight, detox or unwind.
On arrival, guests get a thorough health check with Sister and one
of three in-house GPs, and a chat with the redoubtable Lady de
Saumarez who discusses the reasons for your visit and the dietary
requirements for your stay. These interviews are supposed to
last only 15 minutes but allow a good half hour. The food is
predictably spartan but delicious. 'Breakfast' is brought to your
room – you will never have been so pleased to see a slice of
lemon in a cup of hot water. Those on the full diet have lunch in a
very pretty dining room overlooking the Italian gardens. A typical
lunch consists of home-made soup; six salads – three high- and
three low-calorie; cheese; home-made bread and biscuits.
Supper at 6pm is a thermos of broth; cottage cheese or yogurt;
wheatgerm and honey and fresh fruit. There is a good choice
of extra treatments, including: Pilates (body conditioning in
conjunction with deep breathing); CACI a painless and non-
invasive combination of massage and micro-current therapy,
allegedly undertaken by Delia Smith before a TV series; Faradism
and a range of massages and beauty treatments. Incredibly
invigorating is the Shrublands Sauna followed by a dip into a
freezing plunge pool, which will really make you tingle. There are
lots of interesting villages and places to visit locally, or you could
book painting lessons, go cycling, riding or fishing, or play golf
or croquet. Most guests, however, find that they wind down so
completely that they are incapable of doing anything other than
napping between treatments. Some naughty guests apparently
walk the length of the drive to the nearest pub, where burgers and
chocolate are on sale, but this is frowned upon. Smokers will be
relieved to know that, whilst smoking is strongly discouraged, you
are allowed to smoke in the conservatory.

The clientele is predominantly female, although there are

usually several male guests and the atmosphere is like that of a rather exclusive girls' boarding school, with much giggling and swapping of life histories over supper.

• **COST** *Wednesday to Sunday stay, £476, including bed, full board, initial consultations, service, two main treatments daily and a choice of exercise classes*

• **HOW TO GET THERE** *Take the M25, A12 to Ipswich and A14. Bypassing Ipswich, look for a tall chimney and bear left following the sign for B1113, Great Blakenham. Follow signs to Claydon via a roundabout under the A14 (fourth exit). Go through Claydon and on for 2 miles. Immediately after the fork for Coddenham, you will see the entrance for Shrubland Hall on the right, opposite the Sorrel House Inn. Continue up the drive for ¾ mile; the clinic is on the left*

SCOTLAND

STOBO CASTLE HEALTH SPA

ADDRESS Stobo Castle, Peebleshire EH45 8NY
☎ 01721 760249 **FAX** 01721 760294

An imposing Scottish castle in rolling green countryside 7 miles outside Peebles, Stobo Castle is the ultimate get-away-from-it-all spa. The building dates back to 1805 and, although it is grand and imposing, because it only has 27 bedrooms it manages to be cosy and personal at the same time.

First off, you are given a health check and a chance to discuss the treatments you have chosen. Treatments are available to help you detox, lose weight, start a fitness regime or even give up smoking. The spa area has underfloor heating and a glass room and there is a range of treatments including a Stobo facial – an electric, deep-cleansing facial for an oily combination skin – and ionithermie – a treatment where two different types of electrical currents are applied, through creams and ampoules, to reduce and firm the figure. The effects are increased removal of toxins, improved oxygen supply and inch loss. There's also a detox treatment, which includes treatments like Thalgobodytherm Wrap or Algotherapy, which break down fatty deposits and detoxify the system, a super collagen-lifting facial designed specifically for fine lines and wrinkles, and a CACI treatment, which is a non-surgical face lift that restores facial muscle tone. Another very popular treatment is paraffin wax – warm wax is administered to your back, which brings immediate relief to painful necks and tight muscles. There is an exercise pool, a whirlpool and an aqua aerobics class. There is also a gym, or you can enrol in a Stobo ABC fitness plan, in which you are given your own personal fitness plan. Or try a yoga session or tennis or swimming coaching. And, to finish off, you can have your hair done and a make-up lesson using Guerlain products.

The food is delicious and not too spartan – lots of local produce.

But best of all at Stobo, you have the wonderful grounds to explore – including the Japanese Water Gardens and the lake – and guided walks in and around the estate. Or you can take a mountain bike to explore further afield. As well as tennis, golf, riding and fishing can also be arranged.

- **COST** *£138 per person per night for sharing a twin room. This includes all meals, use of facilities and one body massage per night of your stay*
- **HOW TO GET THERE** *Fly to Edinburgh with Go. A taxi can be organised from the airport or you can travel by bus to Peebles, just 7 miles from Stobo, and take a taxi*

WALES

ST DAVID'S HOTEL AND SPA
ADDRESS Havannah Street, Cardiff Bay CF10 5SD
☎ 01222 454045 **FAX** 01222 487056

Cardiff, at first thought, might not spring to mind as the most glamorous location for Rocco Forte's stunning hotel spa. Modern and space-age, the hotel stands out like a modern bird perched on the banks of Cardiff Bay. If the exterior is dramatic so is reception. You can forget chintz curtains as your normal spa concept: this entrance is absolutely, mindbogglingly stunning. First off, there is an atrium, seeming to extend up for miles into space, and then you check in at one of the smartest minimalist desks. Already, it's easy to feel that all this glamour will rub off and you will walk out again two days later a happier, shinier person too. Amazingly, as well as having your bags brought up to your room, they also offer to unpack them. It's an offer too good to resist as long as they won't find everything too shabby for this oh-so-perfect hotel. Unsurprisingly, the rooms more than live up to the glamour of the entrance. All the rooms are air-conditioned and, best of all, have a deck looking out over Cardiff Bay. The furniture is Italian (well, of course) and you get satellite TV and a minibar, which you should promise yourself not to plunder. Meals are taken at the Tides Bar and Restaurant which is also open to visitors and guests not at the spa. But no need to worry – there are deliciously adapted dishes of the lighter kind for dieters.

The treatments at the spa are designed to harmonise mind and body, with sea products, salts and minerals. Top treatments include: a jet blitz; marine hydrotherapy bath; an ESPA detoxifying algae wrap; and there's an hour-and-25-minute-long ESPA stress-buster treatment, especially designed for men; or even a flight reviver for the jetlagged. As well as all this, there's a 15-metre exercise pool overlooking the bay, gym and salt-water hydro pool. And, to finish off, you can have a Vincent Longo Make-Over, so you come out radiant and truly beautified.

The Special Occasions programme, for example, includes

aromatherapy massage, facial, luxury hand treatment and makeover, light lunch and use of pool, gym and relaxation area.

• **COST** *A two-day programme costs £199 based on two people sharing. This includes accommodation, dinner, spa lunch and a choice of Detox Day, Stress Recovery Day or Special Occasions Day programme*

• **HOW TO GET THERE** *By train from Paddington to Cardiff Central and the spa is 10 minutes from the station by taxi.* ☎ *0345 484950 for rail enquiries*

FRANCE

THALASSA BIARRITZ HOTEL REGINA ET DU GOLF

ADDRESS 52 Avenue de l'Imperatrice, 04200 Biarritz

☎ 0171 584 2841 (Erna Law Consultations Ltd), for reservations

If you want to go for the latest concept in spa treatments, then give thalassatherapy a whirl. Typically, it is something the soigné and chic French, with their more dedicated attitude to making themselves look and feel their best, are already into in a big way.

Thalassatherapy literally means 'seawater treatment', and turns the benefits of a marine environment into beauty treatments. The climate, water, seaweed, sand and 'other substances extracted from the sea' (heaven knows what these might be) are all used in some way or another. The real beauty of going to the Thalassa Centre in Biarritz is that not only will you be improving your form, but you will also feel as though you have a had a real break away from it all. Many of the French are now eschewing the South of France and making Biarritz fashionable again. Stay in the Hotel Regina et du Golf, an Edwardian hotel 300 metres from the Thalassa Centre by courtesy boat.

The range of treatments for an introductory short break visit include a Getting Back Into Shape treatment, which is adapted to your own needs, plus other specific treatments such as Leg Toning, Marine Beauty, and a Bride to Be programme. All the treatments are conducted under the supervision of a qualified medical team. Wonderfully, and this is where the French are really streets ahead of the UK, they run a Post Natal course. If ever there is a time when you just want someone to take over, massage and pamper you and above all give you your old body back, it is after you've had a baby. The programme is aimed at mothers eight weeks or more after giving birth, to help them get back into shape and to help babies with their early learning. Four thalassatherapy treatment sessions per day, designed to help you cope with the aftermath of childbirth and pregnancy: tiredness, backache, slack muscles, excess weight and so on. And, even more wonderfully, and so unlike our own dear country, you can take your baby with you, so you can continue to breastfeed. There is a professional, qualified nursery nurse in the hotel, you can take the baby into the whirlpool, and babies stay for free. Unfortunately, the minimum stay for this is rather longer than a weekend – 6 days. But what the hell, if you've had to put up with stretch marks, surely you can stretch the weekend out a little?

- **COST** *The cost also compares very well with UK spas. A two-night weekend break for two costs 1840F (around £184 at time of writing) per person for bed and breakfast, two complimentary meals for two (your choice of lunch or dinner) and three thalassatherapy treatments per day each for two days. Or 3250F per person for 2 nights, half board including flights from Stansted with Ryan Air*
- **HOW TO GET THERE** *Ryan Air flies from London Stansted into Biarritz, with prices starting at £69.99 return including taxes*

LES THERMES MARINS DE MONTE CARLO

ADDRESS 2 Avenue Monte Carlo, 98000 Monaco

☎ 92 16 40 40 or 92 16 36 36 (offer bookings)

For grand-prix grass widows or those who fancy taking French leave, what could be more glamorous than going to Monte Carlo's blissfully beautiful spa *en bord de mer*? What could be dreamier than looking out to sea while you lie in your treatment bath? This is a super-glam spa with every conceivable luxury: two seawater swimming pools, sauna, restaurants and bar. Treatments include jet spray showers, anti-cellulite, stress control and aqua-gym classes. Get Your Figure Back and Help to Stop Smoking stays are also available.

- **COST** *Discovery of Well-Being package includes accommodation for two nights at Hotel Mirabeau, breakfast, one day with four relaxation treatments, use of spa facilities and a dietetic dinner at La Coupole for 6700F*
- **HOW TO GET THERE** *Fly to Nice and take a helicopter to Monte Carlo (costs £37– £40 per person each way). A taxi will take 35 minutes or so and costs about £40. Regular coach transfers from the airport cost about £10 or you can take the train from the main station in Nice, £3. Once in Monte Carlo, all taxi fares start at £5*

GOURMET WEEKENDS

Let's start off by getting one thing straight – neither of us purports to be a food critic. However, like most people, we've eaten enough meals out to know the excellent from the indifferent. We may not talk knowledgeably about 'reductions' and *jus* or techniques of cookery but we do know when something tastes delicious – whether it's a bag of chips or a nine-course gourmet meal with all the trimmings. Not only that, but eating a good meal is as much about the atmosphere as the food. It's no use eating ambrosia if you have highly irritating waiters, or you feel uncomfortable to be there. Sometimes, high expectations of a restaurant – from a review or the fact that it has a Michelin star – can lead to disappointment. Just serving a dish with great aplomb from under a silver dome doesn't ensure success. Sometimes, it's just the little things that can spoil a meal, rather than the food itself – bad or supercilious service, long waits between courses or uncomfortable chairs. Sometimes, it's the little touches that make it a truly memorable evening: a charming and well-informed manager – the Fat Duck scores here – having a chat with the chef after the meal – the Fat Duck or the Vineyard – or just a delightful waitress serving the most delicious coffee and *petits fours*.

We have based this chapter on the premise that you are making a weekend of going to a particular restaurant or hotel. You may want to go somewhere fabulous to eat and economise on accommodation or you may want to go for the full monty. Some of the places that we have included are obvious and are in here because they did live up to our expectations; some of them are in because they serve simple but delicious meals at reasonable prices.

BERKSHIRE

THE FAT DUCK

ADDRESS High Street, Bray, Berkshire SL6 2AQ

☎ 01628 580333   **FAX** 01628 776188

In the delightful village of Bray, this restaurant looks, on the outside, like a pub (which it formerly was) but inside it is stylish and modern. One of the hottest restaurants on the planet, the Fat Duck really does live up to its reputation and more. It's the chef's restaurant – top chefs like Marco Pierre White, Gordon Ramsey and Nico Ladenis have all made pilgrimages here – and so should you. Manager Nigel, resplendent in Rupert Bear trousers, gives you a very warm welcome and amusingly dissects each dish in intricate detail. The whole point of this restaurant is that each dish is extraordinarily complicated but tastes wonderful – definitely not the sort of thing that anyone in their right mind would attempt at home.

- **CHEF** Heston Blumenthal – self- taught – a wonderfully inventive chef who is also the owner

- **SIGNATURE DISHES** For starters, try crab feuilleté with roast foie gras, marinated salmon, crystallised seaweed, and oyster vinaigrette; or cuttlefish cannelloni of duck and maple syrup with parsley broth and long turnips. Try a main course of roast spiced cod with Castelluccio lentils, braised cockscombs and purée of pea. Puddings are sublime and include délice of chocolate; salted butter caramel with pistachios and peanuts; chocolate and thyme sorbet

- **WINES** The restaurant specialises in French country wine, but ask for advice from enthusiastic sommelier John Walden

- **COST** About £120 for two, depending on wine choices

- **WHERE TO STAY** The Chauntry House, Bray-on-Thames, Berks. ☎ 01628 673991. The Chauntry House is just a short stroll from the Fat Duck. It has a lovely, warm, welcoming atmosphere and it looks out over the cricket pitch in front and has lovely terraces at the back. The bedrooms are comfortable rather than outstanding but staying there is a real pleasure. Breakfasts are a real treat: there is a huge buffet of cereals, fruit salad, compote, croissants, hot rolls, toast, coffee, tea, fruit juice and full English breakfasts made to order. Costs from £102 per room for a single, or £130 for a double room

- **WHAT TO DO** Walk off the excesses of a night at the Fat Duck by going for a good long stroll along the riverside. Or take out a boat: these can be booked through Simon Davies of Rivertime, ☎ 01628 530670; the hotel can also arrange boats for you.

- **HOW TO GET THERE** Take the M4 to Junction 8/9 (Maidenhead). Then follow the A308 to Windsor. You will see a bridge. Just before the bridge, take a left turn to Bray

THE VINEYARD AT STOCKCROSS

ADDRESS Stockcross, Newbury, Berkshire RG20 8JU

☎ 01635 528770 **FAX** 01635 528398

'A bit of California in the Home Counties' sums the Vineyard up perfectly. If you are a person who needs the illusion that you are spending the weekend at someone's country estate, complete with authentically creaking floors and oddly-shaped bathrooms shoehorned into tiny spaces, then the Vineyard is not for you. However, if you are happy to relax in a luxurious, extremely well-appointed hotel, with a terrific restaurant, first-class staff and an amazing wine list then ring immediately. The Vineyard is the pet project of industrialist Sir Peter Michael, CBE, who is passionate about food and wine, so much so that he owns his own vineyard in California. His excellent wines are available nowhere in the UK except in the hotel restaurant.

- **CHEF** *Executive Chef is Billy Reid, who was formerly Executive Chef at L'Escargot, where he earned a Michelin star, as well as having worked at the Ritz, the Waterside Inn and the Box Tree at Ilkley. It is quite possible that you will meet Mr. Reid, as he likes to get out of the kitchen and talk to guests*

- **SIGNATURE DISHES** *The 'fusion' menu includes dishes such as foie gras and chicken liver pâté; tartare of scallops with a hairdo of greens surrounded by truffle oil; and roast loin of lamb, perfectly pink and tender in seven slices, with French beans, butter-sautéed mushrooms and mash*

- **WINES** *A blistering wine list, running to 90 pages. The Californian list is particularly stunning. The two that we tried from Peter Michael's own vineyard were outstanding. The list offers many bottles from extremely small, family-owned estates that are usually available only within 100 miles of the vineyards*

- **COST** *Dinner, bed and breakfast, per person per night: cottage single (not in a separate cottage, but sweetly decorated and tucked up under the eves), £164 weekends. Cottage double, £117 weekends. Luxury double, £129 weekends. Grand double and double suite, £152 weekends. Luxury suite, £199. Grand suites – the ultimate in comfort, with four-poster bed, spacious sitting room and bathroom – £252*

- **WHAT TO DO** *At the hotel, you can now relax in the Vineyard Spa, free to guests, which includes an indoor pool, spa bath, steam room, sauna, gymnasium and treatment rooms. Explore the joys of the countryside and hunt for antiques in small towns nearby. Donnington castle is not far away, and there's Didcot Railway Centre for steam enthusiasts. Our favourite activity was throwing stones in the river at Kintbury and watching the narrowboats there. You can take a narrowboat ride, either motor-driven or horse-drawn*

- **HOW TO GET THERE** *By road, take the M4 to Junction 13 and then take the A34 Newbury bypass to the A4 interchange. At the roundabout, follow the A4 towards Hungerford. At the next roundabout, take the B4000 to Stockcross. The Vineyard is a mile along, on the right. AA-type signs signpost the A4 roundabout for* the Vineyard. By train, from Paddington to Newbury, arriving at Platform 3 or Platform 4 (the ridiculously able concierge confides). You can either take a cab from the station or be picked up in the hotel's Chrysler by prior arrangement

WALDO'S RESTAURANT

ADDRESS Cliveden, Taplow, Berkshire SL6 0JF

☎ 01628 668561   **FAX** 01628 661837

Cliveden is famously beautiful and in a truly stunning setting overlooking the Thames. Waldo's is worth a visit in its own right and, if you can't manage a night staying at Cliveden, then book yourself into somewhere else locally and go for dinner. Do take the trouble to wander around the grounds and terrace before dinner, as it's well worth it. Waldo's is in the basement, in the old kitchen and servant's quarters. The bar is cosy and welcoming in 'country-house library' style and the restaurant is cool and stylish, with some interesting pictures, and not overly grand or intimidating.

• **CHEF** Gary Jones, previously head chef at Homewood Park Hotel and at Richard Branson's Necker Island

• **SIGNATURE DISHES** Velouté of oysters, sea bass and scallops, scented with coriander; fillet of John Dory and clams, with mousseron mushrooms, sorrel and fresh herb bouillon; the chef's signature pudding is fresh jellied orange Muscat terrine, with bitter-sweet chocolate sorbet. For the gourmand as well as gourmet there is the £84, nine-course tasting menu. A typical menu is: ravioli of Cornish crab, scented with ginger; confit of foie gras with apples, sweet bay leaf jelly and brioche toast; oak-smoked salmon, sevruga caviar and warm sour cream blinis; pan-seared red mullet and scallop with brandade, niçoise olives and tomato; lemon verbena sorbet; roast quail with spring cabbage, asparagus and madeira jus; a selection of Europe's finest cheeses with home-made bread; tiramisu with espresso anglaise; coffee and petits fours

• **WINES** The wine list is extensive and ranges from the lower end of the price range (£19 for a bottle of house wine) to the more expensive. You can choose a wine to suit any dish and from all the main wine regions around the world. There is also a large variety of champagnes starting at £39.50

• **COST** Three-course dinner £58, which includes mineral water and coffee and petits fours. Tasting menu is £84. A nice touch is 'service is neither included nor anticipated'

• **WHERE TO STAY** Stay at Cliveden. Prices per night are double room, £290; large double, £360; junior suite, £445; one-bedroom suite, £550. There is also Spring Cottage, a three-bedroom cottage on the bank of the Thames, with exclusive boat and personal butler, which costs £2,400 for two nights mid-week, from £2,800 for two nights at a weekend. See the main entry in Romantic Weekends, page 9, for more details on Cliveden

• **HOW TO GET THERE** Take the M4 out of London and come off at Junction 7 (Slough West). Follow signs for Maidenhead. Follow

this road for 1½ miles to a junction with the B476 signposted
Taplow, Bourne End, Cliveden (opposite garage). Follow this road
for 2½ miles until the gates of Cliveden are on the left. By rail, take
a train to Burnham Station (2 miles from Cliveden) or South Station
(6 miles) and then take a taxi

THE ROYAL OAK

ADDRESS The Square, Yattendon, Berkshire RG18 OUG
☎ 01635 201325   **FAX** 01635 201962

The Royal Oak is a really pretty, wisteria-clad country inn, with
lovely furnishings and real style. The fantastic walled garden is
ideal for drinks or dining al fresco in the evening. Weekends need
to be booked well in advance as its fame has spread far and
wide. Eat in the restaurant, which has a *table d'hôte* menu only,
or in the brasserie, from the *à la carte* menu.

- **CHEF** Robbie McRae, the owner. Before setting up the Royal Oak,
he worked for Marco Pierre White and also for the Roux brothers
at the Waterside Inn, Bray
- **SIGNATURE DISHES** *Caramelised fillet of sea bass, with crayfish
and fresh asparagus and roasted baby plum tomatoes; peppered
tornados of hake, with tarte tatin of chicory and sauce lie de vin;
baked papillote of banana, with caramel and honey-roasted nuts*
- **WINES** *French and New World wines, from £9 upwards, with a
large range between £15 and £25*
- **COST** *Three-course dinner in restaurant £32.50; in the brasserie,
three-course dinner is £21 per head*
- **WHERE TO STAY** *Stay in one of the five bedrooms in elegant old
English style. Rooms, £115 per night. Weekend packages for
£340 per person include accommodation, breakfast, one dinner
in the brasserie and one dinner in the restaurant*
- **WHAT TO DO** *Windsor; Oxford; lots of lovely walks; river trips;
Wyld Court Rainforest, an indoor tropical garden*
- **HOW TO GET THERE** *Take the M4 Junction 12 and head for
Pangbourne. Take the Bradfield turn off and Yattendon is
signposted from there. The Royal Oak is in the main square*

DERBYSHIRE

FISCHERS AT BASLOW HALL

ADDRESS Calver Road, Baslow, Derbyshire DE45 1RR
☎ 01246 583259   **FAX** 01246 583818

A pretty Derbyshire manor house on the edge of the Chatsworth
Estate, Fischer's Baslow Hall is the perfect spot for a 'grande
bouffe' out of London. I was taken there for a surprise wedding
anniversary weekend and it was ideal. Luxurious suites with very
comfy beds mean that you sleep really well after your dinner. And
the food is well worth the journey. The hotel is owned by Max and
Susan Fischer, who bought it in 1988 and have decorated it to

feel like a private house. Max does the cooking and uses the best of local produce, such as Derbyshire spring lamb, Chatsworth venison and wild hare, as well as imported luxuries like *foie gras* and truffles. In 1995, he won Egon Ronay Restaurant of the Year and has one Michelin star.

• **CHEF** *Max Fischer is the chef-patron. He specialises in beautifully executed classic dishes and adventurous newer cuisine*

• **SIGNATURE DISHES** *A sample dinner menu would include canapés and savouries served with pre-dinner drinks; chef's surprise savoury served at the table; among the starters is a choice of roasted sea scallops with truffles and sherry vinaigrette; pan-fried foie gras on brioche toast with citrus sauce; layered chicken, wild mushroom and sweetbread terrine; glazed pig's trotter on pease pudding; crab ravioli with crustacean sauce. This might be followed by tornados of halibut on spring greens; fish of the day; roast pigeon breast with pithiviers of foie gras and Madeira sauce; fillet of naturally reared beef with red-wine sauce; pig's trotter with pommes purée and morel mushrooms; breast of guinea fowl and confit of its leg, with salsify and trompettes de mort mushrooms; Derbyshire spring lamb saddle, with aubergine tian and tarragon sauce; or rabbit saddle wrapped in Parma ham and herb tortellini. Dessert or cheese is followed by coffee, hand-rolled chocolates and petits fours*

• **WINES** *House wines are £13; there is a wine list offering about 70 items*

• **COST** *Set dinner costs £45 per person. Lunch is £20 per person for two courses and £24 for three courses*

• **WHERE TO STAY** *In the hotel. Hideaway breaks cost £180 Standard, or £210 Luxury, per couple per night for two or more nights, which includes accommodation in a double room, bakery breakfast, dinner and a newspaper*

• **WHAT TO DO** *Visit nearby Haddon Hall, Hardwick and Kedleston as well as the market towns of Ashbourne and Bakewell. Don't miss the splendid Chatsworth House and its excellent farm shop, which is rather more like Fortnums than your average farm shop in a shed. Pick up a leaflet in the hotel for where to buy factory bargains direct. If you're on a romantic weekend, you might like to visit the David Nieper factory shop and buy some silk underwear. The John Smedley knitware factory, who supply, among others, Paul Smith, is well worth rummaging around in for bargains*

• **HOW TO GET THERE** *From the M1, take Junction 28 to Chesterfield on the A617. Follow the 'Chatsworth House' signs on the A619 to Baslow. Drive through Baslow village on the A6233 Stockport road. The church is on your left. Baslow Hall is on the right as you leave the village*

HAMPSHIRE

ON THE QUAY

ADDRESS 47 South Street, Emsworth, Hants PO10 7EG

☎ 01243 375592   **FAX** 01243 375593

A delightfully situated, waterside, privately-owned restaurant, with a Michelin star, really excellent food and a superb cellar. The restaurant makes an ideal target for a gourmet weekend break and you could even fit in a visit to the Chichester festival.

- **CHEF** *Ramon Farthings was previously head chef at Harvey's in Bristol for four years. He started his apprenticeship with Chris Oakley at the Pier waterside restaurant in Harwich and later became personal chef at Althorp for the then Earl Spencer, then sous chef at the Castle and head chef at Cacot Manor*

- **SIGNATURE DISHES** *Because of the restaurant's proximity to the harbour, fresh fish is a speciality. Cod and langoustine fritters, served on a smooth potato cream with a langoustine reduction is superb. He also produces excellent puds and his speciality is the 'four-lemon dessert': lemon crème brûlée, lemon parfait, lemon tart and lemon-curd mousse, with lemon biscuits and lemon syrup*

- **WINES** *For a restaurant of its size, the 250-odd-bin cellar being built up and enhanced by the owners is very respectable. It ranges from bottles of house red at £13.50 to over £200 for wines such as Penfolds 'Grange' '95 and '93. The wine list is well laid out and helpful*

- **COST** *£33 per head for à la carte, lunch £16.50 for 2 courses, £19.50 for 3 courses*

- **WHERE TO STAY** *The Brookfield, Emsworth, Hants., ☎ 01243 373363 (a ¾ mile walk) costs £85 per night for a double room including breakfast. The Millstream Hotel, Bosham, Hants., ☎ 01243 573234 (4 miles away) costs from £112 per night for a double room. Crouchers Bottom Country Hotel, Birdham, Hants., ☎ 01243 784995 costs £85 per night for a double room. Or try one of the local B&Bs – the Old Rectory at Chidham, ☎ 01243 472088; Hatpins at Bosham, ☎ 01243 572644 or Tidings, opposite the restaurant, ☎ 01243 374731*

- **HOW TO GET THERE** *By car, take the A3 (but try to avoid travelling south through Hindhead between 5pm and 7pm, as it can be a real bottleneck, especially on a Friday). Then take the B2149/8 to Emsworth. At the Emsworth roundabout, continue south (straight on) and round the square to the end of South Street. By train, travel either from Victoria or the faster line from Waterloo to Havant. Trains from Waterloo will require a change at or a taxi from Havant (2½ miles away). The faster trains from Waterloo to Havant depart up to three times an hour during the day, reducing to an hourly service late in the evening*

ISLE OF WIGHT

THE GEORGE HOTEL

ADDRESS Quay Street, Yarmouth, Isle of Wight PO41 0PE
☎ 01983 760331   **FAX** 01983 760425

Yarmouth's historic George Hotel is a 17th-century town house positioned only a few paces from the ancient harbour. On sunny days, meals can be served outside in the garden. Inside, there is a luxurious dining room and sunny yellow brasserie overlooking the garden and Solent. The George features wood panelling, huge fireplaces and a flagstoned hall. Many bedrooms have sea views, one has a four-poster and two have balconies.

- **CHEF** Kevin Mangeolles
- **SIGNATURE DISHES** *The restaurant has a Michelin star. The food is 'modern British', emphasising seasonality and local produce. The dinner menu includes: a trio of duck tastings (pan-fried duck rillette, ravioli of honey-flavoured duck and pan-fried foie gras on sultanas); rack of new-season lamb with a sea kale and sweetbread ravioli on tomato- and tarragon-flavoured sauce; prunes d'Agen parfait, with an apple and cider sorbet*
- **WINES** *There is an extensive list, with about 200 wines on offer, including five house red and five house white wines, all at £11.50. An Errazuriz Chardonnay, £11.50; Pinot Noir Louis Jadot, £17.50; a red wine from the Côte D'Or and a Château Cissac £35*
- **COST** *The four-course dinner menu is set at £36.75 per person. There is also a brasserie, which has à la carte starters from £4.75– £6.25, main courses from £9.00–£13.95 and desserts at £5.25*
- **WHERE TO STAY** *In the hotel. Accommodation is £95 per night for a standard single, £130 for a standard double or twin or £175 for a Balcony Room – double or twin. These prices include breakfast*
- **WHAT TO DO** *See Weekends by the Sea, Isle of Wight, page 148*
- **HOW TO GET THERE** *See Weekends by the Sea, Isle of Wight, page 148*

KENT

WHITSTABLE OYSTER FISHERY CO.

ADDRESS The Horsebridge, Whitstable, Kent CT5 1BU
☎ 01227 276856

Almost a shack bang on the beach, with nothing between you and the sea except pebbles and sand, in the summer the whole of the front of this restaurant opens up, so you can eat al fresco. Very informal – you can view before you eat, on display in a large holding cabinet, a mind-boggling array of live oysters, lobsters and crabs. There's an eclectic style of décor – with lots of whitewashed walls and bric-a-brac – and lots of scrabble-playing and four-hour lunches are the order of the day. If you get bored with the view you can always pop upstairs to the cinema on the first floor: it's very tiny but shows all the latest films. Don't let its presence deter you from visiting the fishery: it's not at all obvious.

- **CHEF** *Head chef Chris Williams has been at the Oyster Fishery Co. for seven years*
- **SIGNATURE DISHES** *Naturally, all manner of seafood – delicious oysters, lobsters, local and Cornish crab. Cod in beer batter and chips; octopus stew; moules and chips; as well as hake, halibut, lemon and Dover sole, sea bass and so on*
- **WINES** *The house wine (£9.95), a Chilean Chardonnay, Sancerre and Muscadet all team up splendidly with the oysters*
- **COST** *Starters cost between £5 and £12.50, main courses £9.50–£23.00 and desserts £3.95. Book well ahead as there is such a demand. Saturdays are particularly busy*
- **WHERE TO STAY** *In one of six multicoloured converted fisherman's cottages complete with shutters opening onto the beach. They are quite basic but charming. The cottages are owned by the restaurant but booked through the Hotel Continental, 289 Beach Walk, Whitstable, Kent CT5 2BP ☎ 01227 280280. Prices per night range from £90 to £125*
- **WHAT TO DO** *Walk along past beautifully coloured beach huts, to the harbour town and yacht club. Opposite the harbour is a warehouse that sells fresh fish at wholesale prices so you can buy some more fish to take home. Lots of arty-crafty shops, antique shops and a theatre. You can also watch power-boat races and visit nearby Canterbury*
- **HOW TO GET THERE** *The train from Victoria to Whitstable takes about 1½ hours. Then it's a 15-minute walk from the station. By car, go down the A2, then take the M25 and then the M26. At Junction 4, take the A228 towards Rochester and then get onto the M2 Eastbound. At the end of the M2, take the A299 and A290 to Whistable. Once in the town, there is a one-way system. Follow this and look for a car park on the left. The restaurant is on the sea front and the hotel a little further on through the one-way system*

NORTHAMPTONSHIRE

FAWSLEY HALL HOTEL

ADDRESS Fawsley, near Daventry, Northamptonshire NN11 3BA
☎ 01327 892000 **FAX** 01327 892001

A fairly newly opened hotel, housed in a Tudor manor house with Georgian additions, set in 2000 acres of parkland with lots of gargoyles and gables. Good for beating stress and chilling out, very quiet and peaceful with delicious food served in former Tudor kitchens with a lovely fireplace. There are lots of cosy alcoves on different levels, so that larger tables are kept well apart from romantic tables for two. Romantic couples should request the Queen Elizabeth Chamber, with a stately four-poster bed.

- **CHEF** James Haywood, previously the sous chef under his predecessor Tim Johnson
- **SIGNATURE DISHES** Nico Ladenis inspired dishes, including tortellini of goats' cheese on a red-pepper coulis; breast of corn-fed chicken with boudin blanc and morel raviolo; grilled duck breast with potatoes and green peppercorns; and orchard fruits tarte tatin, with plum sauce and caramel ice cream
- **WINES** An excellent selection of wines from as little as £13 for a Muscadet de Sèvres et Maine
- **COST** Dinner from around £30 per person
- **WHERE TO STAY** In the hotel. Weekend break £185 including breakfast for two people
- **WHAT TO DO** Take lots of long walks in the Capability Brown-designed gardens and see the chapel in the grounds
- **HOW TO GET THERE** Take the M40 to Junction 11 (Banbury) and then the A361 to Daventry. The hotel is signposted on the right, 1½ miles after Charwelton

OXFORDSHIRE

THE FEATHERS HOTEL
ADDRESS Woodstock, Oxford, Oxon OX20 1SX
☎ 01993 812291 **FAX** 01993 813158

'There is magic about this place' says manager Martin Godward, who began his career as a commis in the kitchen nine years ago. There is certainly a lovely warm atmosphere about the Feathers and a magic about the food. Charming and comfortable rooms with Penhaligon shampoos, Michaeljohn soaps and emollients from the Ragdale Clinic.

- **CHEF** Mark Treasure, formerly chef at Michael's Nook, Grasmere
- **SIGNATURE DISHES** The Feathers' food is outstanding: on a scale of one to ten, a wow. Head chef Mark Treasure really is a treasure: he has the knack not only of combining flavours in subtle and lovely ways but also of making individual ingredients taste more of themselves. Signature starters include roast scallops with haricot blanc purée, sage, salsify and truffle oil; and chicken and lobster set in a clear basil and muscadet jelly. Followed by pavé or calves' liver, pommes purée, button onions, and wild mushrooms; or canon of lamb rolled in parsley crumb, with caramelised shallots and black olive salsa. For dessert, try a towering concoction of vanilla crème with praline biscuit, chocolate sorbet and dried apples. Or opt for cheese: the Feathers actually presents you with a cheese menu, which saves all that embarrassing questioning your French waiter as to what the cheeses actually are. Cheeses are French, Welsh, East Anglian – all perfectly ripe. There is also a seven-course tasting menu at £48, meant to be served to the whole table
- **WINES** House wines, by George du Boeuf, are £11.95, and the book-sized wine list ranges from £12.50 to nearly £200

- **COST** *Starters range from £7.95–£11.95, main courses from £17.50–£22 and desserts from £6–£8.50*
- **WHERE TO STAY** *Stay in the hotel. Single rooms from £88 per night; double/twin-bedded rooms, £105–£169 per night; suites, £220–£275 per night. Prices include tea and shortbread on arrival, continental breakfast and newspaper*
- **WHAT TO DO** *Not many facilities on site but the Feathers can arrange chauffered punting, hot-air ballooning, fishing (both fly and coarse), gliding, microlighting, light aircraft, golf, quad bikes, shooting, clay-pigeon shooting, tennis, polo and private tours of Blenheim Palace. There is also a pair of mountain bikes*
- **HOW TO GET THERE** *From London and the M25, take the M40 north to Junction 8, then follow the A40 to Oxford. Then take the A44 to Woodstock and Bleinheim Palace. Turn left after the traffic lights in Woodstock. The Feathers is on the left. By Rail: Intercity from Paddington to Oxford 8 miles from Woodstock and then take a taxi, which will cost £10–£15*

THE LEMON TREE
ADDRESS 268 Woodstock Road, Oxford, Oxon OX2 7NW
☎ 01865 311936
Stunning décor, modern with lots of blue glass and ragged walls, massive exotic palms in pots and well designed wicker furniture give the Lemon Tree a contemporary but comfortable feel. There's a lovely garden at the back for drinks before dinner and really charming staff. This appeal seems ageless – young romantic student types, students dining with parents and children all seem happily at home. There's a modern menu and the obliging staff are happy to split starters between children.
- **CHEF** *Robert Engleston, previously at Winteringham Fields*
- **SIGNATURE DISHES** *Aubergine and goats' cheese millefeuille, full of flavour and interesting textures; chicken breast en papillote; crispy duck confit; and pan-fried scallops are all delicious*
- **WINES** *A very extensive range of traditional and New World wines, from house wines at £9.95 up to £65. Matua Valley Sauvingon Blanc, Hawks Crest Cabernet Sauvignon from the Napa Valley, and La Rioja Grand Reserve*
- **COST** *The average for three courses, including wine, is approximately £34 per person*
- **WHERE TO STAY** *The Old Parsonage Hotel, 1 Banbury Road, Oxford. ☎ 01865 310210, costs from £145 for bed and breakfast in a double room per night. Bath Place Hotel – a really charming, city-centre hotel converted from a 17th-century cottage. It is located at 4–5 Bath Place, Oxford, ☎ 01865 791812 and costs from £95 per night for bed and breakfast for two in a double room or £90 for one*
- **WHAT TO DO** *Punts can be hired from the Magdalen Bridge Boathouse at £10 per hour. Punting gives splendid views up and down the River Cherwell and endless opportunities to run over*

ducklings and cygnets. Tour the colleges; Magdalen College costs £2.50 per adult. Visit the University of Oxford Botanical Gardens on the edge of the River Cherwell. See also Cultural Weekends, page 151

• **HOW TO GET THERE** *Take the M40 and leave at Junction 8 (the A40, Oxford and Cheltenham). Follow it to the third roundabout and turn left onto Woodstock road, heading to Oxford City Centre. The Lemon Tree is ¾ mile along, on the left-hand side. Note that the car park requires extreme sobriety to manoeuvre – the word 'ouch' as you come out, to remind you that the single-track driveway takes traffic in both directions, is a timely reminder. By train, go from Paddington to Oxford*

RUTLAND

HAMBLETON HALL
ADDRESS Hambleton, Rutland LE15 8TH
☎ 01572 756991 **FAX** 01572 724721
In a wonderful rural setting overlooking Rutland Water and built in 1881 as a hunting box, this is quite small, with just 15 bedrooms. The interior is beautifully designed and decorated in country-house style, and Aaron Patterson's cooking is sublime.

• **CHEF** *Aaron Patterson started at Hambleton and then trained with Raymond Blanc, where sous chef Simon Hadley also trained*

• **SIGNATURE DISHES** *Essence of tomato with goats' cheese tortellini; sirloin of Dexter beef (reared by a local farmer) with roasted ceps and red-wine sauce; pigeon pot au feu, with ravioli of wild mushrooms and madeira-flavoured jus; vanilla cream with English strawberries; pavé of white and dark chocolate with raspberries*

• **WINES** *Sommelier Dominic recommends with the Dexter beef a Le Gay 1988 Pomerol or a 1995 Gaillat. The wine list is strong on French wines but also has a good selection of Californians*

• **COST** *A la carte from £50–£60 per head. Set menu £35 per head*

• **WHERE TO STAY** *In the hall. Bed and breakfast from £160 to £305 per room per night*

• **WHAT TO DO** *Visit nearby stately homes such as Burghley House or scenic towns such as Stamford where Middlemarch was filmed. Rutland Water offers watersports, cycling, walking, fishing and sailing*

• **HOW TO GET THERE** *Take the A1 north to the A606 Oakham exit. Follow the A606 through Empingham and Whitwell. Look for a turning on the left for Hambleton and Egleton. Continue down this road into the village; the hotel sign is on the right*

STAFFORDSHIRE

THE OLD BEAMS RESTAURANT

ADDRESS Waterhouse, Staffs ST10 3HW
☎ 01538 308254   **FAX** 01538 308157

the Old Beams is well worth the drive out of London; it's in an attractive area on the edge of the National Peak Park and in a convenient spot for local sightseeing. There is a small bar area, with a roaring fire in winter, a restaurant area and a larger conservatory. The staff are extremely welcoming and accommodating. We stumbled upon the Old Beams quite by chance, when we were looking for somewhere to stay with the children to visit nearby Alton Towers. Local pubs were all booked up as it was half term, and, despite knowing nothing about the Old Beams, we booked in. Having stayed there we vowed to go back *sans* children because the food was just so good. Chef-patron Nigel Wallis and his wife, Ann, aimed to create a top provincial restaurant 'not just for recognition in the guide books, but more importantly one that's known for the warmth of reception and the quality of food and service to its customers'.

- **CHEF** *Nigel Wallis reckons that the kitchen is the heart of any restaurant, and he and his team select the best produce available. They have won various accolades for their work*
- **SIGNATURE DISHES** *A typical dinner menu might be: pan-fried smoked haddock on chive and garlic mash, with a mild curry sauce; tart of pigeon, wild mushrooms and spinach, with a rosemary-scented veal jus; ragoût of sea scallops and langoustines in a frothy champagne sauce; open tart of tomatoes and basil with an olive dressing; soup of the day; followed by fresh fruit sorbet; then Old Beams fish of the day; grilled breast of Gressingham duck on a bed of couscous, with a confit leg and spicy sauce; pan-fried Aberdeen Angus fillet steak, with ceps and celeriac crisps on a rich red-wine sauce; corn-fed breast of guinea fowl, gently cooked in vermouth with pan-fried foie gras and spring vegetables; or panache of new-season lamb and vegetables in a truffle-scented broth. A selection from their pudding menu might be: sweet chestnut mousse with pears and chocolate sauce; tart of raspberries and clotted cream; hot soufflé of pistachio with chocolate sauce, or cappuccino of crème brûlée*
- **WINES** *The award-winning wine list contains a selection of wines that Nigel Wallis feels will enhance the dishes on the menu. House wine costs £15.95; both by Jean-Paul Brun, the white is a Chardonnay Beaujolais blanc and the red is also a Beaujolais*
- **COST** *Set three-course lunch, £22. Dinner à la carte. Starters cost from £5.25 to £10.95, main courses about £20, desserts between £6 and £7.25*
- **WHERE TO STAY** *The Old Beams has five rooms of its own, all en-suite with Heal's hand-made beds. The rooms are very comfortable and attractively furnished. The only downside is that they are on*

the other side of a relatively busy road from the restaurant. The full English cooked breakfast was one of the best we have eaten anywhere – delicious local bacon and home-made sausages. The single room is £65 per person per night, the small double £75 per person per night, the three large doubles £89.95 and the four-poster bedroom, £120

- **WHAT TO DO** Alton Towers (of course); Chatsworth House; Haddon Hall; Kedleston Hall and the Potteries, where many of the china manufacturers have tours and shops
- **HOW TO GET THERE** Take the M1 to Junction 25, Leek and Ashbourne. Go through Ashbourne and the road takes you through the centre of Waterhouses

SUFFOLK

THE FOX AND GOOSE

ADDRESS Fressingfield, Eye, Suffolk IP21 5PB
☎ 01379 586247   **FAX** 01379 586688

A traditional, half-timbered country pub in the wilds of north Suffolk, which has established a reputation for serving extremely good food at very reasonable prices. The pub backs onto the churchyard and has everything you would expect a country pub to have: cosy rooms, log fires, friendly staff and a small garden in which to eat when the weather is fine. There is also an excellent children's menu, with exotic touches like crispy Peking duck with cucumber, spring onions and pancakes. The pub will also cook anything your child would like if it is not on the menu.

- **CHEF** Maxwell Dougal
- **SIGNATURE DISHES** Warm goats' cheese, griddled aubergine and ratatouille tart; creamy saffron, garlic and red pepper risotto
- **WINES** What you would expect of a pub
- **COST** Set lunch menu: £9.50 for 2 courses, £12.50 for 3. Midweek dinner £17.50, à la carte around £28 for 3 courses
- **WHERE TO STAY** Stay at Rosemary Willis' B&B ☎ 01379 586254 which costs £47 per night for a double room (£23.50 per person), or with Christina Baxter at Starston Hall, near Harlesden ☎ 01379 854252
- **HOW TO GET THERE** Take the M25 to Junction 12, Ipswich and Colchester. Stay on till you reach the A14 and turn left to Bury St Edmunds. Then turn right on the A140 to Norwich and right again on the B1117 to Eye, Stradbroke and Halesworth. Beyond Stradbroke, take the second left turning for Fressingfield and keep going till you enter the village

THE GREAT HOUSE HOTEL

ADDRESS Market Place, Lavenham, Suffolk CO10 9QZ
☎ 01787 247431   **FAX** 01787 248007

Lavenham is a delightful place to spend a weekend. However, the Great House would be worth a visit, even if it were bang next door to an oil refinery rather than in this scenic medieval town. Rather more a 'restaurant with rooms' than a full-blown hotel, the building dates back to the 15th century and was once the home of Stephen Spender. It faces onto the market square, with its famous Wool Guildhall – the star of many a film or period drama. Owners Regis and Martine Crépy are charming and welcoming and M. Crépy bears more than a passing resemblance to a Gallic Tony Blair.

Start your evening in the bar with a glass of kir while you peruse the menu. Attractively furnished with rush-seated, ladder-backed chairs, comfy sofas and recessed shelving painted Shaker blue, this is a relaxing place to kick-start your evening. The dining room is small and the tables a tad too close together, but the food is well worth it.

This is a totally unpretentious place, serving excellent food in a delightful setting. The service is attentive without being intrusive and the staff friendly and helpful.

- **CHEF** Monsieur Crépy is the chef-patron and has been running the Great House for 15 years. His style of cooking is honest, tasty and unpretentious. 'I like to take the snobbery out of eating' he says
- **SIGNATURE DISHES** M. Crépy feels that having particular signature dishes is restrictive and he likes to be free to try new dishes. 'If anyone asks me what my speciality is, I say women,' he says, in typical French fashion
- **WINES** There is an extensive wine list, with wines from 15–20 different countries. The staff are helpful without being remotely patronising in suggesting suitable wines
- **COST** The set three-course dinner is a very reasonable £18.95 a head
- **WHERE TO STAY** The Great House has five bedrooms above the restaurant, four of which are suites. The twin room has two double beds, so can easily accommodate a family of four, and M. Crépy is at pains to stress that they really do welcome children – and have awards to prove it. They were the 1997 Family Restaurant of the Year. The bedrooms are all prettily decorated with old rugs and antique furniture and all have en-suite bathrooms. If you're feeling a little 'Moll Flanders', then book the room with the four-poster bed. Rooms cost £39 per person per night for a double and £55 per person per night for a superior double, for bed and breakfast. The Great House has a special leisure break rate of £49.95 per person per night for dinner, bed and breakfast for a two-night stay from Tuesdays to Thursdays. Children under 2 stay free, children 3–12 years are charged £15 for bed and breakfast and those 13 and over are charged £20
- **WHAT TO DO** Lavenham itself; Long Melford – antique shops, Melford Hall and Kentwell Hall; Sudbury – home of Sir Thomas Gainsborough. See also Colchester, page 116
- **HOW TO GET THERE** Take the M11, M25 and then A12 out of London. Come off the A12 at Colchester and follow the A134 to Sudbury. Once in Sudbury, take the B1071 to Lavenham

WILTSHIRE

THE GROSVENOR ARMS

ADDRESS Hindon, Salisbury, Wiltshire SP3 5DJ
☎ 01747 820696 **FAX** 01747 820869

An old country village inn, run by Rachel and Paul Suter. Opened in 1998, it has established a great reputation for its food. It's very informal, with a glass, theatre-like kitchen, where you can see exactly what goes on. Book well in advance, especially for Saturday night.

- **CHEF** *Paul Suter, formerly of Gidleigh Park and Bishopstrow House*
- **SIGNATURE DISHES** *Double-baked cheese soufflé; pan-fried saddle of rabbit; caramelised sautéed scallops with rocket and parmesan salad*
- **WINES** *Six different house wines, from £10.75, and about 90 wines on offer*
- **COST** *A three-course meal will cost from about £22*
- **WHERE TO STAY** *The hotel's rooms cost £75 per room, including breakfast. The four-poster room costs from £85 per night*
- **WHAT TO DO** *Salisbury; Shaftesbury; Stonehenge; the castle at Tisbury; riding; golf; clay pigeon shooting; go-karting; flying and gliding; watersports*
- **HOW TO GET THERE** *Take the M3, then the A303 past Wylye and then look for signs for Hindon on the A303. At the traffic lights in Hindon, turn sharp right and then sharp left (the Grosvenor Arms is signposted). The hotel is now on the left*

SCOTLAND

STAC POLLY

ADDRESS Dublin Street, Edinburgh EH3 6NL
☎ 0131 556 2231 **FAX** 0131 557 9779

Run by Roger Coulthard, Stac Polly is a very cosy and inviting restaurant where the staff are both friendly and attentive. It is a very popular place, so make sure you book well in advance; as a result the atmosphere tends to be lively but this doesn't detract from its intimate nature. You feel tucked away from the bustle of the city.

- **CHEF** *James Guldberg*
- **SIGNATURE DISHES** *The food is sensational, with a dinner menu offering such delights as baked filo pastry parcels of finest haggis, set on a sweet plum sauce garnished with chives; or grilled smoked haddock, baby brioche and a poached egg, topped with a light cheese and mustard glaze. Main courses consist of good things such as: roasted saddle of venison, topped with herbed black pudding and served pink, with pickled walnuts and a rich game jus; or baked tail of west coast monkfish, served on a spring onion*

mash, with a citrus-scented sauce and buttered leeks. The pudding menu offers a range of choices such as cheesecake with a fresh raspberry sauce and crème chantilly, or sticky toffee pudding served with a creamy caramel sauce

• **CHEF** *Stac Polly offers a list of house recommendations, with all wines coming from regional France*

• **COST** *Starters cost from £5.95, main courses £13.95 and desserts all at £4.75*

• **WHERE TO STAY** *The Frederick Hotel, ☎ 0131 226 1999 costs between £22.50 and £35 per person per night including continental breakfast. The Malmaison (see Cultural Weekends, Edinburgh, page 189)*

• **WHAT TO DO** *See Cultural Weekends, Edinburgh, page 189*

CULTURAL WEEKENDS

Your aim for a weekend away might be to inject a little culture into your life. Of course, 'culture' is a much-abused word, and can mean different things to different people. One man's highbrow is another's pretentious rubbish. What seems great Art or Literature to some is Painting by Numbers or the Beano to someone else. However, it is generally accepted that going to the opera or visiting a city or area that has a plethora of galleries, museums and interesting historical buildings counts as a cultural experience. All of us can suffer from cultural overkill, and in some instances, such as Florence, it's just not possible to fit in everything in a single weekend without reeling from the shock. In others, you may wish to build a weekend around a 'one off', such as seeing a performance of a particular opera or play, thus leaving the rest of your weekend free for general pottering. Some cities such as York and Bath combine a wealth of museums and sites with less esoteric pleasures such as shopping, where you can still con yourself into thinking that you are improving your mind. We have included a few foreign destinations, which would make great cultural weekend breaks because they are now so accessible. Cheap flights from the likes of Go and EasyJet mean that you can have a weekend abroad without it costing an arm and a leg. In fact, the costs and rate of exchange can mean that you would spend a lot less, even including your flight and accommodation, than you might doing a similar weekend in London.

ALDEBURGH

- **HOW TO GET THERE** *By train, to Saxmundham, changing at Ipswich. By car, take the M25 and A12. Then turn onto the B1094 signposted to Aldeburgh*

WHERE TO STAY

THE CROWN HOTEL
ADDRESS High Street, Southwold, Suffolk IP18 6DP
☎ 01502 722275
See page 61 in Weekends by the Sea.

THORPENESS HOTEL AND GOLF CLUB
ADDRESS Benthill, Thorpeness, Suffolk IP16 4NU
☎ 01728 452176
This club is set in Suffolk heritage coastal countryside only 2 miles
north of Aldeburgh. See page 63 in Weekends by the Sea.

THE WENTWORTH HOTEL
ADDRESS Wentworth Road, Aldeburgh IP15 5BD
☎ 01728 452312   **FAX** 01728 454343
See page 43 in Weekends by the Sea.

WHERE TO EAT

THE LIGHTHOUSE
ADDRESS 77 High Street, Aldeburgh IP15 5AU
☎ 01728 453377
Highly recommended.
● **COST** *Evening meal £13.50 for 2 courses, £15.75 for 3 courses.*
A la carte lunch menu

REGATTA
ADDRESS 171 High Street, Aldeburgh IP15 5AN
☎ 01782 452011
Serves informal local seafood and is excellent for post-concert fare.
See Weekends by the Sea, page 45 for details.

WHAT TO DO

THE ALDEBURGH FESTIVAL
ADDRESS Snape Maltings Concert Hall, Snape, Saxmundham,
Suffolk IP17 1SP
☎ 01728 687110
Aldeburgh, a delightful fishing town on the Suffolk coast, each
year plays host to one of the world's best-known classical music
events, the Aldeburgh Festival, founded more than 50 years ago
by former resident Benjamin Britten. Many works by Britten and
other composers were inspired by Aldeburgh and premièred here.
A mix of contemporary works – one living composer is always

featured – and established work, the festival is a mix of operatic, chamber and orchestral recitals, as well as films, walks and lectures. It attracts top-notch performers such as Dame Felicity Lott and Ian Bostridge, and has an atmosphere all of its own.

This year (2000) the festival will take place from 9–25th June and is followed by the Snape Proms in August, which usually includes a carnival day when everyone has to buy a Chinese lantern for 50p at dusk and take it with them to the beach, where there is a firework display. This year there will also be a spring series of concerts, with an Easter festival predominantly featuring Early Music.

Whilst most tickets are booked in advance, 20 tickets from each concert will be held back until the day of the performance.

ADNAMS CELLARS AND KITCHEN; ADNAMS WINE SHOP

ADDRESS Victoria Street, Southwold, Suffolk IP18 6JW
☎ 01502 727220
Adnams has an extensive range of wines to buy. Adnams is a famous local brewery company, as well as being a distinguished wine merchant. They also give tastings.

ALDEBURGH BOOKSHOP

ADDRESS 42 High Street, Aldeburgh IP15 5AB
☎ 01728 452389
Sells books, art materials and stationery.

BYWAY'S BICYCLES CENTRE

ADDRESS Priory Lane, Darsham, Saxmundham IP17 3QD
☎ 01728 668764
Hire bicycles and visit Aldeburgh, Southwold, Framlingham and Dunwich.
• **COST** £8 a day

BATH

The Romans knew a good thing when they saw one, and Bath has been attracting visitors for over 2000 years, since a Romanised British aristocrat founded Aqua Sulis. Nowadays, the honey-coloured buildings of Bath stone nestling in the softly rolling Cotswold hills make it the perfect city for a weekend break. Bath has all the elements – it's not too far to travel, it has rafts of things to see and do and good places to stay and eat. The surrounding countryside is easily accessible, should you want a jaunt out of town, and, if the weather's fine, then there are plenty of spots to stop and eat a picnic whilst enjoying the scenery. Although Bath has a long history, and a unique heritage, it is by no means pickled in aspic. There are hip shops and buzzy restaurants as well as thriving festivals – of literature, music and film.

• **HOW TO GET THERE** *Take the M4 and exit at Junction 18. Then follow the A46 to Bath or by rail from Paddington to Bath, from £17 return if booked 7 days in advance.* ☎ *08457 000125*

WHERE TO STAY

THE ROYAL CRESCENT

ADDRESS 16 Royal Crescent, Bath BA1 2LS
☎ 01225 823333   **FAX** 01225 339401

The Royal Crescent is at the top of the hill in a half-moon crescent of houses. Today the crescent is so unchanged with beautifully preserved Georgian houses that it would be easy to imagine even now a Jane Austen heroine emerging from one of these elegant houses. In fact, the Royal Crescent looks much more like a period house than a hotel – discreet and luxurious – and eerily quiet. Our suite was through a succession of heavy doors with not a soul to be seen en route. Our room was beautiful and elegant with wide windows leading out to an enormous garden with lots of tables where the most exquisite teas of dainty sandwiches and scones were being served by immaculately-turned-out waiters in snow-white aprons. Tea is a must served on silver salvers while you lose your senses in a page or two of Sense and Sensibility, transporting yourself back in time. A gentle dip is also recommended at the Bath House, the Royal Crescent's brilliant spa which is housed in an ecclesiastical-style building just off the garden that complements the rarefied atmosphere of the hotel. The hotel is very quiet and would be ideal for a couple who want a romantic weekend away in complete privacy. The Royal Crescent also has a hot air balloon with sky-high prices to match and a vintage river launch.

• **COST** *Double rooms from £190 per night. Suites from £380*

THE QUEENSBERRY HOTEL

ADDRESS Russell Street, Bath BA1 2QS
☎ 01225 447928   **FAX** 01225 446065

Four Georgian houses form this charming hotel which is currently being heaped with awards. All rooms are individually decorated, one with a four-poster bed. Two rooms were originally Georgian drawing rooms.

• **COST** *Double room £115 per night, breakfast included (winter break, minimum 2 night stay). Otherwise, double rooms from £120*

APSLEY HOUSE HOTEL

ADDRESS 141 Newbridge Hill, Bath BA1 3PT
☎ 01225 336966   **FAX** 01225 425462

This is a Georgian house built for the Duke of Wellington in 1830, just a mile from the city centre, now a small privately run hotel with

just nine bedrooms. The interior includes many period features and is furnished with fine antiques and oil paintings.
- **COST** *£75 for a double room*

WHERE TO EAT

OLIVE TREE RESTAURANT, QUEENSBURY HOTEL
ADDRESS Russell Street, Bath BA1 2QS
☎ 01225 447928   **FAX** 01225 446065
Definitely the 'in' restaurant in Bath. Very relaxed, informal and friendly and extremely attractive. Mediterranean style food includes Provençal fish soup with sauce rouille and garlic croûtons £7, seared Cornish scallops skewered with rosemary £8.25, roast monkfish with saffron and lemon and lightly spiced puy lentils £16.25.
- **COST** *Set menu, evening £24 per person, lunch £12.50 for 2 courses or £14.50 for 3 courses*

THE FIREHOUSE
ADDRESS John Street, Bath BA1 2JL
☎ 01225 482070
The Firehouse has lots of delicious salads including Caesar and Chinese chicken.
- **COST** *Dinner from £40 a head including wine*

THE MOON AND SIXPENCE
ADDRESS 6a Broad Street, Bath BA1 5LJ
☎ 01225 460962
Just off Broad Street and near Shires Yard, this restaurant has a two-course lunch menu including soup and pan-fried fish cakes with tartare sauce, bruschetta of Mediterranean roasted vegetables and mozzarella.
- **COST** *£6.75 for 2 courses*

CLOS DU ROY, SEVEN DIALS
ADDRESS Saw Close, Bath BA1 1EN
☎ 01225 444450
For smart French food, try this restaurant.
- **COST** *Evening menu £19.50 for 3 courses or £16.50 for 2 courses, lunch menu £13.95 for 3 courses*

SCOFFS
ADDRESS 19–20 Kingsmeade Square, Bath BA1 2AE
☎ 01225 462483
Good place for a coffee.
- **COST** *Standard lunch about £3.50. Cakes from £1*

WHAT TO DO

ROMAN BATHS MUSEUM AND PUMP ROOM

ADDRESS Stall Street, Bath BA1 1LZ

☎ 01225 477785

Nobody should go to Bath and miss the Baths. Imagine un-togaed Romans gossiping in the steamy atmosphere or Jane Austen socialising in the Georgian Pump Rooms.

• **OPENING TIMES** *Apr–Sept, 09.00–18.00; Oct–Mar, 09.30–17.00; Aug 09.00–18.00 and 20.00–22.00*

• **COST** *Adults £6.90, children £4, concessions £6. Family ticket (2 adults and up to 4 children) £17.50*

THE AMERICAN MUSEUM IN BRITAIN

ADDRESS Claverton Manor, Bath BA2 7BD

☎ 01225 460503   **FAX** 01225 480726

Less well known than the Baths and Pump Rooms, the American Museum will take you a good two hours to visit. The museum shows how our early American cousins lived and has galleries devoted to Native Americans, Shakers, Pennsylvanian Germans and Spanish colonists. The museum has 18 authentically recreated rooms, such as the Milliner's Shop, with beautiful hat boxes and displays.

There is an excellent tea room which serves real American cookies.

• **OPENING TIMES** *Daily 14.00–17.00; except Mon, from the end of Mar to the beginning of Nov*

• **COST** *Adults £5.50, children £3, concessions £5.00*

BATH ABBEY

ADDRESS Bath BA1 1LT

☎ 01225 422462

The beautiful parish church of Bath, set in an Italian-style piazza. The Abbey dates from AD 781 and was built largely from stones recovered from Roman ruins. As it stands today, it is an example of the late Perpendicular style and has a beautifully colourful fan-vaulted ceiling. The building has large windows and the ornate west front features relief sculptures depicting the biblical image of Jacob's ladder reaching up to heaven. The Abbey Heritage Vaults tell the story of 1600 years of Christianity.

• **OPENING TIMES** *All year and every day (apart from during the Sunday service), 09.00–18.00 in summer and 09.00–16.00 in winter*

• **COST** *A £2 donation is requested*

THE ROYAL PHOTOGRAPHIC SOCIETY

ADDRESS The Octagon Galleries, Milsom Street, Bath BA1 1DN

☎ 01225 462841

The oldest photographic society in the world founded in 1853 with Queen Victoria and Prince Albert as patrons. There is nearly always an interesting exhibition, from David Bailey to historical exhibitions. Not only that, the Society is a great place for lunch and coffee. You can also buy wonderful calendars and cards.

- **OPENING TIMES** *Daily 09.30–17.30*
- **COST** *Adults £2.50, concessions £1.75, under-7s free. Family ticket (2 adults and 2 children) £5.00*

MUSEUM OF COSTUME AND ASSEMBLY ROOMS

ADDRESS Bennett Street, Bath BA1 2HQ

☎ 01225 477789

An absolute must for anyone even remotely interested in clothes and costume. The museum has fabulous examples of costumes from the 1600s to the present day.

- **OPENING TIMES** *10.00–17.00*
- **COST** *Adults £4.00, children (6–18 years) £2.90, concessions £3.60. Family ticket (2 adults and up to 4 children) £11*

NO 1 ROYAL CRESCENT

ADDRESS Bath BA1 2LR

☎ 01225 428126

A typical Georgian town house, redecorated and furnished to demonstrate what life was like in late 18th-century Bath – for the affluent, that is.

- **OPENING TIMES** *Feb–Oct 10.30–17.00, Oct–Nov 10.30–16.00*
- **COST** *Adults £4, concessions £3.50, groups £2.50, family ticket £10*

BATH BOATING STATION

ADDRESS Forester Road, Bathwick, Bath BA2 6QE

☎ 01225 466407

A superb collection of Victorian boats to look at, as well as punts, boats and canoes to hire.

- **OPENING TIMES** *Apr–Oct 10.00–18.00*
- **COST** *Adults £4, children £3, Senior citizens £3 per hour*

HOLBOURNE MUSEUM AND CRAFTS STUDY CENTRE

ADDRESS Great Pulteney Street, Bath BA2 4DB

☎ 01225 466669

This is a beautiful Georgian building with an impressive collection of fine and decorative art, paintings and work by 20th-century artists and craftsmen and women. There is an award-winning teahouse in the garden.

- **OPENING TIMES** *Mon–Sat 11.00–17.00; Sun from mid-Feb to mid-Dec 14.30–17.30; closed Mon from Nov–Easter*
- **COST** *Adults £3.50, children £1.50, Senior citizens £2.50*

BATH FESTIVALS BOX OFFICE

ADDRESS 2 Church Street, Abbey Green, Bath AG1 1NL
☎ 01225 463362   **FAX** 01225 310377

The Box Office has all the information on Bath's festivals as well as brochures and tickets. Some important festivals for the year 2000 include the Bath Literature Festival in March , the Bath International Guitar Festival in August, the Bath Shakespeare Festival in September, the Royal Photographic Society's Collection 2000 exhibition and the Bach Festival commemorating the 250th anniversary of the death of JS Bach and the Mozart Festival at various venues in November.

SHOPPING

Check out the shops just off Milsom Street in Shires Yard. This is a restored 18th-century carriage yard where there are lots of designer clothes shops and a brilliant interiors shop. There's Image (☎ 01225 447359), which sells lots of designer labels, such as TSE cashmere; and Annabel Harrison (☎ 01225 447578), for designer labels including Armani, DKNY, Nicole Farhi and lots more.

Also visit the Alessi Gallery which has one of the best collections of whacky designer kitchenware in the country. A fairly new shop to Bath is Shoon, 14 Old Bond St, selling lots of funky sportswear such as Oakley glasses, Patagonia outdoor wear, Dockers trousers, walking boots. There's a marvellous hat shop – the British Hatter at 9 Walcot Street. And the Faerie Shop which sells lots of fairy dresses, wings and wands . Christopher Wylde has attractive jewellery in Northumberland Place. Mallorys is an old fashioned but excellent jewellers in Milsom St and Andrew Dando in Gay Street deals in excellent porcelain. Also visit Rachel James for women's designer knitwear in Margarets Buildings which is just off Brock St between the Circus and the Royal Crescent – cashmere and cashmere mixes including TSE and Iceberg.

CAMBRIDGE

TOURIST INFORMATION CENTRE

ADDRESS Wheeler Street, Cambridge CB2 3QB
☎ 01223 322640

Mention Cambridge to most people and they think of carols from King's, Philby, Burgess and Maclean, and the Cambridge Footlights – particularly if they're of 'a certain age'. Although perhaps lacking the glamour of Oxford, Cambridge has a tranquillity and intimacy that make it ideal for a weekend trip.

The centre, where most of the colleges are, is largely pedestrianised, and easy to walk round. Go when the students are 'up' (Cambridge parlance for termtime) for a buzzier atmosphere, or when they're 'down' for a quieter visit. Don't miss visiting a few of the colleges with their beautiful courts or King's College Chapel, of Christmas Eve Carols fame.

As one would expect of a university town, Cambridge has plenty of pubs, mostly untouched by theme-pub chains, where you can stop for a coffee, a pint or lunch. If the weather's fine, take a relaxing punt ride along the Backs, behind the Colleges. In town, it is well worth buying Varsity (about 30p), the student newspaper, which is available in many shops in the town. Despite the pages of student irony and some news, it contains a comprehensive section listing student concerts and plays, many of which are open to the public. For instance the ADC theatre (Park Street) is often worth a visit and served as a training ground for many of today's famous actors and comedians.

There is not enough space here to discuss even a fraction of the interesting historical associations of the Cambridge colleges. It is almost impossible to tour a college, especially an older one, without being impressed by the buildings and atmosphere. Wandering into colleges (those which are open to visitors, and most are) is highly recommended. Indeed, one of the best ways to see Cambridge is to wander with no fixed direction. Most of the colleges are open to the public (except during the exam season) and there is an informative walking tour around the city, which takes in many of the colleges – tickets available from the Tourist Information Centre. Visitors are normally required to enter a college by the main gate, each has a Porter's Lodge and it is worth checking there for their visiting regulations. Porters are invariably helpful; visitors who wander around colleges without having at least made their presence known at the Porter's Lodge are frowned upon.

• **HOW TO GET THERE** *Take the M11 to Junctions 11, 12 or 13 (park and ride facilities available). By train, Kings Cross to Cambridge takes about an hour and is under £20 for an adult return*

WHERE TO STAY

THE CAMBRIDGE GARDEN HOUSE MOAT HOUSE

ADDRESS Granta Place, Mill Lane, Cambridge CB2 1RT

☎ 01223 259988

This is a newly refurbished hotel, containing a fitness centre with everything, a pool, sauna, spa, gym and so on. There is a terrace bar and also the Riverside Brasserie, which has a delicious à la carte menu. Three courses are about £23 and include tartare of smoked salmon with crème fraîche to start followed by a choice of fish, Thai chicken, or fillet steak and half a lobster (a bit more pricy!) and five or six puds to choose from. They have a large selection of wines, starting at £12.50.

• **COST** *To stay for Friday and Saturday nights will cost £154 per double room, including breakfast, but for an extra £25 (£179) it is worth getting a room with a river view*

THE ARUNDEL HOUSE HOTEL

ADDRESS Chesterton Road, Cambridge CB4 3AN
☎ 01223 367701

A pleasant hotel with a conservatory bar looking onto a large garden. There is also a restaurant, where three courses cost £16–£20 per person.

• **COST** *Rooms range in size and view and cost £65–£92.50, including continental breakfast*

THE UNIVERSITY ARMS HOTEL

ADDRESS Regent Street, Cambridge CB2 1AD
☎ 01223 351241

This hotel overlooks Parker's Piece, a large green complete with cricket pitches. Most rooms overlook this space. There is also a restaurant, at £20 for three courses.

• **COST** *A double room costs £135 per night but for £150 you can get an executive suite with your own parking space (a not insignificant advantage in Cambridge, where parking problems are a mainstay of locals' conversations)*

BROOKLANDS GUESTHOUSE

ADDRESS 95 Cherry Hinton Road, Cambridge CB1 7B5
☎ 01223 242035

• **COST** *£42–£50 for a double room*

DE FREVILLE HOUSE

ADDRESS 166 Chesterton Road, Cambridge CB4 1DA
☎ 01223 354993

• **COST** *£50–£60 for a double room*

REGENCY GUEST HOUSE

ADDRESS 7 Regent Terrace, Cambridge CB2 1AA
☎ 01223 329626

Right in the centre of town.

• **COST** *£55–£65 for a double room*

WHERE TO EAT

THE STAR OF INDIA TANDOORI
ADDRESS 71 Castle Street, Cambridge CB3 0AH
☎ 01223 312569
The best curry house in a row of them all the way up Castle Street.
• **COST** *£20 for two including beer*

THE BUN SHOP PUB
ADDRESS 1 King Street, Cambridge CB1 1LH
☎ 01223 366866
A 'traditional' Irish bar, with good value pub grub. There are also two restaurants, one serving Spanish tapas, the other a proper French restaurant.

THE BARON OF BEEF
ADDRESS 19 Bridge Street, Cambridge CB2 1UF
☎ 01223 505022
Supposedly has the longest bar in Cambridge, with bar snacks.

THE GRANTA
ADDRESS 14 Newnham Terrace, Granta Place, Cambridge CB3 9EX
☎ 01223 505016
A good punting start/stop point.

THE MITRE
ADDRESS 17 Bridge Street, Cambridge CB2 1UF
☎ 01223 358403
Serves real ales and good, reasonably priced pub grub, particularly good for Sunday lunch. The Mitre is a good bet for a 'traditional' atmosphere with a dark cavernous interior and candles spilling wax.

THE COUNTY ARMS
ADDRESS 43 Castle Street, Cambridge CB3 0AF
☎ 01223 566696
This pub is not normally filled with students and is particularly recommended for its pub food.

THE PICKEREL
ADDRESS 30 Magdalene Street, Cambridge CB3 0AF
☎ 01223 355068
Down the hill, nestled into Magdalene College on Magdalene Street, is the Pickerel. It is reputedly the oldest pub in Cambridge and has a wonderful snug atmosphere; it serves a limited lunch menu so, although it is not worth visiting for the food, many believe the atmosphere is incomparable. While there, it's worth visiting the Pepys Library in Magdalene College, featuring Samuel

Pepys' books and shelves, which are claimed to be the first bookstacks invented for the purpose. Check at the Porter's Lodge for unpredictable opening times.

PIZZA EXPRESS

ADDRESS 7a Jesus Lane, Cambridge CB5 8BA

☎ 01223 324033

One of two in Cambridge, serving excellent Italian-style pizzas; the restaurant is in an old dining club, with one wood-panelled room. There is also a good, mainly Italian, wine list and other dishes apart from pizza, including ham and eggs, cannelloni and a large tomato and mozzarella salad.

• **COST** *Pizza from £4.50 to £7.65. Starters from £1.45, main courses from £5.50, desserts from £3*

TAI CHEUN

ADDRESS 12 St. John's Street, Cambridge CB2 1TW

☎ 01223 358287

This is a standard Chinese, which often has a good 'all you can eat' Sunday menu.

• **COST** *Prices range from £4–£5 a dish up to £28 per person for the set menu*

MICHEL'S BRASSERIE

ADDRESS 21–24 Northampton Street, Cambridge CB3 0AD

☎ 01223 353110

This is a good-value French restaurant, with a commendable wine list and tasty food. A typical menu might be carpaccio of peppered salmon, followed by pan-fried medallions of pork, served with braised lentils *jus* and crispy carrot, with iced strawberry and mascarpone parfait with peppered strawberries to finish. The *à la carte* menu offers similar-style dishes, a favourite being char-grilled tuna steak with Szechuan pepper, oriental-style risotto and pak choi.

• **COST** *There is a set menu at £21.95 per person. A la carte dishes are between £9.95 and £15.50*

BROWNS

ADDRESS 23 Trumpington Street, Cambridge CB2 1QA

☎ 01223 461655

Browns has a breezy, brasserie-style atmosphere with plants everywhere and big ceiling fans. They don't take dinner reservations though, so you may have to wait with a glass of wine for a while.

• **COST** *Three courses will cost £15–£20 and there is a real mixture of dishes, including fresh fish on a daily basis and bargain specials*

MIDSUMMER HOUSE

ADDRESS Midsummer Common, Cambridge CB4 1HA

☎ 01223 369299

This is said to be the best restaurant in Cambridge, with top-notch French/International cuisine which might include: marbled terrine of poached chicken and *foie gras*, wild mushrooms and shallot cream; or seared sea scallops, celeriac purée, truffle vinaigrette *à la* Jean Bardet; followed by pan-fried tranche of salmon, cauliflower purée, *trompettes de mort*, with braised celery and langoustines butter sauce; or pot-roast guinea fowl, tarragon mousse, *pommes fondantes*, caramelised shallots, baby carrots and *essence des cèpes*. The wine list is plentiful and the puddings are equally desirable.

• **COSTS** *Dinner costs £39.50 for three courses. If the dinner looks too ambitious, there is a luncheon menu at £19.50 for three courses which is also very impressive. 3-course Sunday lunch £27.50*

THE THREE HORSESHOES

ADDRESS High Street, Madingley CB3 8AB

☎ 01954 210221

Just a taxi ride away from Cambridge, near the American War Cemetery, this is a very good restaurant with a monthly-changing menu, which tends to have specific themes. Along Japanese lines, the starters might be: salmon, prawn and avocado sushi roll, with apple, cucumber, mooli salad and saké dressing; whilst the main courses remain international, with wild mushroom cannelloni and twice-baked spinach and ricotta soufflé for the vegetarians there are also various fish and meat dishes such as roast partridge stuffed with goats' cheese. Puddings include warm chocolate fondant with milk-chocolate ice-cream and Jack Daniels sauce.

• **COST** *Starters at £6.50, main courses between £13.50 and £15.75 and puddings for £5.50. There are six or seven house wines at £9.75, which are supplemented by many more expensive ones*

WHERE TO DRINK

Cambridge pubs, like those of most other cities, are gradually being taken over by large chains, but many of them still retain some level of independence that makes them individual and often quirky. Bene't Street, off King's Parade, features the Eagle and the Bath Ale House; being close to the centre of town (and King's College) they are popular with tourists during the day and students in the evening. Although prices tend to be higher than elsewhere, both are very comfortable and offer a good central location to rest tired feet in pleasant surroundings.

West of Trumpington Street, Silver Street crosses the Cam (near the colleges of Peterhouse and Queen's). From there, a number of easily accessible pubs nestle up to the river, including the Anchor, which is large and popular with students. On the other side of the river, on Newnham Terrace, is the Granta; this is an ideal place for a summer visitor as the beer garden looks over the river. There are punt rental locations at this part of the river and it is from this point that a punt can be dragged over a weir to follow the river into the countryside. Visitors should be warned that, at the end of the summer term, after exams have finished (early July), these pubs and the open areas around them can become filled with celebrating (drunk) students. However, during the earlier part of the summer term, while the students tend to be locked in libraries, the area is blissfully quiet (note the other side of the coin: most colleges are closed to visitors during the exam season).

WHAT TO DO

GEOFF'S BIKE HIRE
ADDRESS 65 Devonshire Road, Cambridge CB1 2BL
☎ 01223 365629
Cambridge is ideal for walking and cycling (being largely flat).
• **COST** *Bikes can be rented from £7 per day*

SCUDAMORE'S BOATYARD
ADDRESS Magdalene Bridge and Mill Lane, Cambridge
☎ 01223 327280
A very calm and picturesque way to see the colleges is to punt along the 'Backs', where the river winds along the back of and through the property of many of Cambridge's oldest colleges. Punt yourself (which takes a little practice but can be mastered in a couple of hours), or hire a guide (many of whom are current students) to punt for you and provide an interesting commentary on the history of the colleges you pass.
• **COST** *Punts available at varying prices. Hire from £10 per hour. Tours £8 per person (reduction for children)*

THE ORCHARD TEA GARDENS
ADDRESS Mill Way, Grantchester CB3 9ND
☎ 01223 845788
This is where many Cambridge alumni, Rupert Brooke, Bertrand Russell, Wittgenstein and others, would take afternoon tea in the sprawling orchard. For something stronger, there are a few pubs including the Red Lion and the Green Man. Also worth a visit is the church.
• **HOW TO GET THERE** *The brave can punt upstream to Granchester (which takes 3–4 hours), a beautiful ride which takes you past meadows and overhanging trees which line the river; it takes less time to come back, being downstream. The less brave walk (about one hour from town centre via Newnham), cycle (30 minutes) or take a taxi*

SHOPPING

Cambridge has always been a market town and the main square (opposite King's College) has a regular market selling everything from fruit and veg to second-hand books and clothes. There is also a regular craft fair in All Saint's Gardens, Trinity Street, open on summer weekends and at Christmas and Easter. The city has a variety of clothes shops, numerous bookshops (including the Cambridge University Press bookshop, which has been continuously trading since 1581).

KING'S COLLEGE

ADDRESS King's Parade, Cambridge CB2 1SJ

☎ 01223 331100

Founded by Henry VI in 1441, famous alumni include Rupert Brooke and Robert Walpole. It has some magnificent buildings, most notably the Gothic chapel (completed in 1547) which is open to the public. The best way to see the chapel is to attend evensong, normally sung by the famous King's College Chapel Choir.

- **OPENING TIMES** *For information on college opening times and chapel services, call the Tourist Liaison Officer* ☎ *01223 331212*
- **COST** *Adults £3.50, children £2.50, under-12s free*

ST JOHN'S COLLEGE

ADDRESS St John's Street, Cambridge CB2 1TP

☎ 01223 338600

Founded in the early 13th century by students from Paris and Oxford and refounded in 1511, famous alumni include William Wordsworth. The college covers a large area and there is a very good visitor route which passes through all the most interesting parts of the college. In particular, it features the Bridge of Sighs (a replica of the Venice original) and a clock tower with no clock – the result of a lost bet with Trinity College!

- **OPENING TIMES** *Easter to November*
- **COST** *Adults £1.75, children, students and concessions £1*

TRINITY COLLEGE

ADDRESS Trinity Street, Cambridge CB2 1TQ

☎ 01223 338400

The largest Cambridge college, founded by Henry VIII in 1546. The Prince of Wales was an undergraduate there and, amongst others, Newton, Tennyson, A.A. Milne and Nehru were alumni. Even if you don't enter the college to do the tour, it is worth peering through the main gate (when it is open) to see Great Court, which is wonderfully imposing, but otherwise walk through this always impressive college to see Christopher Wren's library.

- **COST** *Adults £1.75, children, students and concessions £1*

PETERHOUSE
ADDRESS Trumpington Street, Cambridge CB2 1Q7
☎ 01223 338200
This is reputedly the oldest and the smallest college and has buildings dating back to the 13th century.
- **COST** *Free admission*

CLARE COLLEGE
ADDRESS Trinity Lane, Cambridge CB2 1TL
☎ 01223 333200
Features little besides a lovely 17th-century Old Court, and delightful, tranquil gardens (although access can be restricted).
- **COST** *March to September adults £1.75, children £1*

QUEEN'S COLLEGE
ADDRESS Silver Street, Cambridge CB3 9ET
☎ 01223 335511
The old part of Queen's College and in particular the old dining room is thought by many to be one of the loveliest sights of Cambridge. Don't miss the famous Mathematical Bridge which according to legend was once held together with no fixtures. It was dismantled in order to learn the secret; it eluded all however and so subsequently was screwed back together.
- **COST** *Adults £1, children free*

MUSEUM OF ARCHAEOLOGY AND ANTHROPOLOGY
ADDRESS Downing Street, Cambridge CB2 3DZ
☎ 01223 333516
- **OPENING TIMES** *Tues–Sat 14.00–16.30; closed Sun & Mon*
- **COST** *Donations requested*

MUSEUM OF CLASSICAL ARCHAEOLOGY AND ZOOLOGY
ADDRESS Sedgwick Avenue, Cambridge CB3 9DA
☎ 01223 335153
- **OPENING TIMES** *Mon–Fri 10.00–17.00; Sat (during term time) 10.00–13.00*
- **COST** *Donations requested*

THE FITZWILLIAM MUSEUM
ADDRESS Trumpington Street, Cambridge CB2 1RB
☎ 01223 332900
The Fitzwilliam Museum is certainly worth a visit, housing a fine collection of ancient, classical and modern works.

- **OPENING TIMES** *Tues–Sat 10.00–17.00; Sun 14.15–17.00; closed Mon*
- **COST** *Free, but a donation is suggested*

KETTLE'S YARD
ADDRESS Castle Street, Cambridge CB3 0AQ
☎ 01223 352124
An intriguing museum, this is the home lived in by artists Jim and Helen Ede, preserved as it was when they lived there. It has the atmosphere of a lived-in house and contains the Ede's art collection, whilst also housing a more recently attached gallery.

- **OPENING TIMES** *Tues–Sat 11.30–17.00; house 14.00–16.00; closed Mon*
- **COST** *Free*

ELY CATHEDRAL
ADDRESS Chapter House, The College, Ely, Cambs CB7 4DL
☎ 01353 667735
15 minutes from Cambridge by train, Ely Cathedral started as a monastery in AD 673, with work on the buildings as we now know it starting in 1083. Oliver Cromwell lived and plotted just down the road and his house is now the Tourist Information Centre (29 St Mary's Street, ☎ 01353 662062)

- **HOW TO GET THERE** *Coming from Cambridge, take the 109 bus, which leaves from the bus station on Drummer Street every hour and takes an hour. Alternatively, take the train, which takes only 15 minutes*

GARSINGTON

GARSINGTON OPERA
ADDRESS Garsington Manor, Garsington, Oxford OX44 9DH
☎ 01865 361636 **FAX** 01865 361545
Even if you think that opera is a lot of overweight women singing like strangulated cats, you should go to Garsington if you possibly can. Even more exclusive than Glyndebourne, although of the two it is the younger, it is smaller, more intimate and makes a perfect English evening. The house itself is Jacobean and extremely beautiful and the setting pure magic. Owners Leonard and Rosalind Ingrams have created their very own opera house in their back garden and the semi-open-air performances are of an exceptional standard. Strictly speaking, you should be a member to get tickets and although there is a three-year waiting list it is sometimes possible to get returns. The Season in 2000 will run from 11th June to 9th July. Productions usually include works by Mozart, Rossini, Haydn and Strauss and Mr Ingrams usually attends every performance.

Just like Glyndebourne, black tie and floaty dresses are *de rigueur* and so is a picnic, which can be eaten in the grounds or in the marquee if it's raining. If you wish to eat more formally, then book a table in the Great Barn, but don't expect masses of elbow and leg room in this tad-too-cosy room. There are four menus: a vegetarian, £32.50 for three courses; a hot menu with three main courses such as stuffed chicken breasts with sun-dried tomatoes and paprika sauce or fillet of beef with a tarragon, shallot and red-wine sauce, £37.50; and a cold menu, £32.50; a simple menu, £28.00 for two courses includes gravadlax or asparagus and Gruyère tart. Picnics can also be provided, with proper china, for £29.50 per person.

- **COST** *Tickets from £60 to £100*
- **HOW TO GET THERE** *Take the M40 and exit at Junction 7, signposted Wallingford. At Stadhampton, turn right onto the B480 to Oxford*
- **WHERE TO STAY** *The Old Parsonage in Oxford city centre (see Oxford on this page)*

OXFORD

Oxford is divided into town and gown. If you were gown then you probably know as much as there is to know about Oxford. But as well as being a university town, Oxford has lots to offer the visitor for a weekend break. Apart from undergraduates running around in college scarves pushing bicycles, it really is a city of dreaming spires, honey-coloured buildings and walks by the Isis. Take a tour of the University colleges which are open at various times of the day for example. Much of Oxford will be familiar from various episodes of Inspector Morse – take a punt from the Cherwell bridge, or browse among the bookshops looking for *Zuleika Dobson*. Go for the 1st May, when the boys sing madrigals from Magdalen tower. Or use Oxford as a base for touring the surrounding countryside, visiting places like Woodstock or Blenheim along the way.

- **HOW TO GET THERE** *By train from Paddington station. Make sure you get a fast train otherwise you will stop everywhere from Didcot to High Wycombe. By car it's an easy zip down the M40 all the way to Oxford*

WHERE TO STAY

THE OLD PARSONAGE
ADDRESS 1 Banbury Road, Oxford OX2 6NN
☎ 01865 310210   **FAX** 01865 311262
Situated between Keble and Somerville Colleges, the Old Parsonage is within walking distance of all the main sights. It is a wisteria-covered 17th-century town house at the top of St Giles. Choose one of the deluxe bedrooms in the original part of the house or one of the rooms

overlooking the garden. There is an attractive roof garden where guests can have breakfast and a car park which is useful in Oxford's busy city centre. Guided tours of Oxford can be arranged. Its reputation however really excels when it comes to food. The Parsonage Bar serves up delicacies such as salmon fishcakes with oriental seasoning and chargrilled quail and there is an excellent wine list.

- **COST** *From £145 to £195 for a double*

BATH PLACE

ADDRESS 4–5 Bath Place, Oxford OX1 3SU

☎ 01865 791812

Located in the heart of the city centre, Bath Place is a stone's throw from Oxford. Guests stay in a cluster of 17th-century cottages complete with original oak beams where Dante Gabriel Rossetti and Edward Burne-Jones stayed to pursue their art. Some rooms have four-poster beds.

- **COST** *Doubles from £95*

WHERE TO EAT

LE PETIT BLANC

ADDRESS 71–72 Walton Street, Oxford OX2 6AG

☎ 01865 510999

This Raymond Blanc eaterie north of the city centre is the epitome of stylishness with its Conrad-designed multicoloured décor. The menu is modern French with Asian accents. Confit of guinea fowl leg and pan-fried John Dory with saffron mash and aubergine caviar are the kinds of exotic dishes being created here. Children are particularly welcomed – they love the bright primary colours of the restaurant. They also have a choice of comics at the bar as well as their own menu which steers well clear of fish fingers and baked beans. Youngsters can educate their tastebuds as well as their minds by ordering potage maman blanc, crêpes and tiramisu. The set menu might include haddock soufflé with green bean and tomato salad and pan-fried salmon in a sorrel cream sauce.

- **COST** *For adults, two courses from £12.50; children's menu is £5.95 for two courses*

THE LEMON TREE

ADDRESS 268 Woodstock Road, Oxford OX2 7NW

☎ 01865 311936

It's hard to miss this restaurant with its striking ochre frontage and Chinese-style roof . Situated in North Oxford, it is a fashionable hang-out for romantics with its elegant spacious interior, stained glass windows and soft spotlights over each table in the evening which makes a nice rest from a day of culture in the city. The menu is a mixture of Mediterranean with a modern British twist. Organic and free-range products are used wherever possible. Choose from chargrilled squid and tuna loin steak amongst others. It's a tight squeeze as you come out of the car park so perhaps it's better not to have that last drink.

• **COST** *Three course meal with wine: £33 a head*

THE GRAND CAFE

ADDRESS 84 High St, Oxford OX1 4BG
☎ 01865 204463

This teashop has the most heavenly décor and impeccable but relaxed service from welcoming staff, who keep smiling no matter how run off their feet they are. Light-as-a-feather scones with jam, cream and fresh strawberries, an excellent selection of coffees and teas and, best of all, hand-made chocolates for sale individually (40p each). Worth going to Oxford just for tea.

• **COST** *Cream tea is £6.50; grand high tea including sandwiches and champagne, £12.50*

THE TROUT INN

ADDRESS 195 Godstow Road, Lower Wolvercote OX2 8PN
☎ 01865 302071   **FAX** 01865 302072

Oxford and the surrounding area has lots of good pubs where you can enjoy a pint or stop for a bite to eat. The Trout is just outside the town on the banks of a weir stream just off the main river and is *Inspector Morse's* local. It's a very scenic spot, particularly in summer, when you can sit quietly by the water sipping your Pimms. The building itself dates from 1646 and has leaded casement windows and walls of Cotswold stone. The interior is cosy and welcoming with panelled walls. There's a good menu of the usual pub variety as well as some surprises such as lamb with white onion sauce.

• **COST** *Starters from £2, main courses from £6.95 and desserts £2.75*

• **HOW TO GET THERE** *Take the A40 out of Oxford towards Burford and turn off at the Wolvercote roundabout*

WHAT TO DO

THE OXFORD INFORMATION CENTRE

ADDRESS The Old School, Gloucester Green, Oxford OX1 2DA
☎ 01865 726871

The information centre organises walking tours of the city and the colleges. Oxford past and present takes you on a stroll with a qualified guide through Oxford's historical past. It leaves the Information Centre at 11am and 2pm every day. There are also *Inspector Morse* Walking Tours on Saturdays from 1.30pm from March until October.

• **COST** *Tours: adults £4.90, children £3*

MAGDALEN COLLEGE
ADDRESS Magdalen Bridge, High Street, Oxford OX1 4AU
☎ 01865 276000
- **COST** *Adults £2.50, under-16s £1.25*

CHRISTCHURCH COLLEGE
ADDRESS Christchurch, Oxford OX1 1DP
☎ 01865 276150
The largest college, famously built by Henry III. It was headquarters for the Royalists in the Civil War.
- **COST** *Adults £3, children £2*

CHRISTCHURCH CATHEDRAL
ADDRESS Within the grounds of Christchurch College
This is one of the smallest cathedrals in England. It is thought to be on the site of the nunnery of St Frideswide, patron saint of Oxford.

THE ASHMOLEAN MUSEUM
ADDRESS Beaumont Street, Oxford OX1 2PH
☎ 01865 278000
It has excellent collections of antiquities and paintings and an outstanding Egyptology section.
- **OPENING TIMES** *Tues–Sat 10.00–17.00; Sun 14.00–17.00; Closed Mon*
- **COST** *Entrance free but a donation of £3 each is requested*

UNIVERSITY OF OXFORD BOTANICAL GARDENS
ADDRESS Rose Lane, Oxford OX1 4AZ
☎ 01865 276920
These gardens, with their exotic glasshouses, are well worth a visit. With some 8000 species, they are the oldest botanical gardens in Britain, right on the edge of the River Cherwell.
- **OPENING TIMES** *Winter 09.00–16.30; Summer 09.00–17.00; Last admission 16.15 all seasons*
- **COST** *Adults £2, under-12s free. Winter admission free*

CARFAX TOWER
ADDRESS Corner of St Aldates and High St, Oxford
If you want to see superb views of Oxford's famous spires visit the Carfax Tower. The 72-foot high tower has 99 steps to climb and offers fabulous views of the city.
- **OPENING TIMES** *Apr–Oct 10.00–17.30*
- **COST** *Adults £1.20, children 60p*

MAGDALEN BRIDGE BOATHOUSE

ADDRESS C Howard and Son, High Street, Oxford
☎ 01865 202643

Rowing boats can be hired per hour for up to four people. There are splendid views up and down the River Cherwell, with masses of ducklings and cygnets on the river. Don't miss Parson's Pleasure – a stretch of the river where it's permissable for men to swim nude.
- **COST** *£10 per hour for up to four people; £25 deposit and identification*

THE OXFORD STORY

ADDRESS 6, Broad Street, Oxford
☎ 01865 790055

This is a permanent exhibition – the Oxford story tells you about Oxford's scientists, poets, astronomers and comedians and is particularly popular with children.
- **OPENING TIMES** *Daily 10.00–16.30*
- **COST** *Adults £5.50, concessions, children and students £4.50. Family ticket £16.15 (two adults, two children)*

UNIVERSITY OF OXFORD SHOP

ADDRESS 106, The High Street, Oxford
☎ 01865 247414

See the official University of Oxford Collection of books in its entirety.

BLENHEIM PALACE

ADDRESS Blenheim, near Woodstock, Oxon
☎ 01993 811325

Any visit to Oxford should include a trip to Blenheim Palace, about half an hour from the city centre. It is glorious just to walk around the grounds even if you don't have time to visit the palace itself. It was built for John Churchill, the 1st Duke of Marlborough in recognition of his great victory over the French at the Battle of Blenheim in 1704. The Palace was designed by Sir John Vanbrugh. Set in 2100 acres of parkland landscaped by Capability Brown, the palace is one of the first examples of English baroque.
- **OPENING TIMES** *Mon–Sun 10.30–17.30; park open all year from 09.00–16.45*
- **COST** *Adults £8.50, children 5–15 £4.50*

STRATFORD-UPON-AVON

Stratford is the ultimate tourist destination for many overseas visitors, particularly our American cousins. For that reason, it's largely given a wide berth by us Brits, apart from, possibly, a trip to the RSC. However, Stratford is a great place for a weekend – apart from the almost obligatory theatre trip and visit to Anne Hathaway's cottage, there are interesting pubs and the surrounding countryside is arguably some of the most attractive in the country. And if you want to visit the theatre and sites but don't want to stay in the centre of town, there are plenty of other choices, from Georgian manor houses in the Cotswolds to farmhouses in Warwickshire, that are no more than half an hour away from Stratford.

• **HOW TO GET THERE** *Take the M40 to Junction 15, to Stratford on the A46, then left on to the A3400 to the town centre. At the same junction, you will find Warwick and Royal Leamington Spa in the other direction. By train, Paddington to Stratford takes 2¼ hours and costs £22.40 for an adult return*

WHERE TO STAY

GLEBE FARM HOUSE

ADDRESS Loxley, Warwick CV35 9JW
☎ 01789 842501
This farmhouse is set in 30 acres of countryside, with lovely views from every room. All rooms contain four-poster beds and have en-suite facilities.

• **COST** *£85 per night for double room and full English or continental breakfast. Dinner can be provided*

• **HOW TO GET THERE** *Leave the M40 at Junction 15 and follow sign to Stow and Wellesbourne A429. Go through Barford and over all three roundabouts. The road narrows and then turns sharply to the right. Glebe Farm House is the next drive on the right. By train, go to Stratford station and from there take a taxi, or transport can be arranged to meet you*

UPPER COURT

ADDRESS Kemerton, near Tewkesbury, Glos GL20 7HY
☎ 01386 725351
A really lovely Georgian manor house, with six bedrooms – some with four-poster beds – in the house and courtyard cottages in converted stables in the grounds. Heated swimming pool, tennis court, croquet and 15 acres of gorgeous gardens. Clay pigeon shooting and lots of areas for barbecues and picnics.

• **COST** *Double room, £75 per night, cottages £175 for three nights (cottages only available in low season)*

ALVESTON MANOR

ADDRESS Clopton Bridge, Stratford CV37 7HP
☎ 0870 400 8181
This hotel is in the town centre and is built within an Elizabethan manor house; the first performance of *A Midsummer Night's Dream* took place in the gardens. The hotel's restaurant, the Manor Grill, has won a number of awards, with three courses at £25.

• **COST** *Prices start at £140 per double room per night and rise to £240 for a suite. Weekend leisure break £160 for 2 people including dinner, bed and breakfast*

THE SHAKESPEARE

ADDRESS Chapel Street, Stratford CV37 6ER

☎ 0870 400 8182

This hotel is a 17th-century timbered inn, complete with two ghosts. Award-winning Gordon Inglis is the Head Chef at the hotel's Garrick Restaurant, serving traditional British fare, £19.50 for three courses.

• **COST** *Double rooms start at £150 per room per night and go up to £240 for a suite*

SWAN'S NEST

ADDRESS Bridgeford, Stratford CV3 7LT

☎ 0870 4008183

With a river frontage, this hotel is an ideal place to stay for theatre-goers, with a pre-theatre dinner menu at £37 for three courses at its Cygnet Restaurant and 24-hour room service if you still feel peckish when you get back.

• **COST** *Double room prices range from £85–£125. Weekend specials £148 dinner, bed and breakfast in a standard room, £178 for an executive suite*

MALLORY COURT HOTEL

ADDRESS Harbury Lane, Bishops Tachbrook, Leamington Spa CV33 9QB

☎ 01926 330214

For those visitors looking for a quiet retreat in the countryside, this Lutyens-style hotel, with an award-winning restaurant, lighter bar meals, and extensive gardens is the perfect place.

• **COST** *A double room starts at £230 per night, including room, early morning tea/coffee, newspaper, full English breakfast and three-course set dinner with coffee. There are also rooms at £250 and £300*

• **HOW TO GET THERE** *Take the M40 to Junction 14, follow the A452 to Leamington. Continue past first island, but at second turn right into Harbury Lane (signposted Harbury and Bishops Tachbrook). Over staggered crossroads, Mallory Court is 200 metres on the right. By train, go from Marylebone Station to Leamington Spa and from there take a taxi*

WHERE TO EAT

THE OPPOSITION

ADDRESS 13 Sheet Street, Stratford CV37 6EF

☎ 01789 269980

The Opposition is a long-standing restaurant with a varying European *à la carte* menu. There is a wide range of dishes from soup to king prawns to start, followed by dishes such as lasagne or fillet steak, then a variety of puddings.

• **COST** *A three-course meal with wine will cost between £25 and £30*

THE HOWARD ARMS

ADDRESS Lower Green, Illmington, Shipston on Stour CV36 4LT

☎ 01608 682226

This won the 1998 Dining Pub of the Year in Warwickshire award. The pub serves excellent wine and dishes such as oak-smoked salmon with a warm potato galette and sour cream and chives, or potted trout and olive oil toast; followed by calves' liver, buttered onions, crisp bacon and balsamic dressing; or fillet of pork Wellington with apples and sage. Puddings include organic ice cream and warm chocolate brownies.

- **COST** *Starters are about £4.50, main courses about £9.50 and puddings £3.95. It also does bed and breakfast at £55 for a double room. There is also a two-night weekend break, £42.50 per person per night, which includes bed and breakfast and £15 supper allowance*
- **HOW TO GET THERE** *Outside Stratford, along the A3400 to Chipping Norton and Oxford, then to the right, in a pretty little village*

THE BLUE BOAR

ADDRESS Temple Grafton, nr Alcester B49 6NR

☎ 01789 750010

The Blue Boar is in a pretty little village just off the A422 to Worcester, to the left. Good wine and food and rooms too. Typical à la carte dishes include mushroom and sweet pepper stroganoff and fillet steak. There is also a traditional bar menu, featuring steak and kidney pie and so on, with prices from £6.95.

- **COST** *Sunday lunch inclusive menu, three courses and coffee, £11.95. A la carte menu dishes are priced from £6.95 to £14.75. House wine is £8.95 for a litre carafe but prices rise to £30, with a choice of fifty wines. Bed and breakfast, double room with en-suite £59.50 per room per night, single £39.50*

WHAT TO DO

THE ROYAL SHAKESPEARE THEATRE

ADDRESS Waterside, Stratford-Upon-Avon CV37 6BB

☎ 01789 295623 (Box Office)

The Royal Shakespeare Company regularly performs Shakespeare's plays, and others, in his home town, with guest performers taking some of the lead roles. There are also theatre tours and a theatre fair in the summer, providing practical workshops, tours and demos for all ages.

SHAKESPEARE'S HOUSES

☎ 01789 204016

There are five houses associated with the Bard. You can purchase a full ticket for these, or a ticket for the three in the town centre.

These houses include Shakespeare's birthplace, Henley Street, which houses the main exhibition; Anne Hathaway's Cottage, Shottery, 2 miles west of Stratford, which is still owned by her descendants, and contains her bed (left to her in William Shakespeare's will); Mary Arden's house, Wilmcote, 4 miles north of Stratford, which was his mother's house before she married his father, John; Nash's House and New Place, Chapel Street, once owned by Thomas Nash, the husband of Shakespeare's grand-daughter, outside of which lies the site of Shakespeare's final home; and Hall's Croft, Old Town, owned by Shakespeare's son-in-law. All these houses are 16th-century.

- **OPENING TIMES** *Summer, daily 09.00–17.00; Winter, Mon–Sat 09.30–16.00; Sun 10.00–16.00*
- **COST** *For a ticket covering all five houses, prices are: adults £11, concessions and students £10, children 5–16 years £5.50. Family tickets £26. For the three houses in the town centre prices are: adults £7.50, concessions and students £6.50, children 5–16 £3.70. Family groups, £18. Children under 5 free*

HOLY TRINITY CHURCH

ADDRESS Old Town, Stratford-Upon-Avon CV37 6BT
☎ 01789 266316
This church, on the riverside, is also worth a look, being the final resting place of Shakespeare himself.

THE TEDDY BEAR MUSEUM

ADDRESS 19 Greenhall Street, Stratford-Upon-Avon CV37 6LF
☎ 01789 293160
Houses hundreds of teddies from around the world, past and present.

- **OPENING TIMES** *All year, 09.30–18.00*
- **COST** *Adults £2.25, children under 14 £1*

STRATFORD AND AVON CRUISES

ADDRESS Swans Nest Boathouse, Swans Nest Lane CV37 7LS
☎ 01789 267073
Take a half hour trip down the Avon.

- **OPENING TIMES** *Every 20 minutes 09.30–19.00*
- **COST** *Adults £3, children £2*

THE SHAKESPEAREAN

ADDRESS St Michaels Stud, Meerend Road, Meerend CV8 1PU
☎ 01676 532222
This guided tour on a horse-drawn omnibus begins and ends outside the main theatre.

- **OPENING TIMES** *All year round*
- **COST** *Adults £3.50, children £1.50, concessions £2.50. Family ticket £9*

WARWICK CASTLE

ADDRESS Warwick, Warwickshire CV34 4QU

☎ 01926 406600 (24-hour information line)

2 miles from Junction 15 of the M40, this castle dates from William the Conqueror and became one of the finest and most well kept castles in Britain. Now owned by the Madame Tussauds Group, which has made it more entertaining to visit. Warwick is only a short journey from Stratford and is well worth visiting. Most visitors are bussed in by tour companies, go round the centre and leave, so the town itself is relatively unspoilt. The main street has an indoor antique market with lots of stalls selling interesting bargains such as jugs, tapestry screens and old textiles. Leave time to wander round after visiting the castle.

- **OPENING TIMES** *Daily 10.00–17.00; closed Christmas Day*
- **COST** *Adults £9.50; children 4–16, £5.80; under-4s free, concessions £6.85; family of four £27*

KENILWORTH CASTLE

ADDRESS Kenilworth CV8 1NE

☎ 01926 852078

Beyond Warwick, Kenilworth Castle is an Elizabethan castle with rooms used for Queen Elizabeth I's visits. The X18 coach runs from Warwick town and pulls up right outside the castle itself.

- **OPENING TIMES** *Daily 10.00–16.00; closed Christmas holidays and New Year's Day*
- **COST** *Adults £3.50, children 5–16 £1.80, under-5s free, concessions £2.60*

YORK

For centuries, York was the capital of the North, a centre of commence, Christianity, learning and the arts, and much of the richness of that time has lingered. The city walls, built on Roman foundations, and their beautifully preserved gates, the magnificent Minster, the winding streets lined with elegant Georgian mansions and shopfronts, along with York's open welcome for visitors, make it a delightful destination for a weekend a million miles from London.

Waves of history have washed over York. Since a legion of the Roman Army first established a fortress here in AD 71, the city has been Roman, Anglo-Saxon, Danish by way of the Vikings, Norman, and has been at the crossroads of much British history. In medieval times, York was the richest city in the country after London, and its glorious Minster dates from that time. The city declined along with the wool trade and was never one of the great manufacturing centres of the Industrial Revolution, so it has been charmingly preserved. It is compact, so leaving the car in London and strolling the streets of York is a pleasure.

- **HOW TO GET THERE** *York is within easy reach of London. Going via train on GNER from Kings Cross takes from just under two*

hours to two hours and twenty minutes, and costs from £26 return.
☎ *0345 484950 for schedules and fares. Trains leave hourly on*
the hour from Kings Cross and at odder intervals from York station,
so check the schedule for return

WHERE TO STAY

MOUNT ROYALE HOTEL

ADDRESS The Mount, York Y24 1GU
☎ 01904 628856   **FAX** 01904 611171

We cannot recommend the Mount Royale too highly. There are
certainly grander hotels in the area, but you would be hard pressed
to find one with a warmer welcome or friendlier atmosphere. It is
made up of four conjoined town houses outside the city walls.
The décor is entirely in the Northern mode, which is to say, every
surface is decorated, especially in the lobby area: figured carpets,
figured wallpaper, frilly plants, ornately framed prints and repro-
type paintings. There are dogs. It is a million miles from the
capital's cool minimalism or home-counties country-hotel grandeur,
and as such is a cultural experience in itself.

The one-acre garden is likewise an explosion of shape and
texture. There are espaliered fruit trees, palms, a wishing well,
topiary, a heated outdoor pool, plastic Wendy house, all in
exuberant colours. This is a direct descendant of the Victorian style
of overkill in decoration. While at first it seems merely tasteless,
after exposure for a few hours it seems full of passion and fun.
It grows on you.

Our room was number 10, costing £140, a two-room suite
facing the quiet garden. The built-in furniture is Scandinavian style,
not retro, lovingly cared-for from the 70s. There is a flowered suite
in the bedroom and two double beds – presumably to accommodate
some kind of provincial wife-swapping. Bottled water, fruit bowl,
kettle, cookies, silver packets of hot chocolate and Horlicks are all
provided. Actually, the whole place is extremely comfortable.

If you are eating in the hotel, last orders for dinner are at 8pm,
which may be tricky if you are travelling up on a Friday evening
after work. However, they are very accommodating and will
stretch the point or serve you in your room.

First off, they have a truly great children's menu, encompassing
all the regulars, plus a few specials. They'll serve everything with
chips. Spaghetti bolognese came with lovely big shavings of
Parmesan and criss-crossed with chives. Corn on the cob had fresh
herbs scattered over the top. The strawberry ice cream tasted
home-made. £7.45 for three courses.

The grown-up menu was almost like a parody of Northern fine
dining: slices of Galia melon fanned out, shrimp cocktail. Starters:
the filo basket with wild mushrooms and brandy-cream sauce was
fine, but over-salted. The chicken-liver parfait with onion chutney
was first rate. The smoked haddock fish cakes were better than

okay and their sauce was very good indeed. The local duck was served Yorkshire style – twice-cooked and falling off the bone. Nice. Nicer still was rack of lamb, served pink with a hugely flavoursome sauce. Veg was two kinds of spuds, mange-tout, and red cabbage. The room service is on-the-spot, friendly and helpful. Starters: £5.75. Main course £18.50. The wine list has selections from all over the world, including the Lebanon and dazzlers like Chateau Petrus 1981. No real surprises and no real bargains, but no ripoffs, either.

• **COST** *Single from £85, double from £95, suite £140, including full English breakfast and VAT. Also, two nights' dinner, bed and breakfast from £260 for two people*

DEAN COURT HOTEL

ADDRESS Duncombe Place, York YO1 7EF

☎ 01904 625082

You'd never know this was a Best Western from the outside, with its three Georgian town houses stunningly located just across from the front of York Minster. But once inside, breeding shows. It has a very comfortable motel-like atmosphere, recently refurbished. On the other hand, do you really want the full Georgian experience, or do you want en-suite baths, colour television, in-house movie channel, hair dryer and kettle?

• **COST** *Singles from £80, doubles from £120, suites from £150. The grand Langley Room has a four-poster bed: £160. All prices include tax and breakfast. Weekend breaks from £140 per person including dinner and breakfast for a two-night stay*

THE JUDGE'S LODGING

ADDRESS 9 Lendal, York YO1 8AQ

☎ 01904 638733

The most central hotel in York. It was originally a private house built in 1710, and later became the Assize Court Judge's residence, hence the name. Rooms are roomy and slightly overdecorated in the northern flouncy style.

• **COST** *Singles from £75, doubles from £100, suites from £130. All prices include tax and breakfast*

WHAT TO DO

There are three huge attractions in York itself, and a host of others worth your time and attention.

NATIONAL RAILWAY MUSEUM

ADDRESS Leeman Road, York YO26 4XJ

☎ 01904 621261, recorded information ☎ 01904 686286

The National Railway Museum is trainspotters' heaven. Really. It has just opened a £4 million refit of its shed and it is truly spectacular, if you like this sort of thing. Home of the world's fastest steam engine, the beautiful blue Mallard, which set a world record, never beaten, of 134mph on 4 July 1938. Stephenson's Rocket is here, which sort of started it all. An amazing model train set built over 55 years by one man, who was such an anorak that, in the interests of exactitude, he built it one centimeter too big to fit onto any existing model railway track, so the museum have got to come up with the readies to create an entirely new train track to run the set. Views over York station, with their actual switching computers on line so you can see how the pros keep the engines from bumping into each other. Steam train rides, play area, picnic area, interactive learning centre, terrific gift shop.

- **OPENING TIMES** *Daily 10.00–18.00; except on Christmas Eve, Christmas Day and Boxing Day*
- **COST** *Adults £5.90, children free*

YORK MINSTER

ADDRESS Deangate, York YO1 7FJ
☎ 01904 557216

Its twin towers impose an ecclesiastical reminder over the whole town that York has been one of the most important Christian centres in Britain for more than a thousand years. This medieval building was built over a span of 250 years and contains half of the world's store of medieval stained glass. If that sounds like a yawn to you, you will be enthralled by the reality. The South Transept was struck by lightning in 1984 and it has been sympathetically and beautifully rebuilt. The remarkable thing that the fire brought to attention is just how little the environs of the Minster have changed over the centuries. It's like a village of medieval workshops of stonemasons, wood carvers, plasterers, scaffolders, all beavering away day and night to maintain the ancient fabric of the building in authentic style.

The Foundations and Treasury, showing the Roman and Norman ruins and the silver collection, the Chapter House, Central Tower and the Crypt are open by admission.

- **OPENING TIMES** *Summer 07.00–20.00; winter 07.00–18.00*
- **COST** *Admission free, but a donation of £3 is suggested*

JORVIK VIKING CENTRE

ADDRESS Coppergate, York YO1 9UT
☎ 01904 643211

Building works in the 70s uncovered a row of four Viking buildings along with remarkably well-preserved clutter, including boots and pins. There is a sort of indoors non-thrilling fairground ride where you get into a little cart and are taken back in time to experience the sights, sounds and smells of the Jorvik settlers. It would seem to be a really good school trip, and if you have children between the ages of 4 and 12 it is probably a good stop. The museum attached to it is better because it houses real, actual stuff that the

Vikings used and left behind, and the antiquity of it makes the hairs stand up on your neck.

- **OPENING TIMES** *Daily 09.00–17.00*
- **COST** *Adults £5.35, children aged 5–15 £3.99, students and senior citizens £4.60. Family ticket £17 (2 adults and 2 children)*

THE WALL

Maybe the most fascinating tourist attraction is the wall that remains around York. The Romans first built the wall, and the Anglo-Danish kings reinforced what remained with an earthenware bank. Medieval-era wall is what mostly remains, encircling the old city. It was the Normans who built the lovely gates, or 'bars', and four of them remain: Micklegate Bar, the monarch's entry, where traitors' heads were piked, Bootham Bar, on the North Road, Monk Bar, with a working portcullis, and Walmgate Bar, with its authentic funnel-like Barbican. About three miles of it remain, there is a hardy group who walk it daily for exercise, but just to climb it and let your imagination drift backwards gives a sort of historic thrill. Imagining that our civilisation once depended on the bravery of men standing atop a stone wall with little more than pointy sticks is a powerful thought.

'Gate' is the old Danish word for 'street' and the city gates are called bars, because they can admit you or bar your way. So York likes to say it is the place where the streets are gates, the gates are bars and the bars are pubs.

WHERE TO EAT

BETTY'S

ADDRESS 6–8 St Helen's Square, York YO1 8QP

☎ 01904 659142

Once upon a time, everyone who was anyone in York ate at Betty's lovely wood and mirrored restaurant. Betty's opened here on 1 June 1937 and the place still retains the atmosphere of the Second World War, who used Betty's as a centre of ops and scratched their names on the mirrors by the bathrooms. Nowadays, it seems to be mainly the tourist trade who are happy to queue for half an hour or more to get a seat on one of the banquettes. Betty's has seating on two floors, but the basement seemed dreary; better to wait for one of the tables with a view through the huge glass windows to the pedestrianised St Helen's Square. A selection of twelve teas and nine coffees complement the Swiss-based menu. The ham and Gruyère sandwich had a hint of honey. The Swiss rösti was excellent. But it is the dessert trolley which will stick in your mind, if not on your thighs. Children are extremely well catered for. There is also a bakery and teashop adjoining, so you can continue the indulgence at home.

- **OPENING TIMES** *Daily 09.00–21.00; (08.30 on Sat)*
- **COST** *Sandwiches from £3.40, starters from £3.60, main courses from £5.95. Cream Tea, £4.80, and The Ultimate Afternoon Tea, £9.60. Set menu, 2 courses £9.95, 3 courses £13.45*

THE BLUE BICYCLE
ADDRESS 34 Fossgate, York YO1
☎ 01904 673990

A local favourite, especially for supper. Grilled halibut with rosemary butter and chocolate pavé are specialities. Booking advised.

- **OPENING TIMES** *12.00–14.30; 19.00 till late in the evenings*
- **COST** *£28–£35 per head for 3 courses including wine*

THE PARSONAGE COUNTRY HOUSE HOTEL
ADDRESS Main Street, Escrick YO19 6LF
☎ 01904 728111

This will require a taxi trip out of town, but the food is worth it. Run by wonderfully eccentric Kenny Noble. 'Posh English' is how they describe their food.

- **OPENING TIMES** *12.00–13.45; 19.00–21.00*
- **COST** *Dinner £19.75 for 2 courses, £24.50 for 3*

EDINBURGH

TOURIST INFORMATION CENTRE
ADDRESS 3 Princes Street, Edinburgh
☎ 0131 473 3800

A genteel, serene city with grand architecture. Almost everything revolves around Princes Street, with the dramatic Edinburgh Castle perched on a hill at one end and, at the other end, the Balmoral Hotel and North Bridge which spans across the old town. Now Scotland's official capital, Edinburgh has become a sophisticated city and home to the much acclaimed Edinburgh Festival and Edinburgh Tattoo – a military musical extravaganza.

There aren't many green spots in Edinburgh although the Royal Botanical Gardens, Inverleith Row, are spectacular with huge Victorian Palm Houses and many interesting sections. If you are feeling bold, you could always climb on the top of Arthur's Seat, the big volcanic mountain south of the city.

- **HOW TO GET THERE** *King's Cross to Edinburgh from £37 return if booked 7 days in advance with Great Northern Eastern (☎ 0845 722 5225) or Euston to Edinburgh overnight for £79 return if booked 7 days in advance with Scotrail (☎ 0845 7550033). Fly GO from £55 return from Stansted (☎ 0845 6054321)*

WHERE TO STAY

THE MALMAISON

ADDRESS 1 Tower Place, Leith Docks, Edinburgh EH6 7DB
☎ 0131 468 5000

The Mal commands a stunning position overlooking the regenerated Leith Docks – now a lively area for young professionals, full of trendy cafés, restaurants and hotels, along with the new residential development in old buildings. The Malmaison is extremely chic, with lots of weird and whacky touches – the oversized, high-back chairs in reception – which set the tone for the rest of this highly desirable hotel. The French-style brasserie has friendly young staff. The rooms are brilliant and even the mini-bar is a design statement, with boxes of Bloody Mary and G&Ts and loads of munchies. A Bows sound system, CDs and bathrooms with the Mal's own bespoke toiletries.

- **COST** *Weekend rate from £99 per room per night, up to £150 for a suite*

THE HOWARD HOTEL

ADDRESS 34 Great King Street, Edinburgh EH3 6QH
☎ 0131 557 3500

The Howard is on a wide Georgian street in the heart of New Town, minutes' walk from George Street and Princes Street. Along with its smart public rooms, with cosy fire places, it has very luxurious bedrooms and suites. The restaurant '36' is one of the leading ones in Edinburgh, with chef Malcolm Warham providing Scottish/International cuisine, at high prices.

- **COST** *£245 for a double, £325 for a suite*

DRUMMOND HOUSE B&B

ADDRESS 17 Drummond Place, New Town EH3 6PH
☎ 0131 557 9189

This is also set in New Town, looking over a beautiful cobbled square, with private gardens.

- **COST** *Double £90–£110, including full Scottish breakfast (haggis and black pudding as well!)*

WHERE TO EAT

EST, EST, EST

ADDRESS George Street, Edinburgh
☎ 0131 225 2555

Est, Est, Est had the distinction of recently having to turn away Mick Jagger because they were full. It's an Italian restaurant with excellent food. Tables are well spaced out and prices very reasonable.

- **COST** *Starters £2–£4; main courses £6; desserts £3*

STAC POLLY

ADDRESS 29–33 Dublin Street, Edinburgh EH3 6NL

☎ 0131 556 2231

Serves traditional Scottish fare made from best-quality ingredients, such as Angus beef and smoked salmon. It has such a good reputation that it is often very difficult to get a table here. (See also Gourmet Weekends, page 156).

• **COST** Dinner is about £20–£25; main courses start at £13.95

'36' AT THE HOWARD HOTEL

ADDRESS Great King Street, Edinburgh EH3 6QH

☎ 0131 556 3636

This is one of the top gourmet restaurants in Scotland and, although pricey, it serves up the most perfectly presented and equally tasty food. The set lunch might consist of: baked goats' cheese and potato tart with cucumber relish; braised leg of rabbit, with garlic, thyme and Madeira, set on a red-onion 'mash'; caramel cream pot with a maple syrup and pecan nut biscuit. For dinner, the menu is à la carte, with starters like red wine, lobster and prawn risotto with its own sauce; or puy lentil salad with roast celery and a coriander and sesame oil dressing; followed by loin of venison with creamed Scottish chanterelles and tarragon, set on a rösti potato and gin sauce; or steamed fillet of sea bass, set on basil mash potatoes, with vermouth cream sauce and spinach salad; puddings include dark chocolate and peppermint soufflé, with a champagne sorbet, and grapefruit panacotta with an aniseed *tuile*.

• **COST** Lunch is £16.50 for two courses, including coffee, and £19.50 for three. A la carte starters are about £6.95, main courses £16.95 and puddings £5.25

THE WITCHERY

ADDRESS 352 Castlehill, Royal Mile, Edinburgh EH1 2NF

☎ 0131 225 5613

An offbeat restaurant by the castle, full of candles at night. Lots of tapestries and ancient panelling make it slightly spooky but fun. This restaurant is right by the castle entrance at the top of the Mound. Pre- and post-theatre menus are very reasonable, with a choice of three dishes for each course. A typical menu might be: sautéed chicken livers with pesto and spinach; followed by corn-fed chicken breast with orange, lemon, coriander and chick-peas; and one from a selection of puddings, including warmed chocolate tart with lime ice cream.

• **COST** One course £9.95, 2 courses £12.95, 3 courses £14.95

THE WATERFRONT

ADDRESS Dock Place, Leith EH6 6LU

☎ 0131 554 7427

Fantastic for fish. This is set in an old wooden-panelled fisherman's cottage, overlooking the water, providing great food and warmth in the cold winter months. They have two different menus, one for lunch at about £16 for three courses, including salmon tartare and elderflower dressing or smoked haddock kedgeree with pitta bread as starters; then baked cod fillet wrapped in parma ham on roast leek with tomato and olive coulis or chargrilled loin of tuna on tabbouleh with red chilli jam; then a selection of desserts and cheeses.

- **COST** *Three course lunch for £16. Dinner is about £20–£25*

WHAT TO DO

THE EDINBURGH FESTIVAL AND FRINGE

ADDRESS The Hub, Castlehill, Edinburgh EH1 2NE

☎ 0131 473 2010 ☎ 09065 500 678 for a copy of the official Fringe programme.

From 8th–30th August Edinburgh is completely transformed into a theatrical city for the largest arts festival in the world, with a real carnival atmosphere. It includes the International Jazz Festival, Military Tattoo, and Book and Film Festivals. The main festival includes big stars of the classical music world, at the Usher Hall, who normally do the same thing at the Proms. Mainstream theatre companies do their stuff in the Traverse Theatre and at the Festival Theatre, along with ballet and other dance troupes. This will also tell you about Hogmanay – the New Year celebrations, which are truly spectacular.

At the Fringe, scores of Britain's top comedians like Alan Davies do stand-up. There are over 600 performances and over 1000 different shows in 200 venues. Most shows cost no more than £5 and lots of events are free. You need to book well ahead as Edinburgh is packed at Festival time.

EDINBURGH CASTLE

ADDRESS Castle Hill, Royal Mile, Edinburgh EH1 2NG

☎ 0131 225 9846

There is much more to see than just the festival. The Castle is definitely worth a visit, housing the Scottish Crown Jewels and much history. It also has the best views in the city, looking right over the Firth of Forth to Fife.

- **OPENING TIMES** *Summer 09.30–18.00; closes at 17.00 in winter. Last ticket 17.15 summer, 16.15 winter*
- **COST** *Adults £6.50, children £2, under-5s free*

CITY TOUR

☎ 0131 556 2244

The Guide Friday open-top bus tour is definitely worthwhile, taking an hour and showing you this compact city, with stops at all the tourist attractions.

- **TIMES** *Mon–Fri 09.30–15.45; Sat 09.15–16.00*
- **COST** *£8*

ROYAL MUSEUM OF SCOTLAND

ADDRESS Chambers Street, Edinburgh EH1 1JF

☎ 0131 247 4219

The new wing of the museum is a magnificent piece of architecture and, along with the Scottish artifacts, there is also a brand-new, very nice restaurant on the top floor, The Tower, ☎ 0131 225 3003. They also do a pre-theatre menu at £12 for two courses, although the main menu is on all night, at about £25–£35, with oysters and other crustacea on the menu, including lobster claw, crab or *plateau de fruits de mer* for two people, with lobster at £18. The main dishes include grilled calves' liver and various other meat dishes, but this is an obvious choice for fish eaters.

- **OPENING TIMES** *Mon, Wed–Saturday 10.00–17.00; Tues 10.00–20.00; Sun 12.00–17.00*
- **COST** *£3, concessions £1.50, children free*

THE ROYAL YACHT BRITANNIA

ADDRESS Ocean Drive, Leith EH6 6JJ

☎ 0131 555 5566

The Royal Yacht is now docked on Ocean Drive in Leith and is worth a visit, although you must phone first.

- **OPENING TIMES** *Mon–Fri 11.30–15.30; Sat–Sun 10.30–16.30; but times vary with the seasons*
- **COST** *Adults £7.50, children £3.75*

GLASGOW

For so long, Glasgow has been the butt of jokes about yobbish drunks and thick incomprehensible accents. But the reality is very different from its image. Recently cultural city of Europe, Glasgow has a plethora of hip and happening art galleries and restaurants full of Scottish joie de vivre. Dating from the time when civic pride in Glasgow was at its height, its public buildings, described by Sir John Betjeman as the finest specimens of Victorian architecture in Europe, are some of the most magnificent you will see. And there is nothing stuffy about its art galleries and museums. So forget about traditional tartan, shortbread, hackneyed haggis and bagpipes – Glasgow is far more than that – it's a friendly and lively city that will keep you reeling with excitement.

- **HOW TO GET THERE** *British Airways (☎ 0345 222111) fly to Glasgow from Heathrow eight times a day. Fare from £57 return. Suckling Airways (☎ 0870 606 0707) fly to Glasgow four times a day from London City Airport. Fares from £58 return*

WHERE TO STAY

ONE DEVONSHIRE GARDENS

ADDRESS 1 Devonshire Gardens, Glasgow G12 0UX
☎ 0141 339 2001

Ken McCullock's stunningly designed hotel set in a tree-lined Victorian terrace looks for all the world like a row of private houses – there are only three houses in all. The difficulty is deciding which one to go into, but when you do you are greeted by one of their exceptional staff – the young man who greeted us in a long apron was charming and friendly in equal measure. The atmosphere is formal and restrained and the service quite exceptional. You really feel pampered and cared for in a friendly, unfussy kind of way. The rooms are beautifully and individually decorated and the only bizarre layout is that you have to leave one town house and re-enter through another front door to get to the bar. This hotel is so discreet it's the perfect spot to go if you are with someone you shouldn't be with.

- **COST** *Double room from £170 per night; weekend rate from £130–£185 per room per night*

MALMAISON

ADDRESS 278 West George St, Glasgow G2 4LL
☎ 0141 572 1000   **FAX** 0141 572 1002

Much more hip and contemporary is the Malmaison – an outstanding hotel with stylish rooms all of which have been individually designed. Luxuries include your own hi-fi system with CD player, in-house movies and two telephone lines. The hotel has its own brasserie and more recently acquired Café Mal which with its sky-lit area contrasts effectively with the brasserie's more cosy clubbiness. All in all it is a great hotel which still manages to have affordable rates.

- **COST** *Double room costs £99 per night*

NAIRNS

ADDRESS 13 Woodside Crescent, Glasgow G3 7UP
☎ 0141 353 0707

Celebrity chef Nick Nairn and his brother Topher own this terrific place which has a restaurant serving up Scottish fare in an attractive, contemporary setting. It has four gorgeous bedrooms – each individually designed with large bathrooms and names like Nantucket, Vermeer, Silver and Amber.

- **COST** *Double room costs £110–£140*

BRUNSWICK HOTEL

ADDRESS 106–108 Brunswick St, Glasgow G1 1TF
☎ 0141 552 0001

Contemporary, minimalist hotel with every landing painted
in a different colour. Rooms are bright and cheerful with
Japanese-style beds.

• **COST** *Double room costs £65 and includes full continental breakfast*

BABBITY BOWSTER

ADDRESS 16–18 Blackfriars St, Glasgow G1 1PE
☎ 0141 552 5055

This late 18th-century town house is set in the Merchant City and
is renowned for its hospitality. With only six rooms, a sense of
intimacy is inevitable and guests are made to feel very welcome.
Lots of fine Scottish fare including haggis and stovies. Eat on the
patio in the summer.

• **COST** *Double room costs £70 including breakfast*

WHERE TO EAT

THE UBIQUITOUS CHIP

ADDRESS 12 Ashton Lane, Glasgow G12 8SJ
☎ 0141 334 5007

The ethos of this restaurant is 'bringing Scotland's endangered
cuisine out of the home and into the restaurant'. Situated in a
cobbled mews in Glasgow's West End, it has an airy courtyard-
style setting and excellent Scottish fare. Really buzzy, nice
atmosphere with charming staff. The three-course set menu dinner
includes dishes such as venison, haggis and neeps and Scotch
salmon smoked in Darjeeling tea. On Sundays, enjoy a wonderful
three course set lunch which includes starters such as Sauternes
jelly studded with a medley of fish, shellfish and herbs, main
courses such as roast pork, stovies, braised greens and for dessert,
apricot strudel. Other puddings include glazed banana and
custard tart and lemon meringue ice-cream.

• **COST** *£32.95 for three course set menu dinner; £16.60 for three
course Sunday lunch*

NAIRNS

ADDRESS 13 Woodside Crescent, Glasgow G3 7UP
☎ 0141 353 0707

Even if you don't get to stay here (see page 194), you should try
out the food. The food centres around fresh, Scottish produce and
is cooked with a modern approach. The delicious three course set
menu features dishes such as seafood pakora, onion and chilli jam
and dressed leaves, chargrilled sirloin with horseradish mash and
Nairn's chocolate tea cake.

• **COST** *Three course set menu is £27.50*

THE WILLOW TEAROOMS

ADDRESS 217 Sauchiehall St, Glasgow G2 3EX

☎ 0141 332 0521

A visit here really is a must. Designed by Charles Rennie Mackintosh, this tearoom is the sole survivor of four teahouses created by the famous architect. Over 30 blends of loose leaf tea, scones, sandwiches and cakes. Afternoon tea costs £7.75.

• **OPENING TIMES** *Mon–Sat 09.30–16.30*

WHAT TO DO

GALLERY OF MODERN ART

ADDRESS Queen St, Glasgow G1 3AZ

☎ 0141 229 1996

Housed in the former Stirling library, there are lots of controversial works here like 'Happy & Glorious' a rather cruel statue of the Queen in the entrance hall with carpet slippers, a copy of Sporting Life and a corgi. Other contributions are from the likes of Craigie Aitchison and Ken Currie. There is a fab café on the top floor with brightly coloured murals, very much in keeping with the rest of the gallery. Excellent shop downstairs selling innovative and unusual objets d'art.

• **OPENING TIMES** *Mon–Thurs 10.00–17.00; Fri & Sat 11.00–17.00*

POLLOCK HOUSE

ADDRESS 2060 Pollock Shaws Road G43 1AT

☎ 0141 616 6410

The Burrell collection and Pollock park are ten minutes by train from Queen Street station in rural parkland. A modern gallery housing the eclectic collections of William Burrell, there is a distinct preference for medieval works but artifacts range from the Roman empire to Rodin. There is a self-serve café and restaurant on the ground floor. The parks are certainly worth a wander through and Pollock House contains works by Goya, El Greco and William Blake.

• **OPENING TIMES** *Daily, summer 10.00–17.00; winter 11.00–16.00*
• **COST** *Free in winter; summer adults £4, children up to 17 free*

THE GLASGOW SCHOOL OF ART

ADDRESS 167 Renfrew St, Glasgow G3 6RQ

☎ 0141 353 4500

Scottish architect and designer Charles Rennie Mackintosh had an enormous influence on contemporary design and Glasgow is the very best place to see examples of his work. The School of Art is a stunning example and definitely worth a visit on your weekend.

- **OPENING TIMES** *Guided tours are available from 11.00–14.00; Sat from 10.30*
- **COST** *Adults £5, children and students £3. Under-10s free*

MACKINTOSH HOUSE
ADDRESS University Avenue, Glasgow G12 8QQ
☎ 0141 330 5431
See where the great Charles Rennie Mackintosh lived.
- **OPENING TIMES** *Mon–Sat 09.30–17.00*
- **COST** *Free, donations only*

SHOPPING
Shopping in Glasgow is unrivalled by anywhere North of the Border and at the weekends you'll frequently see an influx of students from Edinburgh or other University towns eager to buy the latest trends. Glasgow boasts the largest density of retail outside of London. Shops range from the usual chain stores such as Oasis or Jigsaw to those including designer labels such as Katherine Hamnet and Jean-Paul Gaultier. Princes Square with its art-deco shopping centre is also well worth a visit. There is a restaurant on the top floor, cafés beneath and a basement courtyard. Here you can find Scottish crafts, designer jewellery, candle shops and more, all contributing to its sophisticated elegance. Buchanan Galleries is one of Scotland's largest and most recent shopping centres, with shops such as John Lewis, Mango, East and Viyella.

FLORENCE

If you're thinking of a fabulous and mind-improving place for a weekend, then Florence has to be one of the don't-miss destinations. If your idea of heaven is wandering down little cobbled alleys and suddenly stumbling on the most beautiful church, pausing for a delicious *latte* while you people-watch, visiting mindblowingly wonderful galleries and also squeezing in a spot of shopping, Florence has the lot. The best time to go is probably either spring or autumn, when there are marginally fewer tourists, the temperature is pleasant and the real Fiorentini are not at the seaside or in their country retreats. Cheap airfares, reasonably priced *pensione* and good-value restaurants mean that it needn't cost you billions of Lire, although you may find that you end up spending a not-inconsiderable sum on things to bring home. There are several very good websites on Florence. Two that you might want to browse are at www.fionline.it and www. florence.ala.it.
- **HOW TO GET THERE** *GO flies from Stansted to Bologna (from £80 return, ☎ 0845 605 4321. From Bologna Airport, take a taxi to the station and then a fast train to Firenze Santa Maria Novella – a journey of about an hour*

WHERE TO STAY

BEACCI TORNABUONI

ADDRESS via Tornabuoni 3, Florence 50123

☎ 055 212 645

A delightful old-fashioned *pensione* right in the town centre with antiques, huge dramatic flower arrangements and a sweet roof terrace with views over the terracotta rooftops. The entrance hall is rather uninspiring, but it's a different matter once you're inside. Very central and an easy walk or bus ride from most of the sights.

• **COST** *Double room L300,000–L340,000; single room L200,000–L220,000; suite L500,000–L700,000, breakfast included*

RESIDENZA

ADDRESS via Tornabuoni 8, Florence 50123

☎ 055 284197

Another small hotel on the same street with a warm, cosy atmosphere on the top floors of an old *palazzo* (where in Florence isn't?). Simple bedrooms and a delightful roof terrace, along with its central location, make this a good place to stay.

• **COST** *Double room L300,000; single room L180,000 per night, including breakfast. There is a 20% reduction on prices during the off-peak season*

LIANA

ADDRESS via Alfieri 18, Florence 50121

☎ 055 245 303

A little out of the way (about a quarter of an hour's walk from Piazza del Duomo) and not in the most interesting part of Florence, the Pensione Liana does, however, offer good value for money. The building was, at one time in its existence, the British Embassy, and there are still some elements of faded grandeur to it.

• **COST** *Double room L240,000 per night including breakfast. Single occupancy L210,000 per night*

GRAND HOTEL VILLA MEDICI

ADDRESS via il Prato 42, Florence 50123

☎ 055 238 1331. Book through Leading Hotels of the World Reservations Department, Toll Free 0800 81 123.

If you fancy staying in a larger hotel, try the Hotel Villa Medici, which is an easy walk from the Arno in one direction and Santa Maria Novella in the other. Less personal than the *pensione*, this hotel is grand and opulent, with large chandeliers and lots of brocade and damask on the walls. It has a sweet garden for breakfast in fine weather and an outdoor swimming pool which would be a blessing in high summer. The staff were all delightful and very helpful – particularly the concierge.

• **COST** *Double room L510,000 per night*

WHERE TO EAT

There is absolutely no shortage of good, reasonably priced
restaurants in Florence, and, even if you take pot luck, you would
be very unlucky to stumble across a duff one. The ones we've
mentioned are particular favourites. There are also plenty of good
places for a snack or a cup of coffee. Be aware of the fact that you
will pay almost double if you sit at a table rather than stand at a
bar. In most small bars, you need to queue up at the till and pay
and then hand the receipt to the barman to get your order.

IL CINGHIALE BIANCO

ADDRESS Borgo San Jacopo, Florence
☎ 055 215 706
A popular, intimate restaurant just the other side of Ponte Vecchio,
which serves traditional Florentine cooking. Very friendly staff and
good value food. Try crostini – chicken-liver pâté on toasted local
bread – wild boar stew with polenta, ubiquitous tiramisu, vin santo
and biscotti di Prato, washed down with a robust Chianti.
• **COST** *Around L35,000 a head for a three-course meal*

ZA–ZA

ADDRESS Piazza del Mercato Centrale 21/r, Florence
☎ 055 215 411
A good place to stop if you're sightseeing round the San Lorenzo
market area. This is a small restaurant on two floors, serving
traditional local food. Try a typical Florentine soup, such as pappa
al pomodoro or ribollita, which is made by leaving bread to soak
in minestrone and then literally 'reboiling'.
• **COST** *Around L30,000 a head for three courses*

PAOLI

ADDRESS via dei Tavolini, Florence
☎ 055 216 215
One of the oldest restaurants in Florence, serving an extensive
menu of Italian specialities. You do need to book as it's quite
popular.
• **COST** *Around L55,000 per head*

LATINI

ADDRESS via Palchetti 6, Florence
☎ 055 210 916
Very famous and popular Italian trattoria. Bookings are only taken
between 7.30 and 7.45pm. Your best bet is to get there in good
time – around 15 minutes before opening – and queue.
• **COST** *Around L55,000 per head*

ENOTECA PINCHIORRI
ADDRESS via Ghibellina 87, Florence
☎ 055 242 777
One of Florence's most famous restaurants and one of the best in
Italy. The prices are not cheap, but are commensurate with the
standard of food.
• **COST** *Around L150,000 per head*

PROCACCI
ADDRESS via Tornabuoni, Florence
A good place to stop on via Tornabuoni, famous for its *panini
tarafati* sandwiches.

GIACOSA
ADDRESS via Tornabuoni, Florence
Another stopping spot on via Tornabuoni, which is good for a
quick lunch of pasta and salad.

CAFFE GILLI
ADDRESS Piazza della Repubblica, Florence
Piazza della Repubblica is probably the most central spot for
all the cultural sights, as it's almost equidistant from the Duomo,
Piazza della Signoria and the Ponte Vecchio. There are several
bars in the square with not much to choose between them. Gilli is
a fine example of late 19th-century elegance and a good place to
stop either for a mid-afternoon *latte* or an early evening apéritif. If
the weather is warm, sit outside and watch the world go by.

BAR CUCCIOLO
ADDRESS via Cimatori, Florence
This is where to go for the best *bomboloni* (Florentine doughnuts
with either confectioner's custard or jam) in town.

WHAT TO DO
The problem with Florence, if there is one, is that there is just so
much to see and do; you have to be very selective if you are only
there for a weekend. Everyone will have different ideas of things
that they feel they just can't miss, but there are some obvious buildings
and works of art that you really do have to see – Michelangelo's
statue of *David*, Brunelleschi's dome on the Duomo, Botticelli's *Birth
of Venus* for example. You do also need to build some 'down-time'
into your schedule or your brain will overload. The following is by
no means a comprehensive guide to Florence, or even a complete
list of all there is to see, but more our personal view of things to see
in a weekend. It's a good idea to pick up a leaflet from your hotel
on museum and gallery opening times, as they are sometimes shut
for restoration or for setting up exhibitions.

GALLERIA DEGLI UFFIZZI

ADDRESS Loggiato degli Uffizzi 6, Florence

☎ 055 213 440

The Uffizi is one of the world's most famous galleries, with a huge collection. We found it easier to start with a short visit and then go back again to look at specific paintings, as there is just so much to see. Not only is there the obvious collection of 14th- and 15th-century paintings, but also work by more modern artists such as Chagall.

• **OPENING TIMES** *Tues–Sat 09.00–19.00; Sun 09.00–13.50; Last entry 45 minutes before closing*

• **COST** *L12,000 per ticket*

GALLERIA DELL'ACCADEMIA

ADDRESS via Ricasoli 60, Florence

☎ 055 23885

Founded in 1784 to provide students at the Academy of Fine Arts with the opportunity to study work by past masters, the Accademia is most famous for housing Michelangelo's statue of *David*. Sunday morning is a good time for a visit.

• **OPENING TIMES** *Tues–Sat 09.00–19.00; Sun 09.00–13.50; Last entry 30 minutes before closing*

• **COST** *L12,000 per ticket*

PALAZZO PITTI

ADDRESS Piazza Pitti, Florence

☎ 055 23885, 055 294 883 (bookings)

A monumental palace on the other side of the Arno, built by a Florentine merchant called Luca Pitti, who wanted to outdo the Medicis. Visit the State Rooms, the Gallery of Modern Art, and the Palatine Gallery, which has over 500 paintings by artists such as Raphael, Michelangelo, Filippo Lippi and so on. Be prepared to feel as though you are visiting a gigantic Christmas card display! Behind the Palazzo Pitti are the Boboli Gardens – a good spot for a picnic. Much frequented by young Florentines, foreign students and flashers.

• **OPENING TIMES** *Palatine Gallery, Tues–Sat 09.00–19.00; Sun 09.00–13.50; State Rooms 09.00–13.00; (closed on Mon). Modern Art Gallery 08.30–15.50 (closed every 1st, 3rd and 5th Mon and 2nd and 4th Sun in every month)*

• **COST** *Palatine Gallery L12,000 per ticket; State Rooms, L12,000 per ticket; Modern Art Gallery, L8,000 per ticket (also includes entry to the Costume Museum)*

PALAZZO VECCHIO

ADDRESS Piazza della Signoria, Florence

☎ 055 276 8325

A magnificent civic palace built between 1298 and 1314. Beautiful public rooms, including the Salone dei Cinquecento, with frescoes by Vasari of *Lives of the Artists* fame. The Palazzo Vecchio is set in the Piazza Signoria, one of Florence's largest squares. Set into the ground is a plaque to show where Savonarola was burned in 1498. The Piazza Signoria is a good spot to stop for a coffee or an early evening drink while you contemplate a copy of Michelangelo's *David* outside the Palazzo and the statues by Giambologna and Benvenuto Cellini in the Loggia.

- **OPENING TIMES** *Mon–Sat 09.00–19.00; closed on Thurs; Sun 09.00–13.00. Last entry 45 minutes before closing*
- **COST** *L10,000 per ticket*

PALAZZO MEDICI-RICCARDI

ADDRESS via Cavour 1, Florence
☎ 055 276 0340
Commissioned by Cosimo di Medici and the main residence of the famous Lorenzo 'Il Magnifico', this palazzo is a two-minute walk from Piazza Duomo. Nip in here to see the Benozzo Gozzoli *Voyage of the Magi*, which features the Medici family as the Kings. Take along a pair of binoculars to get a really detailed view.

- **OPENING TIMES** *Mon–Sat 09.00–13.00 and 15.00–18.00; Sun 09.00–13.00. closed Wed*
- **COST** *L6,000 per ticket*

PALAZZO DAVANZATI

ADDRESS Piazza Davanzati, Florence
☎ 055 238 8610
A relatively little-known museum that is set out as it would have been when it was inhabited. A lovely building to stroll around pretending you're a 15th-century Florentine. (The Palazzo has been closed for restoration, and is due to re-open Easter 2000.)

- **OPENING TIMES** *Mon–Sat 09.00–14.00; Sun 09.00–13.00*
- **COST** *Admission free*

THE DUOMO

ADDRESS Piazza del Duomo, Florence
The Duomo is almost as much a symbol of Florence as Michelangelo's statue of *David*. The dome was designed by Filippo Brunelleschi, the Bell Tower by Giotto and two of the fabulous Baptistry Doors by Lorenzo Ghiberti. The interior is imposing and austere – particularly after looking at the multicoloured outside. Don't miss the Michelangelo *Pietà*.

SANTA MARIA NOVELLA

ADDRESS Piazza Santa Maria Novella, Florence
One of Florence's most famous churches, Santa Maria Novella was built for the Dominican order. Amongst other things there are fabulous frescoes by Ghirlandaio.

SANTA CROCE
ADDRESS Piazza Santa Croce, Florence
A Franciscan church containing Michelangelo's tomb with frescoes by Giotto and Cimabue's Crucifix, which was badly damaged in the 1966 flood.

SANTA MARIA DEL CARMINE
ADDRESS Piazze del Carmine, Florence
This church is not one of the most frequently visited as it's slightly out of the way. However, it's worth a trip, not least to look at the Brancacci chapel, with its fantastic frescoes by Masaccio, who died in 1428 when he was only 27 years old. The whole area around Piazza del Carmine and Piazza Santo Spirito, which is known as San Frediano, is a great place for a general wander about. This is the area where the craftsmen work and, if you stroll around during working hours, you can see paintings and furniture being restored and gilt frames and silver items being made.

PONTE VECCHIO
The Ponte Vecchio is Florence's most famous bridge across the Arno, with jeweller's shops built into each side. Go in the early evening, when you can look longingly into the jewellers' windows as well as buying from the traders who spread out their wares on blankets on the pavement. The view from the bridge is stunning at any time of day.

PIAZZALE MICHELANGELO
Take a bus from the centre to this Piazza on the outskirts of Florence for one of the best views of the city. Yet another copy of Michelangelo's *David* dominates the square.

FIESOLE
A Roman village a few miles outside Florence, easily reached by cab or bus. Visit the Roman amphitheatre and have a cappuccino overlooking another great view of Florence and the Tuscan hills.

PASSAMANERIA TOSCANA
ADDRESS Piazza San Lorenzo 12/r, Florence
You could combine a stop here with a visit to the Palazzo Medici-Riccardi and the San Lorenzo market as they are all very close together. The shop is stuffed (almost literally) with beautiful cushions, throws, trims and tassels. Choose cream silk damask cushions with tigers or leopards or buy amazing edging for making your own cushions or lampshades.

GUCCI

ADDRESS via Tornabuoni, Florence

Fashion victims will want to make a pilgrimage to the starting place of the Gucci empire. Very stylish interior and charming staff – we went in on a very rainy day, loaded down with carrier bags, and almost instantly our rather tatty bags were whisked away and put into two smart Gucci bags. Things are slightly cheaper here than in London, but you still need to take out a second mortgage to buy anything.

AMARZOTTI

ADDRESS Borgo degli Albizi 86/r, Florence

Go here to buy Florentine paper and paper goods. The shop has been going since 1980 and is housed – as are many Florentine shops – in an old palazzo, originally built in 1558.

FARMACIA SANTA MARIA NOVELLA

ADDRESS via della Scala 16, Florence

This amazing shop is hardly identifiable as such from the street – it feels as though you are going into an apartment block, but persevere. This is the place to buy scent, soaps and aftershave. Inside, the store looks as though it hasn't changed for several centuries. The merchandise is displayed in breakfronted mahogany shelves and is beautifully packaged. Go for lovely soaps in violet or lily of the valley or aftershave in pomegranate. They even have their own range of products for babies and children. This shop is so beautiful that it's worth a visit even if you have no intention of buying anything. You could go here after a trip to Santa Maria Novella church, which is just around the corner. For another similar shop also try Antica Farmacia de San Marco, via Cavour 146.

MERCATO SAN LORENZO

ADDRESS Piazza San Lorenzo and via dell'Ariento, Florence

An open-air market that runs along several side streets near the Duomo. Florence is famously good for leather, so this is the place to invest in a leather or suede jacket, belts, gloves in a hundred different colours, or handbags in every style imaginable. Visit the Mercato Centrale, which is the indoor food market. Downstairs are the butchers and fishmongers, whilst the first floor houses the fruit and veg stalls. Makes Harrods and Fortnums fresh displays look paltry by comparison.

• **OPENING TIMES** *From around 10.00 to about 19.00 every day except Sun and Mon (depending on season). The market is also open on the first Sun of every month*

MERCATO NUOVO (PORCELLINO)

ADDRESS Loggia del Mercato Nuovo, Florence
Sells similar articles to the San Lorenzo market, as well as Florentine straw items, hand embroidery and wooden goods. Expect to see more touristy tat as well, such as rather hideous onyx chess sets. Stroking the nose of the Porcellino (the bronze statue of a wild boar) means that you will return to Florence.

- **OPENING TIMES** *Daily 08.00–19.00; closed Sun & Mon mornings*

MADRID

Madrid is a great city and eminently do-able in a weekend. You can fly there in just over two hours and in twenty minutes be whisked by fast taxi to the heart of the city. A million miles away from the Costa del Sol and lager louts, Madrid is a glamorous and exciting city with plenty of culture and vibrant nightlife. During your weekend you'll have time to sample remarkable museums, down Rioja and change your mind about sherry. But be prepared to adjust to Spanish hours. You may find yourself eating lunch from three to six in the afternoon and not even contemplating dinner until after ten at night. So if you want to weekend where there's no down time, where the streets are often busier at two in the morning than they are at two in the afternoon, then this is for you. Your feet may hurt at the end of it but you are sure to have gained some Spanish soul.

- **HOW TO GET THERE** *GO airlines fly to Madrid three times a day. Fare from £90, ☎ 0845 605 4321. Kirker Holidays offer a range of weekend packages to Madrid from £275 for a three night stay at the Londres to £582 for a three night stay at the Ritz, ☎ 0171 231 3333*

WHERE TO STAY

THE RITZ

ADDRESS Plaza de la Lealtad, Madrid
☎ 91 521 2857
Situated right in the centre of the city near Ratiro Park facing the Prado Museum. The Thyssen-Bornemisza museum is also near by. Lots of Belle Epoque splendour; very pretty public rooms and a beautiful terrace which makes a lovely stop-off point for tea after a museum-packed afternoon or a lazy Sunday lunch treat.

- **COST** *Double rooms from 58,000ptas*

HOTEL VILLA REAL

ADDRESS Plaza de las Cortes, Madrid
☎ 91 420 3767
Also ideally placed for the museums the hotel has a classic interior and a brilliant collection of AD Roman mosaics.

- **COST** *Double room from 39,700ptas*

HOTEL SANTO DOMINGO
ADDRESS Plaza de Santo Domingo 3, Madrid
☎ 91 547 9800
Smart small hotel just off the top of the Gran Via in the heart of
the city.
- **COST** *Lovely bedrooms from 22,000ptas*

LONDRES
ADDRESS Calle Galdo 2 (just off Calle Preciados), Madrid
☎ 91 531 4105
Located in the shopping area by the Corte Ingles department store
in the fashionable Puerta del Sol disctrict. Simple but comfortable
and excellent value for money.
- **COST** *Double rooms from 9,700ptas*

WHERE TO EAT AND DRINK
The best tapas bars are to be found around Plaza Mayor, a
beautiful square with 17th-century buildings which during the
Inquisition was used for executions; today it is still used for fiestas
and bullfighting. It's a great hangout at lunchtime. At night, head
for the tapas bars in Plaza Santa Anna.

LA MODERNA, VIVA MADRID
ADDRESS Plaza Santa Anna, Madrid
A really good bar with fabulous wall tiles, music and a beautiful
carved old ceiling.

LOS GABRIELES
ADDRESS Plaza Santa Anna, Madrid
A former brothel, again with wonderful floor to ceiling tiles.

RESTAURANT BOTIN
ADDRESS Calle de Cuchilleros, Madrid
☎ 91 366 4217/91 366 3026
Just off the Plaza Mayor, this is quite simply a must. It is one of
Madrid's most famously authentic restaurants and dates back to
1725. Dark and cavernous, it is buzzing with life and serves up
delicious suckling pig or perfectly roasted Aranda lamb. A typical
set course dinner would be gazpacho, roast suckling pig and ice
cream; bread, wine, beer or mineral water is also included in the
price. Remember to reserve a table at least a few days ahead of
your visit as it gets very booked up.
- **COST** *Set course meal costs about 4,300ptas*

POSADA DE LA VILLA
ADDRESS Cava Baja 9, Madrid
☎ 91 366 1860
A lovely old Castillian inn, also near the Plaza Mayor. Specialities include roast lamb baked in clay and straw ovens. Cocido de puchero is a wonderful stew and highly recommended.
- **COST** *Set menu around 5,000ptas*

CAFÉ CHINITAS
ADDRESS Torija 7, Madrid
☎ 91 547 1502
Restaurant with 'tablao' (flamenco). Book ahead.
- **COST** *Flamenco show and dinner 9,800ptas*

WHAT TO DO

THE PRADO MUSEUM
ADDRESS Pasea del Prado, Madrid
☎ 91 330 2800
One of the finest museums in the world, it houses such masterpieces as Velasquez's Las Meninas, Bosch's Garden of Earthly Delights and Goya's 3rd of May 1808.
- **OPENING TIMES** *Daily 09.00–19.00; closed Tues*
- **COST** *Entrance fee is 500ptas; free on Sat from 14.30–19.00*

VILLAHERMOSA PALACE
ADDRESS Paseo del Prado, Madrid
☎ 91 420 3944
Home to the Thyssen-Bornemisza Collection with 900 works ranging from the Venetian primitives to modern masters, the collection takes you from 13th-century paintings right through to modern day works. Walk your way around and you will see works by all the greatest artists – Picasso, Matisse, Chagall – just one or two works by each artist. With its pink walls and floor-to-ceiling shuttered windows, there's an intimate atmosphere; it's rather like walking through someone's house and it makes a nice contrast to the loftier grandeur of the Prado.
- **OPENING TIMES** *Tues–Sun 10.00–19.00*
- **COST** *700ptas*

REINA SOFIA ART CENTRE
ADDRESS Santa Isabel 52, Madrid
☎ 91 467 5062
This is the old San Carlos Hospital. See works by Miró, Gris and Dalí, as well as one of Picasso's most famous works, Guernica.
- **OPENING TIMES** *Mon–Sat 10.00–21.00; Sun 10.00–14.30*
- **COST** *500ptas*

ROYAL PALACE IN CALLE BAILEN

ADDRESS Calle Bailen, Madrid
☎ 91 542 0049
Beautifully preserved, it represents two centuries of history and has
fabulous furnishings, chandeliers, paintings and much more.
• **OPENING TIMES** *Mon–Sat 09.00–18.00; Sun 09.00–15.00*

SHOPPING

If you still have time for a little shopping, visit the Salamanca area
which has the most exclusive shops. The Puerto del Sol is also
worth visiting. You can find items ranging from bullfighters
costumes, fans and espadrilles to guitars, porcelain and antique
furniture. For fans, visit the Amoraima at the Plaza Mayor; for
clothes, try Mango at Goya 83 and find the famous Spanish line
Zara at Gran Via 32. El Corte Ingles is the main department store
and has branches in Calle Preciados (the pedestrian area just off
the Puerto del Sol). On Sunday morning, visit the El Rastro flea
market which sells everything from brightly coloured caged birds
to bric-a-brac and antiques.

PRAGUE

CZECH AND SLOVAK TOURIST CENTRE
☎ 0171 794 3263/4

Prague's beauty demands that you walk its streets and so
fortunately the centre is very compact. If you have just a weekend,
then concentrate your sightseeing around the Old Town and the
Castle areas, which are on the east and west banks of the Vltava
river. Staromestske Nameste (Old Town Square) is an enchanting
mix of medieval and baroque architecture and thankfully untouched
by modern development. Gables, spires, cherubs and a famous
clocktower all conspire to give it a fairy-tale atmosphere, as if you
had landed in the set for a Brothers Grimm story. The cobbled
square is full of cafés and market stalls, but also explore the side-
streets, especially at dusk, when deep-set windows glow with
candlelight and crooked stone steps lead to cellars and graceful
glass foaming with the world-famous Staropramen beer – and
every other table seems to have young men passionately
discussing poetry and politics.
• **HOW TO GET THERE** *Flights with GO from Stansted on their new
Prague route from £100 return inc. taxes,* ☎ *0845 605 4321.
Reach the airport by trains from Liverpool Street running every
40 minutes. Coaches leave Victoria and cost £6 return with a
GO fare*

WHERE TO STAY

If you're really stuck for somewhere to stay, or just turn up hoping to find somewhere, then you shouldn't really have a problem. Look out for locals offering private rooms for the night – usually these are cheap and cheerful, although not always very central, so ask before you accept.

THE PALACE HOTEL

ADDRESS Panska 12, Praha 1-Nove Mesto

☎ 24 09 31 11

This is perfectly located just off Wenceslas Square, in the heart of the old centre. This hotel is built in the Viennese art nouveau style and years of renovation have restored it to its original splendour.

- **COST** *Rooms cost from 5000kc*

U TRI PSTROUSU HOTEL

ADDRESS Drazickeho namesti 12, Praha 1

☎ 57 32 05 65

Its location, just off the Charles Bridge, and original beams and wooden floors can't be bettered.

- **COST** *Not cheap at 5400kc for a room but it's worth it for the location*

DUM U VELKE BOTY PENSION

ADDRESS Vlasska 30, Praha 1

☎ 57 31 11 07

This is the ultimate hideaway pension, crammed with tasteful period furniture and situated in the cobbled backstreets below the castle.

- **COST** *Slightly cheaper than the other hotels*

WHERE TO EAT

Prague isn't exactly a haven for vegetarians, nor is it a gourmet's paradise, but most Czech fare is wholesome and good value. Tourist menus are easy to find, but are occasionally overpriced and substandard. Good restaurants, however, line the Diouha and Celenta streets and dishes such as dumplings and pancakes are certainly worth sampling.

VIARNA V ZATISI

ADDRESS Betlemske nam, Praha 1

☎ 22 22 11 55

A favourite establishment with the locals. The kitchens are famed throughout the Republic for their chocolate mousses.

- **COST** *From 675kc*

BELLEVUE RESTAURANT
ADDRESS Smetanovo nab, Praha 1
☎ 22 22 14 38
There is a champagne jazz brunch with music in the old Prague tradition. Stunning views of the castle make a good backdrop for dishes like yellow-fin tuna and pan-fried quail in Drambuie.
• **COST** *Menus from 790kc*

ZOFIN ZOFIN
ADDRESS Zofin Island, Praha 1
☎ 292 044
Hidden away on the river island of Slovansky Oxtrov and just five minutes from Charles Bridge, Zofin Zofin is a 150-year-old restaurant.
• **COST** *400kc*

WHAT TO DO
Prague's sights are quite breathtaking and it can be difficult knowing where to start. For information on opening times and so on, telephone the Prague Tourist Board, ☎ 02 54 44 44.

THE CASTLE
ADDRESS Hradrany, Praha 1
This is an obvious choice, immortalised by the writer Franz Kafka. The castle houses the government buildings, has great views of Prague, is worth the walk to get there and also has Prague's Cathedral within its walls and one of the best modern art galleries in the world.
• **COST** *80kc*

THE MUNICIPAL HOUSE
ADDRESS Obneci Dom, Praha 1
This has a delightful art nouveau café, with palms, original Alphonse Mucha murals and a live orchestra to finish off the perfect atmosphere.
• **COST** *free*

WENCESLAS SQUARE
ADDRESS Wenceslas Square, Praha 1
Just a few minutes from the Old Town, Wenceslas Square is majestic. It is regarded as the birthplace of Czechoslovakian democracy, the place where the Velvet Revolution started in 1990 leading to the overthrow of the communist regime.

CLASSICAL CONCERTS
Music enthusiasts are very well catered for in this city. Catch classical concerts in the Tyn Church, St Niklaus and in the glorious

St Agnes Convent to the north of the Old Town. In any case, it's easy to buy tickets for one of hundreds of concerts going on every evening – leaflets advertising them are handed out all over town.

CHARLES BRIDGE

The romantic bridge is understandably popular and often overcrowded; however, its beauty is undeniable so don't miss it. To avoid the crush, go at midnight and listen out for a little light impromptu opera singing.

WALLENSTEIN PALACE

ADDRESS At the foot of Castle Hill and Malostranke Nameste (Little Town Square, on the west bank).

The walled gardens of the Palace are worth a visit. There is also a good jazz club in the square and St Nikolas Church on the same square has some of the best classical music concerts in the city. Cafés line the river banks – spot them from the bridges then find a path down to them.

WEEKEND BREAKS IN FRANCE

Whilst it is true to say that we Brits have been hopping across the channel for centuries, the opening of the Channel Tunnel has suddenly made this a really easy option for a weekend – or even just for a day trip. Whether you choose to go by rail, by ferry or on Le Shuttle, the French coast is now easily accessible and only a few hours away. And, however close it may be geographically, it's a million miles away in many other respects. As soon as you get to the other side of the Channel, the scenery is different and the people are different, as are the shops and the food. Of course, you can get superb food on our side of the water, but you'd be unlucky to have a really duff meal on the other side and, not only that, but most places represent really good value for money.

There are many reasons to choose France as a destination for a weekend. First, it really feels as though you've been away for longer than a couple of days if you've been somewhere 'foreign'. Second, the huge *supermarchés* are great places for stocking up on all sorts of delicacies that are hard to find or very pricey over here. Also, it's worth going just 'because it's there'.

WHAT TO BRING BACK FROM A WEEKEND IN FRANCE
Wines and beers – even now that Duty Free has ended, they are
  still appreciably cheaper in French supermarkets
Jams and preserves
Foie gras and pâtés
Cheeses
Tins of white tuna
Luxury items, such as salmon caviar
Sirops or French squash
Crème de cassis/framboise/pêche/myrtille, for kirs
Luxury and cooking chocolate
Large tubs of Nesquik chocolate powder
Children's T-shirts and underwear (available in the supermarkets)
Tins or bottles of *confit de canard* or *oie* as well as *cassoulet*
Bottles of fish soup and rouille

HOW TO GET THERE

Take a Connex train from Victoria to Dover for £20.60 return
☎ 08706 030405
Sea France Ferries ☎ 0990 711711
P&O Ferries ☎ 087 0600 0600
Eurotunnel ☎ 0990 353535
Hoverspeed ☎ 0990 240241
Rent a car at the Calais terminal for £63 for three days.
Hertz ☎ 21 96 3 6 84

Now, by the miracles of modern technology and engineering, you have two choices. You either go over or under the Channel. Both options have their attractions. The Tunnel saves nearly an hour on crossing time and involves 10 minutes' less driving from most of south and west London. 'Disembarkation' from the Shuttle is so much faster than the ferry and there are no delays at the terminal exit – you simply drive straight through onto the N1 motorway.

The Shuttle trains that carry cars through the tunnel have no facilities – other than lavatories and an in-board radio station which broadcasts the sort of warnings about all sorts of possible perils that makes you wonder why you bothered to leave home in the first place. Probably the best way to pass the 35-minute trip is sitting in your car with the traditional sandwiches and thermos – and newspaper. By contrast, when using the ferry, you'll hit the motorway nearly an hour and a quarter later, but having had the chance of a proper meal, some shopping and a stretch of your legs on board. Be warned, however. At peak times, the ferries swarm with kids of all ages – including middle-aged ones trying to drink the bar dry before arriving in port – even at ten in the morning. It can be pretty grim.

If you want to escape from the hordes, most ferries have a Club Class Lounge. Using this will add around £15 per person to the round trip – or more if you haven't booked in advance. An alternative is to eat in the more civilised waiter-service restaurant. On P&O, this used to be excellent value, but it is less so these days. For quick meals, ferries have one or more self-service cafés, but these are real bunfights.

There is of course a choice between P&O and Sea France ferries on the Dover/Calais run, but there is really not much to choose between the two. If you want a more pleasant crossing, choose a time when the ferries are less crowded and try to get on one of the original P&O boats. However, if you're going over for a weekend, you are liable to hit peak time.

Both ferry companies are in a state of transition, as they come to terms with the huge loss of revenue from Duty Free sales. Fares are already increasing but, on the positive side, there will with any luck be fewer people on board who cross merely to buy cheap Duty Free booze.

Typically, a weekend ferry fare for a car, driver and one passenger between June and September is £110. At other times of the year it is about £30 to £40 less. By travelling very early or late in the day it may be possible to reduce the cost, and in winter there are often special deals.

Your choice of route to the Channel ports depends on where in London you start. South and west Londoners are advised to find the shortest route to the M20. For those in the north and east, it is usually quicker to use the M2. In either case, it's hard to avoid the dreaded M25, so allow extra time, especially on a Friday afternoon or evening.

From the centre of London, you can take your choice of motorways, since reaching either is a long haul through endless south London suburbs. From Marble Arch, for example, allow at least 2½ hours to Dover or Folkestone at quiet times. Don't even consider it in rush hour. From Balham, allow 1¾ hours and from Hammersmith, 2 hours.

Don't forget that you must arrive half an hour before your booked departure time. Cutting it much finer could result in being put on the next available boat or shuttle. This normally results in a delay of only ½ or ¾ of an hour, but, at busy times, it could be much longer. Arriving without a reservation is risky, except at times when you are sure that there will only be a few passengers.

The Sea Cat catamaran, operated by Hoverspeed, has much to commend it, although it is generally more expensive than the ferries. However, like the Hovercraft, it has a drawback: in rough weather it becomes uncomfortable and will be cancelled in a storm. When this happens, passengers are transferred to the next available ferry from Dover, which can easily waste a couple of hours.

For speed and excitement, the Hovercraft is hard to beat, and there are sometimes cheap fares to be had if you book at the right time. Those with sensitive tummies may wish to avoid it on a choppy day, and it can be very noisy.

If you have chosen to use the Tunnel, using the M20 to get there has definite advantages. The terminus is right next to the motorway at Folkestone, about 8 miles before Dover East Docks, where the ferries leave. Although the M20 now ends less than a couple of miles from Dover's ferry port, the small saving in driving time with the Tunnel is welcome on a weekend break.

At the French end, the Tunnel also scores by being next to the N1. This is the fastest route to destinations south of Calais, including Boulogne, Le Touquet and Abbeville.

If you are travelling as a foot passenger, you will need to get a boat train from Victoria, which will take you either to Folkestone or Dover. Do make sure that you get off at the port and not in the town centre.

BOULOGNE

TOURIST INFORMATION BUREAU
ADDRESS Forum Jean Noël, quai de la Poste BP 187
☎ 03 21 31 68 38

Boulogne has altogether more character than neighbouring Calais,
and you could easily spend a weekend here alone. It used to be
a popular seaside resort for Edwardian cross-channel travellers
and there are charming streets through which to wander, although
nowadays it is predominantly a port rather than anything else.
The Haute Ville is still scenic, with 13th-century ramparts, an 18th-
century Hôtel de Ville and the Imperial Palace – Napoleon's HQ
when he was planning to invade us. The beach is sandy and clean
and a pleasant spot to sit and enjoy the sun in fine weather.
- **HOW TO GET THERE** See page 214

WHERE TO STAY

Hotels actually in Boulogne are not great and you might be
better to book yourself into one outside the town (see Wimereux,
page 232). However, if you don't have a car, these are the
best of the bunch.

HOTEL LE METROPOLE
ADDRESS 51 rue Thiers, 62200 Boulogne-sur-Mer
☎ 03 21 31 54 30
A mid-priced hotel on a quiet shopping street in central Boulogne.
It is small – 26 bedrooms – and has an attractive dining room.
- **COST** From 350F to 460F per night

HOTEL IBIS CENTRE VILLE
ADDRESS boulevard Diderot, 62200 Boulogne-sur-Mer
☎ 03 21 31 21 01
Part of the national chain and not exactly full of character, this
hotel is, however, reasonably priced, well run and not far from
Nausicaa (see below) and the old town.
- **COST** 210F per room per night

WHERE TO EAT

LES PECHEURS D'ETAPLES
ADDRESS 31 Grande Rue, 62200 Boulogne-sur-Mer
☎ 03 21 30 29 29
Small local fish restaurant. Typically, they might offer herring
terrine, salmon with garlic sauce and chocolate mousse.
- **COST** Good value set menu at 95F

LA MATELOTTE

ADDRESS 80 boulevard Ste Beuve, Boulogne-sur-Mer

☎ 03 21 30 17 97

A very long-established fish restaurant, nearly opposite Nausicaa (see below). Specialities include warm lobster salad and roast turbot with thyme butter.

• **COST** *Menus at 98F, 140F, 180F and 220F*

WHAT TO DO

NAUSICAA CENTRE NATIONAL DE LA MER

ADDRESS boulevard Ste Beuve, Boulogne-sur-Mer

☎ 03 21 30 99 99

You may, like us, have trudged your way round your fair share of windswept, boring Sealife Centres at various locations round the British coast, and have since decided that you just don't do Sealife Centres. However, don't forget that this is France and the great thing about Nausicaa is that it manages to be incredibly stylish, well designed and amazingly interesting. The displays are brilliantly done, with atmospheric background music and beautiful etched glass panels and there are information boards in both English and French. The sharks are impressive, the tropical fish tank mesmerising and even the sea lion pool has a chic blond wood decking. Add to this a shop with marine-related gifts as well as Breton T-shirts and sweater and a restaurant that people visit for the food, not just because they happen to have been looking at the fish, and you can easily spend two to three hours in here. It's good for all ages, from small children who will like the touch pool, where rays come to the surface to have their tummies tickled, to adults who will start wanting some of the display materials as the décor for their bathrooms.

• **OPENING TIMES** *Weekdays 10.00–18.00; Weekends 10.00–19.00*

• **COST** *Adults 53F, Children 36F, under-3s free*

LAND SAILING

ADDRESS Char à Voile Club Côte d'Opale, 272 boulevard Ste Beuve, Boulogne-sur-Mer

☎ 03 21 83 25 48

A land-sailing club right on the beach, next door to Nausicaa. They run children's beginner lessons, rides and courses, adult weekends and week-long courses as well as renting sail-carts and speed-sails. The instructors speak enough English to make themselves understood.

• **COST** *10-hour courses with individual tuition 600F per person; 1 hour 80F*

CHATEAU MUSEE

ADDRESS rue Bernet, Boulogne-sur-Mer

☎ 03 21 10 01 20

A very well preserved château, completed in 1231. The château contains a whole raft of diverse items: Egyptian artefacts, Greek pottery, porcelain, glass, objects from Africa and the Pacific Islands and, for some reason, the largest collection in Europe of things Alaskan.

- **OPENING TIMES** *09.30–12.30 and 13.30–18.15 mid-May to mid-Sept. Open 10.00–12.30 and 14.00–17.00 the rest of the year*
- **COST** *Adults 20F, children 13F, under-12s free*

SHOPS

AUCHAN HYPERMARKET

ADDRESS On the N42, direction St Omer

Those who want to forego all thoughts of culture and worship at the altar of conspicuous consumption can't miss Auchan. The most pleasant and well-laid-out supermarket in the area, Auchan will tempt you into buying trolley loads. Even if you give the wine and beer section a miss, don't bypass the massive cheese counter. The staff will happily let you try the cheeses before you make your selection. The same is true on the *charcuterie* counter where you can buy fabulous rillettes, pâté, *tête de veau* and salamis and *saucissons*. There is a whole aisle devoted to chocolate alone, with a massive choice of milk, plain and cooking chocolate and so forth. Many of the items are a fair bit cheaper than in our supermarkets and the choice is almost overwhelming. As well as food, you can buy reasonably priced kitchenware, such as Le Creuset pans, and a good selection of china and glass. The children's clothes section is also worth looking at, particularly for Petit Bâteau underwear.

- **OPENING TIMES** *Mon–Sat 08.30–22.00; Closed all day Sun*
- **HOW TO GET THERE** *Follow the signs from the centre of Boulogne to St Omer (A42). The supermarket itself is well signposted from the centre, and is just by the slip road to join the motorway to St Omer*

FROMAGERIE OLIVIER

ADDRESS 43–45 rue Theirs, Boulogne-sur-Mer

☎ 03 21 87 58 53

You can smell Fromagerie Olivier almost before you spot it. This cheese shop is now famous throughout Europe and, if you like cheese, a very good bet. M. Olivier supplies many of the top hotels and restaurants throughout France as well as in the UK. As in most French shops, you can try the cheese before you buy. Just try to keep your purchases somewhere relatively cool until you get home.

- **OPENING TIMES** *Tues–Sat 09.00–19.00; closed for lunch 12.00–14.30*

IDRISS

ADDRESS 24 Grande-Rue, Boulogne-sur-Mer

☎ 03 21 30 54 59

For all manner of preserved fruits, from dried pears and apples, glacéd exotic fruits and lemon and orange peel for Christmas pudding, as well as nuts and spices.

- **OPENING TIMES** *Tues 10.00–12.00; Wed–Sat 15.00–19.00*

COMTESSE DU BARRY

ADDRESS 35 Grande-Rue, Boulogne-sur-Mer

☎ 03 21 87 19 20

A French chain selling beautifully packaged tins of *foie gras*, pâtés, cassoulets, preserves and other yummy delicacies that make good presents or store-cupboard standbys for making a gourmet meal out of nothing at short notice. The shop has an attractive livery and is nicely laid out inside.

- **OPENING TIMES** *Tues–Sat 09.00–12.00 and 14.00–19.00*

CALAIS

TOURIST INFORMATION BUREAU

ADDRESS 12 boulevard Clemenceau, Calais

☎ 03 21 96 62 40

For many people, Calais is merely their point of entry into France, and they steam past *sans jettant un coup d'oeil*. Although it isn't the greatest place to stay, Calais does make a good base for touring the surrounding area, and is very convenient for getting to and returning from.

- **HOW TO GET THERE** *See page 214*

WHERE TO STAY

FORMULE 1

ADDRESS Avenue Charles de Gaulle, Coquelles

☎ 03 21 96 89 89

If you are really on a strict budget and don't mind very basic accommodation, then these hotels are very good value. Formule 1 is a large national chain. The hotels are unstaffed and the rooms are very small. Each one does, however, have an en-suite shower and TV in the room.

- **COST** *The cost per night is 139F–149F per room. Breakfast is 22F per person and each room sleeps up to 3 people – 1 double bed and 1 single*

HOTEL GEORGE

ADDRESS 36 rue Royale, 62100 Calais
☎ 03 21 97 34 73

A more traditional hotel right in the centre of Calais, with 43 rooms. Interestingly, the tourist board literature lists this as having 'soundproof rooms'.

- **COST** *From 300F to 400F per room per night. Breakfast is 47F per person*

HOTEL HOLIDAY INN

ADDRESS 6 boulevard des Alliés, 62100 Calais
☎ 03 21 34 69 69

A typical large chain hotel, very convenient for the Channel Tunnel and the ferry ports.

- **COST** *From 592F to 690F per room per night. Breakfast costs 68F per person*

WHERE TO EAT

HISTOIRE ANCIENNE

ADDRESS 20 Rue Royale, 62100 Calais
☎ 03 21 34 11 20

Delightful French bistro in the city centre. Run by Claire and Patrick Comte. Patrick trained at Le Crillon and also the Byblos in St Tropez and serves up excellent fish and grilled meat. Scallops with garlic butter and pigs' trotters are specialities.

- **COST** *A la carte, 60F; three courses with wine, 160F to 190F*

LE COQ D'ARGENT

ADDRESS 1 Digue Gaston, Berthe, Calais
☎ 03 21 34 68 07

The place to visit for classic fish dishes is right on the beach. Of course, there is meat on offer but their speciality is local fish and fruits de mer.

- **COST** *Set price menus from 98F to 220F*

WHAT TO DO

CITE DE L'EUROPE, COQUELLES

To be honest, this is all that many people see of Calais, or indeed the whole of northern France. This huge indoor shopping complex is a magnet for shoppers looking for bargains. The Carrefour hypermarket is a large supermarket, but look out also for shops selling everything from men's and women's clothing, lingerie and jewellery, to chocolates, kitchen goods and so forth. You will also find familiar names such as Victoria Wine and Tesco Vin Plus.

There are cafés where you can have a coffee and look at your purchases, or eat a meal, if you want to make a whole day of it.
- **OPENING TIMES** *Shops open Mon–Thurs 10.00–20.00; Fri 10.00–21.00, Sat 09.00–20.00*
- **HOW TO GET THERE** *The centre is well signposted off the A16 and is right next door to the Channel Tunnel exits*

HONFLEUR

TOURIST INFORMATION BUREAU
ADDRESS Place de la Port de Rouen, 14600 Honfleur
☎ 02 31 89 23 30

The picturesque and historical town of Honfleur is just 20 kilometres away from the docks at Le Havre. Much visited by artists such as Monet, Courbet, Sisley and Turner, it's a pleasant alternative to the Calais and Boulogne areas if you want to spend a more scenic weekend, and aren't going for a French supermarket shopping jaunt; it's well worth the slightly longer journey time. It was from here that The White Ship set off and foundered, causing years of wrangling over the succession to the English throne.

- **HOW TO GET THERE** *Take the overnight P&O ferry from Portsmouth which leaves at around 10pm, arriving at Le Havre the next morning. P&O's prices vary according to how long you stay. The cheapest fare quoted is £29 (car and driver) plus £1 per each additional passenger for off-peak sailings and just 12 hours in France. We paid £156 return for a car and three passengers with an overnight cabin there and back for a five-day trip. It really is worthwhile to pre-book an overnight cabin, as spending the night in a reclining chair – particularly if the weather is rough and your fellow passengers suffer from motion sickness – can be a very off-putting experience. Drive out of Le Havre in the direction of Paris, then cross the spectacular bridges over the Seine and the ship canal to enter Normandy. Turn right at the first roundabout along the coast road and you soon reach Honfleur. The overnight return ferry to Portsmouth leaves at around 11pm, arriving at 7am the following morning*

WHERE TO STAY

HOTEL DU CHEVAL BLANC
ADDRESS 2 Quai des Passages, Honfleur
☎ 02 31 81 65 00
A typical Normandy 3-star hotel dating from the 15th century with views of the harbour.
- **COST** *494F, 629F or 827F per room per night, including breakfast, but depending on the room*

HOSTELLERIE LE CHAT

ADDRESS Place Sainte Catherine, Honfleur
☎ 02 31 14 49 49
A very scenic old 3-star hotel in the centre of Honfleur.
• **COST** *Double room 450F to 500F per night. Breakfast 50F per person*

HOTEL L'ECRIN

ADDRESS 19 rue Eugène, Boudun, 14600 Honfleur
☎ 02 31 14 43 45
Importantly for Honfleur, this is a hotel with private parking.
Nice conservatory overlooking the garden where you can
have breakfast.
• **COST** *390F per night for a twin room with en-suite bathroom; up to 950F for a suite. Continental breakfast 50F per person, English breakfast* à la carte

LE MANOIR DE BOUTIN

ADDRESS Phare du Boutin, Honfleur
☎ 02 31 81 63 00
A delightful small hotel with 9 bedrooms set in pretty grounds.
Typical Normandy-style with half-timbered walls.
• **COST** *640F to 1970F per night*

LA FERME DE ST SIMEON

ADDRESS rue à marais, 14600 Honfleur
☎ 02 31 81 78 00
A restored farmhouse just outside Honfleur, once the retreat of
artists such as Bouding, Monet and Corot who painted the garden
in return for a free meal. Now it is a hotel with a beauty centre,
bio-sauna and body treatments, solarium and jacuzzi.
• **COST** *Rooms 990F to 2190F per night*

WHERE TO EAT

L'ASSIETTE GOURMANDE

ADDRESS 2 Quai des Passagers, Honfleur
☎ 02 31 89 24 88
Near to the old port, this restaurant serves delicious food. The set
menus are particularly good value. Be sure to book your table well
in advance as this is a very popular spot. A typical 258F menu
would include dishes to choose from such as red mullet pâté with
escabeche fillet, smoked salmon tart with fresh herb coulis, foie
gras, roast lamb, calf sweetbread Chartreuse, lobster omelette (a
house speciality) followed by a cheese plate and a dessert of choice.
• **COST** *150F to 400F per menu*

LE CORSAIR

ADDRESS Place St Catherine, Honfleur
☎ 02 31 89 12 80
Good value restaurant with a wide choice of set menus. The
cheapest at 89F might include a seafood platter, cheese or dessert.
- **COST** *From 89F*

PETIT MEREYEUR

ADDRESS 4 rue Haute, Honfleur
☎ 02 31 98 84 23
Another good seafood restaurant using locally caught fish. The
house speciality is bouillabaisse (although this is not strictly a
Normandy dish), oysters and scampi fritters.
- **COST** *Set menu 120F*

WHAT TO DO

MARINE MUSEUM

ADDRESS Quai St Etienne, Honfleur
☎ 02 31 89 14 12
- **OPENING TIMES** *Tues–Sun 10.00–12.00 and 14.00–18.00;
closed Mon*
- **COST** *55F per ticket*

EUGENE BOUDIN GALLERY

ADDRESS Place Eric Satie, Honfleur
☎ 02 31 89 54 00
- **OPENING TIMES** *Mon–Sun 10.00–12.00 and 14.00–18.00;
closed Tues*
- **COST** *28F per ticket*

SHOPS

Honfleur has plenty of delightful small shops to wander around and
look at with lots of exquisite things to buy, particularly for foodies.
Go for cheese, wine, chocolates or nautical souvenirs to take home.
Hats are one of those things that you either love or loathe. Some
people have cupboards full of them and eagerly anticipate the
slightest chance of an appropriate occasion to wear one, whilst
others only put one on when etiquette absolutely demands it. If
you're one of the former, then this is one shop that you'll adore.
Novuaiande at 10 rue St Antoine is brim full of exciting creations,
many of them made in the atelier on the premises; this is a hat
emporium with something for any occasion. Little winter cloches in
velour jostle for position with large Ascot hats in straw or silk with
veiling or extravagant flowers. There are sensible hats to keep off
the rain as well as witty little confections that serve no useful purpose
other than to look gorgeous. They also have a large range of men's

hats including a good selection of panamas for that Death in Venice look. Prices start at a very reasonable 250F for a velours cloche up to 1000F for a large Ascot number.

LILLE

TOURIST INFORMATION BUREAU
ADDRESS Palais Rihour, BP205, 59000 Lille
☎ 03 20 21 94 21

Lille is an easy hop on the Eurostar or a mere one hour's drive from Calais. Like many northern French cities, the outskirts are industrial sprawl and best avoided. The station itself is not particularly prepossessing with derelict wasteland to one side and the city's mammoth hypermarket Euralille to the other. However, once you are safely ensconced in the old centre, Vieux Lille, just five minutes' walk away, the charms of the city become apparent. Flemish-style narrow buildings flank the wide open boulevards, gourmet delights fill the shops along the pedestrianised network of cobbled streets and magnificent squares are lined with enticing cafés. The inhabitants of Lille, though not an overly-stylish lot, are friendly and obviously enjoy the good life.

- **HOW TO GET THERE** *Take the Eurostar from London, a journey of about 2 hours. Alternatively take a ferry to Calais or the Channel Tunnel to Coquelles. From either Calais or Coquelles, take the A15 and the journey should be about an hour's drive. Lille is well signposted*

WHERE TO STAY

CARLTON
ADDRESS 3 rue de Paris, Lille
☎ 03 20 13 33 13
An elegant hotel for those feeling flush.
- **COST** *Double rooms from 1200F*

THE BRUEGHEL
ADDRESS 5 parvis Saint Maurice, Lille
☎ 03 20 06 06 69
This good value two star hotel has attractive Art Deco-style reception rooms.
- **COST** *Double rooms from 345F per night*

MISTER BED CITY
ADDRESS 57 rue de Bethune, Lille
☎ 03 20 12 96 96
An exotically named place to stay for the financially challenged.
- **COST** *Double rooms from just 230F per night*

WHERE TO EAT

THE COQ HARDI
ADDRESS Place du General de Gaulle, Lille
☎ 03 20 55 21 08
A popular restaurant serving traditional regional dishes such as
Waterzoi de Volailles and *Flamiche aux Mareilles.*
- **COST** *Regional menu fixe from 88F*

AUX MOULES
ADDRESS rue de Bethune, Lille
☎ 03 20 57 12 46
Healthy portions of mussels served with mushrooms, cream or the
house speciality, a curry sauce.
- **COST** *Around 60F per serving*

PAUL
ADDRESS rue des Manneliers, Lille
☎ 03 20 78 20 78
Tempting fairy tale strawberry and almond tarts and waffles beckon
you in from the windows of this local patisserie, or for fabulous
chocolates try Au Chat Bleu on the opposite side of the street.
- **COST** *Cakes from 18F for one or a whole cake for six, 80F–90F*

WHAT TO DO

PALAIS DES BEAUX ARTS
ADDRESS Place de la République, Lille
☎ 03 20 06 78 00
The Palais des Beaux Arts is France's most important gallery after
the Louvre. It houses a large collection of old masters and more
contemporary art including works by Goya and Rubens.
- **OPENING TIMES** *Mon 14.00–18.00; Wed, Thurs, Sat–Sun
10.00–18.00; Fri 10.00–19.00; closed Tues*
- **COST** *30F*

VIEUX LILLE
Wandering through the old town is one of the attractions of Vieux
Lille. Don't miss the beautiful rose and yellow façade of the Vieille
Bourse, built in Flemish Renaissance-style whose atmospheric
courtyard now plays host to booksellers, flower sellers and chess
players perched on the stone steps. Look up at J Dimey's modern
and colourful mural just off the rue de Bethune or savour the
tranquillity of nearby St Maurice church with its elegant stained
glass windows.

LOISINORD (SPORTS)

ADDRESS rue Leon Blum, 62290 Noeux-les-Mines

☎ 03 21 26 84 84

Those who have over-indulged might want to slope off to the dry piste just outside Lille to burn off some of the excess. There are also facilities for volleyball, water-skiing, swimming and kneeboard.

- **OPENING TIMES** *Daily 10.00–18.30*
- **COST** *50F for an hour's 'membership' card*
- **HOW TO GET THERE** *An hour's drive from Lille. Take the A1 towards La Bassée, then towards Vermelles, then Mazingarde. The centre is signposted and is next door to the LeClerc supermarket*

SHOPS

Le Marché de la Porcelaine, rue de la Vieille Comédie: a good source of cheap and stylish Limoges porcelain. Nocibe, rue de Bethune: perfume and cosmetics up to 30% cheaper than over here. Lucia Esteves, rue Lepelletier: excellent for superb linens. Rue Lepelletier is the best area for antique shops and designer boutiques as well as some of Lille's finest architecture. Wazemmes market, rue Gambetta: a real foodies' paradise which takes place on Sunday mornings. Sebastopol, place du Concert: a smaller fruit and veg market on a Saturday morning.

MONTREUIL

TOURIST INFORMATION BUREAU

ADDRESS 21 rue Carnot, Montreuil

☎ 03 21 06 04 27

A small, fortified town with an attractive Upper Town of cobbled streets and 16th-century timbered houses. There are 3 km of ramparts to walk around, giving stunning views of the countryside below. This was the setting for Victor Hugo's *Les Miserables* and nearby is the battlefield of Agincourt, although it's best not to mention that too loudly.

- **HOW TO GET THERE** *From either Boulogne, Calais or the Channel Tunnel, take the N1 motorway south. Montreuil is signposted from the motorway.*

WHERE TO STAY

HOTEL DE FRANCE

ADDRESS rue du Cocquempot, Montreuil-sur-Mer

☎ 03 21 06 05 36

To say that this hotel is laid back would be an understatement – it's virtually horizontal.

The vestibule and bar looked like Miss Havisham's house pre-fire – sombre, overfurnished, underlit and probably cobwebby, but by candlelight in the evening it looked quite magical.

All the bedrooms were comfortable, with individual decorative touches and that strange French habit of wallpapered ceilings, which can make you feel as though you have been gift-wrapped.

Breakfast was perfectly acceptable, continental version, but if you want lunch or dinner, forget it, as there is no restaurant. However, there is no shortage of local places to eat within walking distance. The décor was on the bizarre side, the service minimal, the house rules nil, but all in all, a unique experience. It's easy to get carried away with the general atmosphere of the place and over-imbibe so keep an eye on your bar bill.

- **COST** *From approximately 500F per room per night, with an extra 45F per person for breakfast*
- **WHERE TO EAT** *An exceptional restaurant in the area is L'Auberge de la Grande Grenouillère* ☎ *03 21 06 07 22, just outside Montreuil*

PICARDY

TOURIST INFORMATION BUREAU
ADDRESS BP 2616 Amiens, Cedex 1, 80011
☎ 03 32 22 33 66

Picardy is the name that is etched into British culture, although many may not know why. The invasion force of the Norman Conquest under William the Conqueror set sail from here, and more recently it was the scene of the appalling carnage of the First World War. Modern Picardy, however, is much neglected. Most of us rush through it on the way to somewhere more glamorous in France and it is true to say that it is not the most scenic part of the country. It does, none the less, have a quiet charm of its own, and being easily accessible from the Channel Ports or Tunnel is an ideal location for a weekend stay.

- **HOW TO GET THERE** *See Chateau de Foncaucart on this page*

WHERE TO STAY

CHATEAU DE FOUCAUCOURT
ADDRESS Foucaucourt-hors-Nesle, 80140 Oisemont
☎ 03 22 25 12 58
This is the most delightful spot to spend a weekend – particularly if you really want to chill out. The house is primarily the home of M and Mme de Rocquigny and their six or seven children (reports differ as to their number!) and is the epitome of Gallic 'shabby chic'. Mme de Rocquigny speaks excellent English having lived in London for many years. Her children are now mostly grown up,

and she takes paying guests in the house and in a small converted stable block at the end of the garden.

After about an hour and a half's drive from Calais, you arrive through pretty wrought iron gates to get your first glimpse of the château – what in England would probably be classed as a country house. Dogs bound up from all directions – Muffin the Bouvier, a Rottweiller puppy, assorted Pointers and a one-eyed Pekinese. Don't make the mistake of wearing white jeans or you'll end up with a load of muddy paw prints all over them. Park your car on the sweeping drive and enter the house through the central door into a hall which houses an aviary of squawking birds. You can expect a very warm welcome from Madame, her children or staff who will rustle up appropriate drinks or snacks on your arrival. Dinner and breakfast are taken in the beautiful 18th-century dining room surrounded by faded grandeur. The dining room table seats about 20, and meals are communal affairs. This may sound off-putting, but in actual fact it is tremendous fun. The food is traditional but simple French country cooking, all made with fresh ingredients – many from the château's kitchen garden. A typical dinner might include Quiche Lorraine, rabbit stew, delicious cheese, and chocolate mousse.

If you have lunch at the château, M and Mme de Rocquigny will make you up a 'bed' on the lawn so that you can sleep if off if the weather is good. The whole place is slightly shambolic but in a rather charming and French way – rather like staying with one's own delightful but slightly batty relations. This is probably not the place to go if you want to keep yourself to yourself, but if you want to sample a slice of French provincial life, then do give it a go.

- **COST** *From 350F per night for bed and breakfast in the main house. From 120F including sheet hire for a room in the stable block, which houses 18 and is pretty basic. Dinner costs 110F per person for 4 courses and carafes of wine*
- **HOW TO GET THERE** *From Calais, take the A16 to Abbeville and then the A28 towards Amiens coming off at the Oisement exit. Take the D936 to Oisement. Go straight over at the crossroads – the Château is signposted in Oisement, but the signs are difficult to see. Follow the road for a mile or so until you see a signpost to the right to the Château. Go past the cemetery on your right and through the village and you will see the Château straight ahead of you. Remember that French motorways have tolls. At the time of writing the cost of the journey was 44F*

WHAT TO DO

The countryside is not the best that France can offer, but there are a couple of nearby coastal towns which are delightful. Mers-les-Bains has a seafront of Belle Epoque houses and a few good seafood restaurants including Les Mouettes which is in a shack on the beach. Prettier still is the little town of St Valery-sur-Somme where you can have a very good plate of moules et frites for around 30F. The opposite of the estuary is Le Crotoy which has a fantastic sandy beach. A steam railway runs between the two in summer. Ask at a local tourist office for the Marchés de Foie Gras which take place occasionally at local farms. Here you can sample and buy the most delicious home-made foie gras entier, mi-cuit and bloc for a fraction of the price in England.

Many people visit Picardy to see the Somme battlefields which are within an hour or so's drive from the hotel. Head to Péronne for the Historical de la Grande Guerre museum or through Doullens to Arras where you can visit remaining trenches or the war cemetery at Aubigny off the N39 out of Arras.

LE TOUQUET

TOURIST INFORMATION BUREAU
ADDRESS Palais de L'Europe, place de l'Hermitage, Le Touquet
☎ 03 21 06 72 00.

Le Touquet, also known as Paris Plage, is an elegant seaside town and a gentle retreat after the bustle of Boulogne and Calais. As you enter the centre of town you pass lots of sandy soil and conifers and see the famous Westminster Hotel, a large building in pink brick on your right. The resort used to be a favourite of Edward VII who used to stay at the Westminster; it was also a mecca for the fast set in the 20s who came from the South Coast to visit the casinos. Then it became an attraction for the yachting fraternity and attracted 50s stars like Yves Montand, who would holiday there. The point of the place is really that it is largely unchanged and its faded grandeur has a real charm. It is still a yachting resort and is also famous for its golf courses, horse riding and with its long stretch of beach, it makes the ideal resort for children. It is also perfect of course for sand yachting. Best of all it has some very stylish shops and cafés – if only English resorts had anything to compare.

• **HOW TO GET THERE** *From Boulogne, Calais or the Channel Tunnel, take the N1 motorway south as far as the junction with the N39. Turn onto the N39 and follow directions to Le Touquet*

SKY-TREK AIRLINES
ADDRESS Lydd International Airport, Lydd, Kent TN29 9QL
☎ 01797 320000
If you literally want to Channel-hop to Le Touquet, take a 20-minute flight from Lydd airport. Sky-Trek Airlines operates a Friday to Monday scheduled service aboard a three-engined Trislander aircraft. Take a flight from Lydd at 5pm on a Friday evening and arrive in Le Touquet only 20 minutes later. Alternatively, you can leave at 9.30am on Saturday morning. The Sunday evening return flight leaves Le Touquet at 6.40pm.

- **COST** *Apex return (must be booked at least 14 days in advance), £54; standard return, £64. Children under 12 pay half and those under 2, 10% of the adult fare*
- **HOW TO GET TO LYDD AIRPORT** *Take the M25 and M20, exiting at Junction 10 at Ashford, and then take the A2070 to Brenzett and then the airport. By train, travel from Waterloo to Ashford International station and then take a £12 taxi ride*

WHERE TO STAY

WESTMINSTER HOTEL

ADDRESS 5 avenue de Verger, 62520 Le Touquet Paris-Plage
☎ 03 21 05 48 48

A beautifully situated hotel with real old-world charm. Faded grandeur by the bucket load and an amazing old glass lift that the children found just as much fun to play in as the beach or the swimming pool in the basement. Along the corridors there is a rogue's gallery of famous stars who have stayed in the hotel and old pictures of the hotel as it was in its swanky heyday.

Le Pavillon is the Westminster's gourmet restaurant. There are over 350,000 sorts of wine. Pouilly Fumé is priced at 200F, Mouton Rothschild from 3,000F. The set menu prices start from 250F which includes an appetiser, starter, main course and dessert. Sample dishes include: *millefeuille de saumon fumé, terrine de foie gras de canard au Sauternes, filets de rouget barbet* (red mullet), *plateau de fromages de Maitre Olivier* and sorbet.
- **COST** *La Belle Epoque package is a two-night stay, 825F per person per day, including dinner. Otherwise, a double room is 825F for the night. Set dinner menus start at 250F per head*

HOTEL LE CHALET

ADDRESS 15 rue de la Paix, 62520 Le Touquet Paris-Plage
☎ 03 21 05 87 65

A small hotel in the centre of Le Touquet, with a family atmosphere.
- **COST** *From 160F to 400F per room per night*

LE RED FOX

ADDRESS 60 rue de Metz, Le Touquet
☎ 03 21 05 27 58

A medium-sized, simple but comfortable hotel. Breakfast is taken at the café next door to the hotel.
- **COST** *440F per night for a double room. Breakfast 40F*

LE MANOIR

ADDRESS avenue du Golf, Le Touquet
☎ 03 21 05 20 22

A Le Touquet stalwart and famous with the golfing fraternity. People return here year after year. Edwardian splendour with lots of Edwardian dressing tables and wardrobes, Turkish carpets and fireplaces. There is a large outdoor swimming pool and tennis courts and a cosy bar. 150F menu includes an *amuse-bouche*, fish casserole with ginger, and a selection of cheeses.

- **COST** *Rooms from 345F per person per night*

WHERE TO EAT

Le Touquet is a real foodies' paradise, and there are thousands of cafés, bistros and winebars all over the town.

LE CAFE DES ARTS

ADDRESS 80 rue de Paris, Le Touquet

☎ 03 21 05 21 55

A must. Mentioned in the Michelin and Gault Millau guides. Really delicious French food. A typical menu would include *foie gras, noisettes d'agneau*, French cheeses and *millefeuilles au chocolat*.

- **COST** *225F for the above menu*

FLAVIO

ADDRESS 1 avenue Verger, Le Touquet

☎ 03 21 05 10 22

Another Michelin-starred restaurant that has been famous in Le Touquet for 50 years. Fish is favoured here, especially lobster. Superb dishes include *poêlée of langoustines* with artichokes. Closed Mondays.

- **COST** *Set menus 195F for 3 courses, 420F 'dégustation' menu. 520F 'lobster' menu (their speciality). A la carte around 450F per person including wine*

LE CAFE DES SPORTS

ADDRESS 22 rue St Jean, Le Touquet

☎ 03 21 05 05 22

An excellent brasserie. Especially good for offal – sweetbreads, brains, kidneys and pigs' trotters. Lots of bustle and good food. Try steak tartare at 88F, a speciality of the house, or sole meunière. The set menu might include *pâté maison*, sliced lamb or cod in butter and lemon, apple pie and cheese.

- **COST** *99F for set menu*

PERARD

ADDRESS 67 rue de Metz, Le Touquet

☎ 03 21 05 13 33

This famous fish restaurant is the home of Serge Perard's famous fish soup which he sells all over the world. You can buy it here and see it being made. Very, very busy.

- **COST** *Set menu 140F. A la carte costs dependent on season and choice*

WHAT TO DO

SAND-YACHTING

ADDRESS Base Nautique Sud, Front de mer, Le Touquet
☎ 03 21 05 33 51
Bertrand Lambert, the world champion, provides lessons on the beach. Within an hour, anyone can learn sand-yachting, which is safe and easy. Speed-sailing is for the slightly more athletic, but if you can ski, you can learn to speed sail.
• **COST** *250F for 2 hours. Hire charge 100F for 1 hour, 250F for 3 hours*

THALASSATHERAPY

ADDRESS Institut Thalassa, Front de mer, Le Touquet
☎ 03 21 09 86 99
Take the opportunity to indulge in a little beauty therapy at the Thalassa Institute. Thalassatherapy is based on the therapeutic qualities of sea water and sea air.
• **COST** *525F per person for a day of treatments*

AQUALUD

ADDRESS Front de mer, Le Touquet
☎ 03 21 05 63 59/03 21 05 90 96
A giant indoor pool, with lush vegetation, giant toboggan, wave machine and all the toys. Kept at a constant ambient temperature of 27 degrees Centigrade.
• **OPENING HOURS** *10.00–18.00*
• **COST** *52F for 3 hours or 70F all day*

MUSEE DE TOUQUET

ADDRESS à l'angle des avenues du Golf et du Château, 62520 Le Touquet
☎ 03 21 05 62 62
This museum has some interesting temporary exhibitions as well as an art collection covering the end of the 19th century to the present day.
• **OPENING HOURS** *Wed–Sun 10.00–12.00 and 14.00–16.00*
• **COST** *Adults 10F, children 5F*

SHOPS

It's just a short walk from Le Westminster to the central rue St Jean where you will find wonderful original little shops. Touquet Fruits sell a range of Philippe Olivier-vetted cheeses and Le Chat Bleu is the most divine chocolate shop where children are given straw baskets to fill with the sweets of their choice. It's a must-visit. Also, don't miss the factory outlet for Le Marché de la Porcelaine in the rue Metz where you can buy Limoges porcelain. Visit Perard's (see Where to Eat on page 230) and buy a jar or several jars of his famous *soupe de poissons*. Also take a trip to the Art Deco covered market which is open on Thursdays and Saturdays.

WIMEREUX

TOURIST INFORMATION BUREAU
ADDRESS Hôtel de Ville, Quai Alfred Girard, Wimereux
☎ 03 21 83 27 12

The buildings in Wimereux have a fantasy feel, with castellations, turrets and extravagant balconies, rather like what Disney might have produced as a seaside town. There is not an awful lot to do, but there are a few good restaurants along the beach front.
• **HOW TO GET THERE** *From Boulogne, just drive a few minutes up the coast*

WHERE TO STAY

HOTEL DU CENTRE
ADDRESS 78 rue Carnot, Wimereux
☎ 03 21 32 41 08
An old-fashioned, traditional, family-run hotel on the main street through Wimereux. The food is particularly good value, especially the set menus.
• **COST** *250F–320F per room per night*

PAUL ET VIRGINIE
ADDRESS 19 rue General de Gaulle, Wimereux
☎ 03 21 32 42 12
A mid-19th-century hotel built round a small cobbled courtyard. Another typically French, family-run hotel, with very friendly service.
• **COST** *200F–400F per room per night*

WHERE TO EAT

LA LIEGEOISE
ADDRESS Hotel Atlantique, Digue de Mer, Wimereux
☎ 03 21 32 41 01
Typical local restaurant, which is filled with businessmen during the week and families at the weekend. The daily set menus are very good value and consistently good.
• **COST** *130F–390F*

INDEX